THE
BOGEY
MAN

BOOKS BY GEORGE PLIMPTON

The Rabbit's Umbrella • *Out of My League*
Paper Lion • *The Bogey Man* • *Mad Ducks and Bears*
American Journey: The Times of Robert Kennedy
(with Jean Stein) • *One for the Record* • *One More July*
Shadow Box • *Pierre's Book* (with Pierre Etchebaster)
A Sports Bestiary (with Arnold Roth)
Edie: An American Biography (with Jean Stein)
Sports! (with Neil Leifer) • *Fireworks: A History and Celebration*
Open Net • *D.V.* (with Diana Vreeland and Christopher Hemphill)
The Curious Case of Sidd Finch • *The X Factor*
The Best of Plimpton • *Truman Capote* • *Ernest Shackleton*
Chronicles of Courage (with Jean Kennedy Smith)
The Man in the Flying Lawn Chair

EDITED BY GEORGE PLIMPTON

Writers at Work: The Paris Review Interviews, volumes 1–9
The American Literary Anthology, volumes 1–3
Poets at Work: The Paris Review Interviews
Beat Writers at Work: The Paris Review Interviews
Women Writers at Work: The Paris Review Interviews
Playwrights at Work: The Paris Review Interviews
Latin American Writers at Work: The Paris Review Interviews
The Writer's Chapbook • *The Paris Review Anthology*
The Paris Review Book of Heartbreak, Madness, etc.
The Norton Book of Sports • *As Told at the Explorers Club:*
More Than Fifty Gripping Tales of Adventure • *Home Run*

THE
BOGEY
MAN

A MONTH ON THE PGA TOUR

GEORGE PLIMPTON

Little, Brown and Company
New York   Boston   London

Little, Brown and Company
Hachette Book Group
1290 Avenue of the Americas, New York NY 10104
littlebrown.com

Originally published by HarperCollins, January 1968
First Little, Brown edition, April 2016

Little, Brown and Company is a division of Hachette Book Group, Inc.
The Little, Brown name and logo are trademarks of Hachette Book Group, Inc.

The publisher is not responsible for websites (or their content) that are not owned by the publisher.

The Hachette Speakers Bureau provides a wide range of authors for speaking events. To find out more, go to hachettespeakersbureau.com or call (866) 376-6591.

ISBN 978-0-316-32626-1
Library of Congress Control Number: 2016932400

10 9 8 7 6 5 4 3 2 1

RRD-C

Printed in the United States of America

Foreword

by Rick Reilly

George Plimpton has nearly gotten me killed eleven times. He's pulled three hammies for me, almost got me gored, gave me quarter-sized heat blisters, made me throw up more times than an Ipecac tester, left me to drop animals into my pants, and inspired me to sign up for more dangerous jobs than the cast of *Jackass*.

Because Plimpton was one of my heroes, I attempted things no sane person should. I crushed six cars in a monster truck, ran with the bulls, tried out for the WNBA, played women's pro football, became a ball boy at the U.S. Open, flew upside down in an F-14, jumped with the U.S. Army parachute team, became a tour caddy, became a rodeo clown, faced Nolan Ryan's fastball, competed in the World Sauna Championships, delved into ferret legging (don't), and, in homage to the book you hold in your hand, played in the Pebble Beach Pro-Am. Twice.

Plimpton had the genius to stop *talking* to the pros who play the sports he loved and start *playing* the sports he loved. The NFL, the NHL, Major League Baseball, boxing, pro tennis. He'd do it, mostly fail at it, and then write about it, hilariously. That was sports writing's Bob Beamon moment. What Walter Mitty dreamed about, Plimpton did. He broke through the wall, which meant I wanted to break through the wall.

Of course, my attempts were junior varsity compared to Plimpton's. He lived in the era of America that historians classify as "Before

Insurance Lawyers Ruined Everything." So when he wanted to play quarterback for four downs as a Detroit Lion? Do it! they said. (He lost 30 yards.) When he wanted to pitch to a lineup of baseball all-stars? Why not? (He nearly dropped dead of exhaustion.) Step into the ring against Archie Moore? Have at it! (Bloody nose.)

He had titanium guts, but that's not my favorite Plimpton body part. My favorite Plimpton body part is his over-caffeinated mind. For a guy who looked about as clenched-teeth, Thurston-Howell-III, summer-in-Maine button-down as a man can be, underneath he was an incurably curious five-year-old who couldn't stop asking questions. In *Bogey Man,* he never stopped being fascinated by the curious carnival life these golfers lived in bad pants on lush lawns, and it's what makes this my favorite Plimpton book.

The things the man found out! For instance, I'm a lifelong golf fan, player, and writer and yet I never knew:

- Arnold Palmer woke up every night at 2 a.m. to have a Coke.
- Jack Nicklaus, as a rookie, would wear the same pair of pants for all four rounds.
- Porky Oliver's caddy would put his money in his shoe, so that if you saw him limping down the fairway, "you knew he was in the chips," as Plimpton wrote.

Oh, and my absolute favorite:

- The caddy for Deane Beman recalling Beman being so cheap that when he paid him, "he look at you like you done stab him in the knee!"

When Beman went on to become PGA Tour commissioner, we wore that phrase out.

Writer 1: Hey, what did Beman say when you asked him about John Daly?

Writer 2: Man, it's like I done stab him in the knee!

There was nothing Plimpton did that I didn't want to do. One time, Plimpton was writing a freelance piece for *Sports Illustrated,* where I worked for twenty-two years. This was in the dark days before email, so freelancers would get the final edit of their piece faxed or mailed to them. But Plimpton was in Europe at the time, and by the time he got the final edit, the piece had gone to bed without his input. When it came out, Plimpton was not happy with the edit. He sent the hard copy back to the office, with these words scrawled angrily up the side in red ink: "Wholesale tin-eared butchery!"

That became our go-to slam among SI writers for years.

Writer 1: How's that new Vanilla Ice album?

Writer 2: Wholesale tin-eared butchery!

That's the other thing. Because of Plimpton, I learned that not only can you make up imaginary people, you should; as it delights the reader and proves quite useful in digging yourself out of holes and/or making fun scenes last even longer.

Man Looking Over My Shoulder: What does that mean, imaginary people?

Me: Well, for instance, in *Bogey Man,* Plimpton invents the "Japanese admirals" to describe the voices that haunt him just before his backswing. It's great fun. We all have them. My friend Skybox read *Bogey Man* and decided he didn't have admirals, he had "demons." He would watch his shank flying towards the lunch shack and declare: "Lord, the demons just wouldn't shut up on that one!"

Man Looking Over My Shoulder: But that's not exactly reporting, is it?

Me: Who cares? Plimpton let his Technicolor imagination take over where the facts stopped. In *Bogey Man,* he paints these wonderful little scenes that play out in his head once the curtain comes down. For instance, he had this ongoing obsession with the fact that golfers measure the ricochet distance of golf balls off people's noggins. So, after reporting one that went a prodigious distance after hitting a caddy, he can just "see" a caddy sitting on a rock, holding his throbbing head in his hands, "while the measuring tapes are being stretched out... 'two feet 10! Got it!'" I giggle just thinking about it myself.

Plimpton was my ideal. He lived the life I aspired to. Live in Paris. Write hilariously and without arrogance. Appear in *The Simpsons*. Be fearless. Do you realize Plimpton was one of the men who wrestled Sirhan Sirhan to the ground after the assassination of Robert F. Kennedy, only a year after this book was first published? Do you realize he remarried at 61 and had twin girls at 64? At 76, Plimpton died in his sleep. In my eyes, the man lived a perfect life.

Leave it to Plimpton to write one of the funniest books about golf when the man hardly knew a thing about it. Plimpton was a disastrous golfer and joined the tour knowing almost nothing about the game. The actual playing of golf, the nuances of how it was done, the realization of how great these players were, was as lost on him as modern art to Stevie Wonder. (At one point Plimpton asked Palmer about the "WPGA" instead of the "LPGA." Yeesh.) But it doesn't matter. The playing of golf is the least interesting part of golf anyway. It's the stories, the battle against the nerves, the laughs, the bets, the caddies, the fans, the utter desperation and redemptive joy of it all.

Plimpton went out and absorbed it into that sponge brain of his. He came back with such an all-you-can-eat buffet of golf and life nuggets that it didn't matter if he shot 125 every day (which he nearly did).

At the end, after he returns from his misadventures on tour, a friend asks him if he's still going to write the book.

Plimpton replies, "Oh, I should hope so."

Thank God.

Hush, hush...the bogey man is coming.

—*English Variety Hall Song*

THE
BOGEY
MAN

CHAPTER 1

My woes in golf, I have felt, have been largely psychological. When I am playing well, in the low 90s (my handicap is 18), I am still plagued with small quirks—a suspicion that, for example, just as I begin my downswing, my eyes straining with concentration, a bug or a beetle is going to suddenly materialize on the golf ball.

When I am playing badly, far more massive speculation occurs: I often sense as I commit myself to a golf swing that my body changes its corporeal status completely and becomes a *mechanical* entity, built of tubes and conduits, and boiler rooms here and there, with big dials and gauges to check, a Brobdingnagian structure put together by a team of brilliant engineers but manned largely by a dispirited, eccentric group of dissolutes—men with drinking problems, who do not see very well, and who are plagued by liver complaints.

The structure they work in is enormous. I see myself as a monstrous, manned colossus poised high over the golf ball, a spheroid that is barely discernible fourteen stories down on its tee. From above, staring through the windows of the eyes, which bulge like great bay porches, is an unsteady group (as I see them) of Japanese navymen—admirals, most of them. In their hands they hold ancient and useless voice tubes into which they yell the familiar orders: "Eye on the ball! Chin steady! Left arm stiff! Flex the knees! Swing from the inside out! Follow through! Keep head down!" Since the voice tubes are useless, the cries drift down the long corridors and shaftways between the iron tendons and muscles, and echo into vacant chambers and out, until finally, as a burble of sound, they reach the control centers. These posts are situated at the joints, and in charge are the dissolutes I mentioned—typical of them a cantankerous elder perched on a metal stool, half a bottle of rye on the floor beside him, his ear cocked for the orders that he acknowledges with ancient epithets, yelling back up the corridors, "Ah, your father's mustache!" and such things, and if he's of a mind, he'll reach for the controls (like the banks of tall levers one remembers from a railroad-yard switch house) and perhaps he'll pull the proper lever and perhaps not. So that, in sum, the whole apparatus, bent on hitting a golf ball smartly, tips and convolutes and lunges, the Japanese admirals clutching each other for support in the main control center up in the head as the structure rocks and creaks. And when the golf shot is on its way the navymen get to their feet and peer out through the eyes and report: "A shank! A shank! My God, we've hit another shank!" They stir about in the control center drinking paper-thin cups of rice wine, consoling themselves, and every once in a while one of them will reach for a voice tube and shout:

"Smarten up down there!"

Down below, in the dark reaches of the structure, the dissolutes reach for their rye, tittering, and they've got their feet up on the levers and perhaps soon it will be time to read the evening newspaper.

It was a discouraging image to carry around in one's mind; but I had an interesting notion: a month on the professional golf tour (I had been invited to three tournaments), competing steadily and under tournament conditions before crowds and under the scrutiny of the pros with whom I would be playing, might result in 5, perhaps even 6, strokes being pruned from my 18 handicap. An overhaul would result. My Japanese admirals would be politely asked to leave, and they would, bowing and smiling. The dissolutes would be removed from the control centers, grumbling, clutching their bottles of rye, many of them evicted bodily, being carried out in their chairs.

The replacements would appear—a squad of scientific blokes dressed in white smocks. Not too many of them. But a great tonnage of equipment would arrive with them—automatic equipment in gray-green boxes and computer devices that would be placed about and plugged in and set to clicking and whirring. The great structure would become almost entirely automatized. Life in the control center would change— boring, really, with the scientists looking out on the golf course at the ball and then twiddling with dials and working out estimations, wind resistance, and such things, and finally locking everything into the big computers; and with yawns working at the corners of their mouths because it was all so simple, they would push the "activate" buttons to generate the smooth motion in the great structure that would whip the golf ball out toward the distant green far and true. Very dull and predictable. The scientists would scarcely find very much to say to each other after a shot. Perhaps "Y-e-s," very drawn out. "Y-e-s. Very nice." Occasionally someone down in the innards of the structure would appear down the long glistening corridors with an oil can, or perhaps with some brass polish to sparkle up the pipes.

That was the vision I had. I began the overhaul myself. I would obviously have to look the part. A month before I left on the tour, I outfitted myself completely and expensively with new golf equipment. I had played golf since I began (which was when I was twelve or so) with a white cloth golf bag that bore the trade name "Canvasback" for some reason; if the clubs were removed it collapsed on itself like an accordion, or like a pair of trousers being stepped out of. It was light as a feather, and caddies always looked jaunty and supercilious under its weight. I often carried it myself. It had a small pocket with room for three balls and some tees. It had eight clubs in it, perhaps nine—two woods and a putter and the rest, of course, irons with two or three missing—an outfit hardly suitable for tournament play.

So I bought the works. Clubs and a new bag. Sweaters. Argyll socks. A small plastic bag of gold golf tees. I bought some golf shoes with flaps that came down over the laces—my first pair; I had always used sneakers. The golf bag was enormous. It seemed a dull conservative color when I saw it in the late afternoon gloom of a Florida golf shop. But when I took it out on a practice round the next day, it glowed a rich oxblood color, like a vast sausage. It was very heavy with a metal bottom with brass studs around it, and when I first went out I felt guilty seeing it on a caddy's back. But the clubs let off a fine chinking sound as the bag was carried, as expensive and exclusive as the sound of a Cadillac door shutting to, and the fact that porters, caddies, and I myself, whoever carried it, were bent nearly double by its weight only seemed to add to its stature.

It was proper to have such an enormous bag. I thought of the caddies coming up the long hills of the Congressional on television, wearing the white coveralls with the numbers, and those huge bags—MacGregors, Haigs or Wilsons, with the pros' names stamped down the front—with the wiping towels dangling, and the bags nearly slantwise across their shoulders, with one hand back to steady it so the weight would be more properly distributed.

Still, I never really got accustomed to my great golf bag. The woods had brown woolen covers on them. In my early practice rounds in the east I used to follow the clubs at quite a distance, and off to one side, as they were carried down the fairway, as one might circle at a distance workmen moving a harpsichord into one's home—self-conscious and a little embarrassed.

I was particularly aware of the big bag on trips—particularly lugging it around in a railroad station or an air terminal, where intense men with briefcases hurry past, and there are tearful farewells going on, and melancholy groups of military people stand around with plastic name tags on their tunics to tell us who they are. A golf bag is such an immense symbol of frivolity in these parlous times, so much bigger than a tennis racket. When I arrived in Los Angeles by plane to head upstate for the Crosby tournament, the terminal seemed filled with soldiers. There had been many on my plane. At the baggage claim counter the gray-green military duffel bags began coming down the conveyor belt, one after another, and the soldiers would heft them off and set them to one side in a great mound. My golf bag appeared among them with its rich oxblood glow, obscene, jingling slightly as it came toward me on the conveyor.

A porter gave me a hand with it. We got it outside to the traffic ramp with the rest of my luggage and he waited while I arranged to rent a car for the long ride up to Monterey.

"You must be going up to the tournament," the porter said.

"Why, yes," I said gratefully. "The Crosby."

"George Knudson just came through a while ago," he said. "And George Archer. Always tell him 'cause he's, man, *tall*."

"That's right," I said. "He's as tall as they come."

He hefted the bag into the trunk of the car.

"They set you up with a new bag, I see."

The bag was so new that a strong odor drifted from it—a tang of furniture polish.

"A great big one," I said. "They're getting bigger, it seems."

I fished in my pocket for a tip.

"Well, good luck up there," he said. He wanted me to tell him my name, some name he would recognize from the tour so he could announce to them back in the terminal, "Well, you know, So-and-so just came through...on his way up to the Crosby."

"I guess I just head *north*," I said. I waved an arm, and stepped into the car.

"Yes, that's where it is. Up the coast." He smiled. "Well, good luck," he said. "I play to a 5 myself."

"No kidding?" I said.

"Well, that's nothing compared to you guys. I play out on the municipal course. And at Ramble Beach."

"A 5 handicap is nothing to be sneezed at," I said.

"I wish it was a 4," he said.

"Sure," I said. "Well..." I tried hard to think of an appropriate golf term.

"Well, *pop it*," I said.

He looked startled.

"I mean really *pop* it out there."

A tentative smile of appreciation began to work at his features. I put the car in gear and started off. As I looked in the rear-view mirror I could see him staring after the car.

CHAPTER 2

The final hours of the drive go through the high country of the Big Sur, the sea lying flat and unroiled to the west. It was calm and warm, which was welcome golfing weather, but unexpected; the vagaries of the weather during the Crosby are famous: in 1962 it snowed; in 1967 gale winds swept in from the sea and made the play of the ocean holes almost a senseless procedure—like a sort of lunatic golf played between the crews of fishing trawlers bobbing in a storm.

I stopped overnight and it was still easy weather by the early afternoon of the next day when I drove onto the scenic Seventeen Mile Drive that winds along the edge of that pine-covered coastal country.

The Crosby is played on the three golf courses of the Monterey Peninsula—Cypress Point (which is a private club within a club, with only one hundred and fifty members); Pebble Beach, where the headquarters of the tournament are set up; and the Monterey Peninsula Country Club, which, while impressive enough, is the least spectacular of the courses and considered the easiest. (In the last year or so a public course named Spyglass Hill—to commemorate Treasure Island's hill and Robert Louis Stevenson, who lived nearby—has been completed and has displaced the Monterey Peninsula Country Club as the third leg of the Crosby.) All the courses are part of a development known as the Del Monte Properties, which was started in 1915 by Samuel Finley Brown Morse, the captain of the Yale 1906 football team and a grandnephew of the telegraph inventor. I met him by chance years ago in his house in Monterey. I can remember the powerful presence of the man, and how odd it seemed that such a man of vigor lived in a home full of delicate Oriental art and compartmentalized by pale-yellow gauze-thin Japanese screens that were slid to and fro on metal runners, just barely audibly, by servants as we moved through the house. He was a very physical man. He thought nothing of ripping a telephone directory apart, and he often challenged his guests to a boxing match. When they demurred, he would groan, and he would say, "Well, all right, then, let's do some Indian wrestling."

He was an inventor in his own right, or at least of an inventive turn of mind: in 1931 he used the guano from the cormorant rocks in Carmel Bay to fertilize the golf courses—a misdirected plan which turned out to be almost fatal to the grass on the courses, but had the pleasant compensation that the more picturesque sea lions took over the rocks, newly cleansed, and would not let the birds back. There the seals remain, just offshore, making a honking, quite derisive sound—clearly audible to the golfers working the ocean holes.

I parked my car and went into the Del Monte Lodge to register. The place was crowded. People were checking in—the amateur contingent of golfers, I assumed, since all of them were keyed up, as if they'd been belting down drinks of Scotch. They seemed everywhere in the lobby, in their gaudy golfing outfits, back-slapping, and calling out to each other: "Hey, old buddy, been out on the track yet? Been out there myself and had a gorgeous round, absolutely gorgeous."

Bing Crosby was standing by the registration desk, very calm in that hubbub, smiling at people, and shaking hands. He was wearing a Scotch-plaid hat with an Alpine brush in the band; he had a very long thin-stemmed pipe in his mouth, which he would take out from time to time to speak his fancy brand of talk, as formal as a litany: "Ah, Brother So-and-so, the authorities inform me that you have ambulated across our fair acres and invited yourself a sizable 7 on the 8th. What transpired, Brother So-and-so? Did you happen to traffic with the cruel sea?"

Close by was Crosby's friend and lieutenant, Maurie Luxford, the man who actually runs the tournament. He has been doing it for twenty-one years. I went up and introduced myself, and we went off to a corner where it was quiet and he talked for a moment or so about his difficulties as a tournament director. In the months preceding he had received over nine thousand applications from those who wanted to play in Bing's tournament. There was only room for 168 amateurs, Luxford said, shaking his head; of that number Crosby had reserved about 120 places for his own friends whose names were from what Luxford referred to as "Crosby's Black Book"—Bing's golfing friends—and that left a maximum of forty-eight places for Luxford to fill from those thousands of applications stacked in the big cardboard containers in the corner of his office.

"It's quite a privilege," Luxford said. "You'd be surprised what people will do to get an invitation to the Crosby. I had a man come up to me in a country-club locker room and offer $20,000 in cash for an invitation. Very embarrassing."

I whistled in awe; I took the opportunity to thank Luxford for sending *me* an invitation. I had written Crosby a few months earlier saying that I hoped to do a series of articles on playing on the tour and how grateful I would be if he were to extend the privileges of his tournament.

"I hadn't realized *what* a privilege," I said. "What a temptation for the unprincipled—to trade off an invitation for some of that hard cash."

Luxford looked at me carefully.

"Oh, I'm who I say I am," I assured him.

"Well, I *hope* so," he said.

When I asked him how the tournament worked, he said that this was the twenty-fifth, the Silver Anniversary of the tournament—what Bing called his "clambake"—and that the proceeds (television fees, entry fees, and the rest of it) were to be split up among local charities.

"The pro-am event is one of the biggest sources of income for a golf tournament," Luxford said. "The entry fee here for the pro-am is $150. For some tournaments it's much more. It costs $1,000 to play in the pro-am of the Florida Citrus Open. So those guys down there are close to $150,000 before they *begin* thinking about income from ticket sales and television."

The Crosby is quite unlike any other pro-am tournament. Most tournaments have a pro-am event on the first day—each professional playing with three amateurs, who play to their handicaps, the four-some's best ball on each hole being recorded. In the Crosby each pro is paired with one amateur and the two play together as a team for the entire four-day event.

"Who's your partner?" Luxford asked.

"I don't know," I said.

"You better go to headquarters and check in."

On the way up to the tournament headquarters, I kept thinking about the television on the last day—my stomach tightening as I thought of being paired with a great professional, which would mean a big gallery following, and someone carrying a sign with the team names on it, and the women sitting on the shooting sticks in rows ready to make clucking sounds if a shot was scraped along the ground.

"I don't suppose I have Hogan, or Palmer, or anyone like that," I said to the ladies behind the tables at headquarters.

"No," they said. "Mr. Hogan is not playing in the Crosby this year. Your partner is—" they looked it up on the pairing sheets—"Bob Bruno."

"Oh yes," I said.

"You're scheduled to go off with him at 10:10 tomorrow morning at the Monterey Peninsula Country Club. Manuel de la Torre is the other pro in your foursome and his amateur partner is Bill Henley."

They gave me Bruno's telephone number. He was staying at a small motel in Monterey. I called him, and we talked briefly. He had finished his day's practice. He would meet me tomorrow on the first tee. I told him about my golf, my 18 handicap, and I said I hoped he wouldn't mind being saddled with such a thing. He sounded very pleasant. He said, No, that for "ham 'n' egging"—that is to say, combining in a good partnership—a player with a high handicap, if he got onto his game, could be tremendously useful.

Afterward I asked around about him. No one knew much except that he was tall. He turned out to be 6 feet 5½ inches tall, about the tallest professional on the tour—up there with George Archer and George Bayer. His best paydays had been a tenth at St. Paul in 1964, where he won $1,675, and a twelfth at Seattle that same year, for which he won $1,100.

Bruno's status as a golfer (and he would admit it, if ruefully) was in the lower echelons of the touring pros—in the category known as "rabbits." These were the golfers on the tour who were beginning their careers, or whose play was erratic or in the doldrums. They had to play in a qualifying tournament, usually held on a Monday, and fight it out among themselves for the available slots in the draw of the regular tournament. In the Los Angeles Open, for example, which preceded the Crosby, there had been about 20 open slots in the draw for which about 250 rabbits had been forced to compete. The PGA published a complete money list every year, which is uncomfortable reading down toward the end: Jim Hart made $11 in 1967; Reynolds Faber, Norman Rach and Arthur Jones each made $4; a golfer named Alex Antonio played in a number of tournaments, often making the Sunday cuts, yet he never won any money at all.

It is expensive to join the tour. Bruno told me later that $250 a week was a conservative figure, and when I looked startled he explained that the average entry fee for a tournament is $50; any motel room with a plain white bedspread and a window looking on the truck park in back is $50 to $60 a week; a caddy would look awfully sour if he didn't get $50 for a tournament's work; and then one had to set aside $8 to $10 a day to eat. That's $230-odd right there—not taking into consideration travel expenses, or a movie and a haircut from time to time. The PGA itself warns any golfer that he cannot expect to play the tour for less than $300 a week.

To make ends meet, most professionals starting their careers on the tour sell stock in themselves—half their winnings over a stipulated time, usually five years, perhaps ten. Backing a pro is a speculative risk, and assistance comes largely from club members or friends willing to help a young club pro without much hope of financial return.

In a sense I was relieved to be paired with Bruno—a relative unknown. It was bad luck for him, but at least the irregularities of my game would not be disturbing a truly great player, someone making a run for the tournament win.

I asked about the pro-ams—whether the professionals minded playing in them. Almost invariably they approved of them—as providing a way, in a symbolic sense, to repay personally the great enthusiasm the public had for professional golf.

Of course, sometimes insupportable things happened. In his first year on the tour Jack Nicklaus played in a pro-am with a golfer who had played only once before. Apparently the man had sent in made-up credentials, which were accepted by the tournament committee—a handicap of 12 when in fact he could barely have scraped around the course in a score of less than 200. The foursome moved very ponderously. They tried to persuade the novice to pick up when he was out of contention for a hole—which was invariably immediately following his tee shot—but he was stubborn, intent on posting his individual score no matter what. An enormous space—four or five holes—opened between the Nicklaus foursome and the one in front, so that it looked to spectators waiting at a particular hole as if the tournament had been truncated and no one else was coming through. They stirred on the picnic blankets and leaned forward on the shooting sticks and peered at the tournament draw. "Ah-hah. Nicklaus!" His was the group due through. They shook their heads. Nicklaus had a reputation of being a slow player. A half-hour went by. The course stretched empty back toward the opening holes. Some spectators walked back up the course and disappeared over a rise. When they returned, they said that there was a foursome coming through, soon enough they felt, though there was something odd about it—people and marshals scuttling back and forth, and sudden short bursts of movement forward, often sideways, and then stopping, as if what was being watched was the progress of a huge leaping frog. Finally, three balls soared over the rise and came to a rest in the fairway. The spectators leaned forward. Ten minutes went by. Another five minutes. Some heads appeared above the rise looking back. Then they disappeared.

Finally, the group came into view. The center of attention, they could see, was a heavy-set man, his face florid under a long-brimmed white fisherman's hat. The marshals were clustered around him, remonstrating apparently, their hands in supplicatory positions. Then all of them jumped back as the man's club rose and fell. There were shouts of alarm, and then the group rushed forward and settled around him, like flies frightened off and returning to a garbage truck, and the entire lively collection moved off at some eccentric angle, and the scene repeated itself. Somehow they were able to persuade the novice to stop at the 9th hole. Perhaps they told him — *convinced* him — that nine holes was all that was required. . . .

Professionals admit to difficulties of this sort, if to a lesser degree, but still they are firmly in support of pro-ams. Bruce Crampton, for example, told me that certainly it is hard to concentrate during the pro-am rounds — the pro has to spend a lot of time poking around in the rough to find his partner's ball. And then, of course, amateurs are often ignorant — they step on the line of the putt, or hit their shots at the wrong time. Still, the best friends Crampton has in the U.S. (he comes from Australia) are those he met during the pro-ams. Fine people, he said they were, and they asked him to stay at their homes when he came through on the tour the next year.

CHAPTER 3

The invitation to the Crosby allowed me to enter, if tentatively, the world of professional golf—to see it first-hand. It was not actually the first chance I'd had to play with top-flight golfers. Five or six years before, I had gone through a head-to-head match with Sam Snead on his winter home course at Boca Raton, on Florida's east coast. But nothing had come of it as far as writing was concerned, not even a paragraph's worth, though I had expected great things. Over the phone Snead had seemed pleasant and he had arranged the match most agreeably. He asked me where I was staying, and when I said Palm Beach, the plush resort twenty miles up the coast from Boca Raton, he said Yes, yes, yes, indeedy.

I drove down to Boca Raton with a large fresh notebook to fill, and a good automatic pencil, with one in reserve. Snead, from what I could gain from reading about him, was sure to provide good copy. He had a lively way with words of advice about golf. I recalled his warning that a club should be held as one would hold a bird—"Lightly, you mustn't hurt it."

We met and walked out to the first tee where we had a long discussion about the terms of a wager whose size, if I lost, made me gulp. Whatever the cost, though, I thought the day's round would be compensation enough—simply the privilege of playing and listening to such a great golfer. But after that first discussion, I saw very little of

Snead. I never got a chance to *talk* to him. We met briefly on the greens and the tees. I made appropriate sounds of awe when Snead whacked his drives off into the distance. He would climb into his yellow golf cart while I set my ball up on its tee. When I made my shot, off at an angle usually, Snead would say, "I reckon you *hedged* somewhat on that one," and he would set off swiftly after his drive. I moved behind his cart, ranging back and forth for my errant shots with my caddy, the pair of us like two sea birds far in the wake of a trawler.

A girl joined us for the second 9. She had waited on the clubhouse terrace. I could see her yellow dress, and saw her wave as we came up the 9th fairway. I introduced her to Snead. She rode with him in the cart, while I continued to range along behind them.

Sometimes she walked with me. "Do you know what Snead asked me?" she said.

"What?"

"He wants to know how much I *weigh*. He keeps asking me."

"Well, at least you got *some* sort of a dialogue going," I said.

Nor was Snead around to talk to when the round was over. He had met with a threesome of Miami businessmen as soon as we had come in from our tour of the course. When I came running over from the 18th green to say good-bye, he was already on his way to the first tee to join them. He waited for me to reach him. "Pigeons," he said, taking me into his confidence. He winked broadly. I forked over the fifty dollars I owed him from the bet.

"Good luck," I said, still breathing hard from the trot up the 18th fairway.

"Yah, we'll have some fun," he said, turning to his group.

"It was that damn cart," I said. We were up on the terrace, where a member of the club had asked us to join him for a drink. "I might have got something out of Snead and the afternoon if it hadn't been for the *speed* of that thing."

A waiter in an orange coat bent over the table and we ordered drinks.

"It's funny you should blame golf carts," the member said, smiling.

He went on to say that Boca Raton has been famous for its golf carts since the club's establishment by the nabobs of the early twenties. He told us that one of the latter, Clarence Geist, played the course in a specially equipped Packard. It was a familiar sight on the fairways, though startling to those seeing it for the first time. The Packard would lurch out of a grove of trees onto the course, and a player back on the tee, looking up from his ball, would call out, "My God, what's that?"

"That's Clarence Geist's Packard."

"Well, yes, but what is it doing out there? Look at the size of that thing! Think of the ruts it must leave in the fairways. Why doesn't the good man—what's his name?"

"Geist."

"Why doesn't he use a rickshaw? Or at the least a Model T?"

They would watch the limousine stop far down the fairway, and then a distant figure being assisted out of the back, the small knot of people standing by the car as if inspecting a road map, cataleptic until the flash of a club swinging, the heads turning to watch the flight of that faraway, invisible ball. Then the group would load up into the Packard again, which would rock off across the undulations of the fairway.

"That's very interesting," I said. I was still petulant about Snead. "Today was a waste. I certainly never got the sense of what it's like to play against a championship golfer."

"Why don't you try Ben Hogan?" the member asked.

He said he'd call him—he was a good friend—and put in a word for me. Hogan was in the vicinity preparing for the Masters, as he did annually at the Seminole Golf Club north of Palm Beach.

I thanked the member, and a few days later, on his say-so, I called Hogan. I explained somewhat haltingly that I wanted to write an article about competing against great professionals. Perhaps a match with him could be arranged. It would be a great privilege.

I can remember his voice in reply—polite and easy. It took me a while to realize that he was turning me down. He said that yes, our mutual friend had described the notion to him. He said he had no objection to playing a friendly match, perhaps in a foursome along with the friend who had put us in touch. A good player, a former Harvard captain, did I know that? Yes, I said. But Hogan went on, if I intended to write about playing against him in a *competition,* well, that was another matter. The conditions would have to be those of a tournament.

"But, Mr. Hogan," I said, "the chances of our meeting in a tournament...how would that ever happen? I'd have to turn professional. My handicap is 18, Mr. Hogan."

"Well, that's your problem," he said.

He was not being unkind or scornful. He had an acute sense of what the great component of his ability was — the competitiveness — and if it was to be described by a writer for public demand, he wanted it to be assessed at its keenest, under the stress of tournament conditions.

I told the Boca Raton member what had happened, and he smiled.

"It didn't work out," I said.

"No. I rather expected that," he said. "Well, you had the chance to find out about that man's pride. That must be worth something."

"Well, sure," I said. "Sure."

CHAPTER 4

After checking in I went around to the pro shop at Del Monte Lodge and inquired about getting a caddy for the tournament. Almost all the golfers, I was told, both professional and amateur, had already checked in, and most of the caddies had been assigned. There might be somebody left out back, they said.

I looked out there, and a somewhat elderly caddy got up off a bench and hurried up and introduced himself. Abe, his name was—a very small man encased in oversized clothes, an extra-long windbreaker over a worn dark sweater, the baggy pants of a top-banana comedian hanging loosely on him and making him look, from afar, like a waif. He had a dark, wind-creased face and a rather gloomy set to his mouth.

He said, "You looking for someone to pack your bag?"

"Absolutely," I said.

He went on to say that I was lucky to get him. Abe wasn't just any "bag-toter." He knew the three Monterey courses from twenty, maybe thirty years' experience and had "packed" bags for some of the "great ones."

"Marty Furgol—packed for him," he said.

"Oh yes," I said.

"You ain't a pro?" he asked hopefully.

"I'm afraid not," I said.

"Who is your pro?"

"Bob Bruno."

George convenes with caddy, Abe. (*Russ Halford*)

"Who's he?"

"Well, for one thing he's just about the tallest pro on the tour."

"Well, that's something," Abe said.

We went out that afternoon to get in as much of a practice round as we could before darkness fell. We played the ocean holes of Pebble Beach under a setting sun. Out in the sea hundreds of whales were moving north, so that sometimes, looking out, one could spot a dozen or so spouts at the same time, a feather of spray, pink in the dying sun, and then the distant dark roll of the body beneath.

Abe said as we walked along that he was originally a seafaring man. He had come west from Massachusetts, and he had been with the sardine fleets out of Monterey in the days when the schools were thick and lay out beyond the kelp beds. He had become a furniture mover after that, caddying when he had the time. In the evening, years before, when the tides were right, he went down to the rocks and beaches where the sea boiled in at the famous oceanside holes of Pebble Beach and, equipped with a long pole and a sack, he scraped around for lost balls, which he would then sell.

He told me that on a good day he would come up out of the sea with his sack full-up with balls. The activity was not quite legal because of the trespassing laws, so he would set out for home across the golf course with his coat buttoned and straining across the bulge of the sack. His odd notion was that the club officials, if they saw him out there, might take him for a pregnant woman out for a stroll in the twilight.

"They'd've had to be pretty nearsighted, Abe," I said, looking at him. We were waiting on the 6th for a pair in front of us. He was so short that he had to carry my golf bag slantwise on his back, like a soldier carrying a bazooka, and I noticed that the clubs often began to slide out as he walked. He smoked incessantly, never flicking at his cigarette, so that it developed long curved ashes that wavered and finally dropped whole to lie on the grass like gray cicada husks. He had a terrific smoker's cough and wheeze.

"What was the best day?" I asked.

"The top day I ever had on the beaches," he said, "was 350 balls. I dragged myself across the course *that* day."

"What would that day be worth to you?" I asked.

"In the golf shops I could count on getting 50 cents a ball if they weren't too sea-logged. Then the price was 20 cents."

The wait continued on the 6th. I asked Abe if he had ever played golf. He thought about it and said that in twenty-five years he had played three holes. In fact, he had played the last of the holes not more than two weeks before. I asked him how it had gone. He said that for someone just keeping his hand in, he wasn't so bad.

Abe said you didn't have to play golf to be a good caddy. You had to know the courses, that was all, and he certainly knew them. He had been involved in the Crosby tournaments for years. One year he had carried a scorer's signboard down the fairways—one of the years of the bad weather, when the wind had ripped in off the Pacific at gale force. "Man, that was an experience," he went on to say. They paid him ten dollars for carrying the board. He hadn't been able to find a bag to pack that year, and he said that carrying the board behind the foursome, which he thought was going to be duck-soup easy, just changing the numbers from time to time to show where the two players and their teams stood in relationship to par, well, it had been worse than packing *two* bags. It was the wind, catching and flailing at the board and turning it in Abe's hands, and then hauling and jockeying him around the fairway, so that in the big gusts he felt like a man controlled by his umbrella in a windstorm. One of the pros' names on his board was Al Besselink; he couldn't remember the other one. When they got to the sea holes of Pebble Beach—the 7th, 8th—the board became almost completely unmanageable; it kept bearing Abe off inland, toward the eucalyptus forests. He would turn the board's edge into the wind and tack back up toward his group, but the wind would catch and turn the board broadside to, like a sail, and Abe would be scurried off before the wind, hauling to and doing what he could. In my mind's eye I could see Abe careering Al Besselink's name through distant foursomes while galleries turned to stare after him. Finally, he lost his foursome completely, so he tried going inland where he thought he had a better chance of getting the board back to the caddy house by traveling through the natural windscreens of the pines.

"I had to get that sign back up there," said Abe. "If I don't come back in with the sign, maybe I don't get my ten dollars."

I had a good first 9 that afternoon, playing relaxed golf, and Abe, when I told him my handicap was 18, whistled and said "we" would have an interesting tournament. He said maybe we'd even get to have someone carrying a signboard behind us! That's what we would have if we were in contention.

Like many caddies, Abe referred to his golfer as "we" when things were going well. After a good drive he would say, "We're right down the middle. Yessir, we're right down the goddam pike." In adversity, the first person "we" was dropped and the second and third person would appear. A caddy would say after gazing at a duck hook: "You're dead. You're off there way to the left." Or in reminiscing to another caddy after a day's round, he would shift gears in mid-sentence: "So we're right down the fairway, lying one, and what does he do but hit it fat."

When we got to the inland holes the deer were moving—materializing in the shadows of the eucalyptus trees, occasionally bounding in quick long stiff-legged leaps across the fairways. Abe said that one year a whole herd of them had idled across the fairway in front of Tommy Bolt, one of the most tempestuous and colorful players on the tour.

"I reckon every deer on the peninsula lined up and passed in front of Bolt," Abe said. "He got good and red in the ears waiting for them, and finally he shouted, 'Hey, get those marshals outa there!'"

It was dark when we got in. Our starting time in the tournament was 10:10 the next morning. Abe said that he would come and fetch me very early for some work on the practice tee. He told me to get a good rest.

A friend at the lodge had seen the two of us walk in from the course. "Who's that little guy with you?" he asked.

"My caddy," I said.

"You're in trouble. He doesn't look like he can lift a golf ball, much less a bag. And what are those noises he makes?"

"He wheezes somewhat," I said, "but he gets around O.K. Hell, he's a professional furniture mover."

"What does he carry, tea tables?" my friend asked. "You remember Ogden Nash's caddy—the one who had chronic hiccups, hay fever, whistled through his teeth, and who had large shoes that squeaked?"

"Yes," I said.

"Well, that's your caddy."

"Not Abe. Not good Abe," I said. "He's been on these courses for thirty years. You wait," I said. "You just wait."

CHAPTER 5

The first evening at the Del Monte Lodge was very lively, with the sort of self-generated excitement that turns up on the eve of any great sporting event. The bars were crowded; the amateurs were there in full force. Many of them, like myself, had promised themselves to rest up for the event the next day and get to bed early, but the drumbeats from the band and the laughter drifting across the Del Monte compound had attracted them like moths, and they circulated about aimlessly and content in that assault of sound.

I saw Dave Marr, the PGA champion, at a corner table. He waved me over. I had met him a few times in New York, and he motioned me to a seat with a big grin. There were three or four other golfers at the table.

"What have they handicapped you?" he asked.

"I have a good sloppy 18 handicap," I said, "that isn't going to bother anyone."

I ordered a drink.

"He probably plays to a 3," one of the golfers said.

"No, I'm really very bad," I said. "I have this problem with my golf. I have these wayward thoughts that pop into my mind at moments of crisis on the course—images quite apart from golf."

Well, what sort of thoughts, they wanted to know.

I told them, somewhat haltingly, about the retired Japanese Navy officers and the great structure they tried to control, and the dissolutes at the joints with their half-pints of rye. The golfers stared at me uneasily.

"Where does all that stuff come from?" Marr asked.

"Well, I guess from those World War II films about the Pacific fighting—those scenes of the Japanese admirals very smug in the control towers of their battleships...and then suddenly the trap is sprung and the water splashes up against the windows from the shell bursts. They rock back and forth and look confused...and frightened. Remember?"

"Oh yes."

I asked if their concentration was ever upset by such wayward thoughts?

Well, yes, they said, but they weren't harassed by any such thoughts as those I had just described. Japanese admirals! However, they would admit to inner voices that cajoled and murmured encouragement. Dave Marr said that, as he stood over his putt on the 16th green during the PGA Championship he won at Laural Valley in 1965, clear as a bell he heard his baby's voice call, "Careful, Daddy, careful!" just as the baby did when he was being tossed joyfully in the air, roughhousing at home. Marr, hearing his son's voice, *was* careful—so careful that his putt ended up short. He two-putted from there. When Jack Nicklaus chipped in a remarkable shot on the 17th and came within two strokes of Marr's lead, the childish voice disappeared, to Marr's relief, and in its place a somewhat more aggressive voice began to cajole, "Don't let him in, dammit, just lock the guy out"—which Marr was able to do on the last hole to win his championship.

Marr went on to say that what good golfers usually see in their mind's eye is not the actual process they must go through to hit the ball, which is what the average golfer sees, but where the ball is going to end up.

"When you're playing at your best," Marr said, "you look down at the ball on the tee and you see the fairway and the spot out there where your shot's going to land. It's almost like looking at those score cards that have a map of each hole, with the play of the hole marked in dotted lines. What you see is the dotted line. Of course, if you're playing bad, what you see are the woods and the traps, Marlboro Country, and more often than not, if that's what you're thinking, that's where your shot is going to end up."

The golfers nodded.

I told them about my premonition that a large insect would suddenly appear on my golf ball just as I was bringing my club down.

"A what?"

"A bug," I said. "Maybe a beetle."

The golfers winced slightly.

"Man, what a thing to suggest! You hang around the tour long enough," one of them said, "and get us golfers worrying about things like bugs, and no one's going to come close to hitting the ball a *foot*. You're dangerous, man, too dangerous."

"Well, I don't know," I said.

"Just don't tell us too many things like that," he said.

"Who's your partner?" one of them wanted to know.

"Bob Bruno."

"Well, he's tall," someone said.

"Yes, I've heard that," I said. "That's about *all* I hear about him."

"A lot of potential there," the golfer across from me said. "He could be a very fine player, a very much better one, if he could retain his composure."

"His what?" I asked.

"Well, his difficulties with golf sometimes get the better of him. You're likely to find out. He's got a temper like a rooster."

"Yes," said Marr. "Particularly if those Japanese Navy people of yours get out of hand and your game goes to pot."

Someone said, "When his self-control goes—fireworks!"

I must have looked concerned.

"Maybe it won't happen—I mean, his flying out of hand," Marr said. "Partner him well, help him with maybe six, seven strokes a side, and the two of you will get along just fine."

"Well, that's comforting to hear," I said.

CHAPTER 6

I made it a practice, starting with that first evening when I returned to my room from the lodge, of dipping into a large green bag full of books on golf, and doing some reading before dropping off to sleep. I had purchased, or borrowed, the books before leaving on the tour, and I brought them with me in a large green laundry bag with a clothesline drawstring. I dipped into it whenever I had the chance, on the principle that saturating myself with the subject of golf whenever possible might have an osmotic effect on my game.

Some of the books were instructive (such manuals as Ben Hogan's *Power Golf,* Sam Snead's *How to Hit a Golf Ball,* Bob Rosburg's *The Putter Book*), illustrated with stop-action photographs of the perfect swing; line drawings of golfers swinging in barrels, red arrows pointing to danger spots such as the crook of the arm, the chin, the hips; metaphorical drawings to associate the golf swing with some other common act. One of these latter showed a man pulling down a window shade with both hands, with the suggestion, I recall, that the motion was the exact facsimile of the correct way to hit *down* into the ball. I also had a copy of Phillips B. Thompson's *Simplifying the Golf Stroke*—a very popular book in the twenties, five pages long, with print the size of the lower levels of an oculist's chart—which both begins and ends with a sentence urging the reader to think of the golf club as a "weight at the end of a string."

Other books were discursive; some were reminiscences. Some I had ordered simply because I was intrigued by the titles in the catalogues: *Super Golf with Self-Hypnosis,* by Jack Heise; *Golf—Reflections on Morals,* by John L. Low; *The Happy Golfer;* J. Dunn's *Intimate Golf Talks; The Nine Bad Shots of Golf and What to Do About Them,* by Jim Dante and Leo Diegel; *Are Golfers Human?* by R. Murray. One group of books by the same author (Fred Beck) had an intriguing progression of titles—*73 Years in a Sandtrap, 89 Years in a Sandtrap,* and finally *To H——with Golf*—which seemed appropriate to my situation—but when the books arrived they turned out to be cartoon collections which did not measure up to the jocosity of the titles.

Golf literature, on the whole, is on a very high level—which is perhaps not surprising considering the antiquity of the game and its popularity among the educated classes. No other sport can offer such fine reading—with the possible exception of exploration, or game hunting. Browsing through the book bag I found myself introduced to the works of Bernard Darwin—an absolutely first-rate writer, so good that one can sit with one's feet up and read about matches that took place a half-century before and skip dinner or delay an appointment to find out how it came out in the end. It was a dangerous practice to begin a chapter by Darwin. He wrote with such dedication and erudition about his subject and yet with such ease that it almost seemed a trick; and then one could see that at the base of his skill was a profound, almost mystical awe of the game. Here he is, for example, writing about his fixation with golf:

> *I write as one who has been perhaps a fond and foolish devotee, and may have done himself little good by it, but I can look back gratefully on many agreeable hours spent—or even wasted in playing. I think not only of quiet corners of many courses, but of many fields where the grass was so long that almost every stroke required a search; I think of a mountain top in Wales and a plain in*

*Macedonia; of innumerable floors on which I have tried to hit the
table legs; I recall rain and wind and mud and the shadows of
evening falling, so that the lights came twinkling out in the houses
round the links, and the ball's destiny was a matter of pure
conjecture. Remembering all these things, I can say that I may have
been an unprofitable practicer of the game, but at any rate I have
been a happy one.*

Bernard Darwin's grandfather was the great naturalist, Charles, but
he is mentioned rarely in the Darwin books; Darwin's maternal grandfather appears more frequently—an affectionate portrait of a man who
for hygienic reasons of his own never wore socks. He was an amateur
phrenologist and had a greenhouse full of skulls with bumps. According
to Darwin he was a champion of lost causes. He had an "infallible rec-
ipe" for growing strawberries, but annually the strawberry patch would
be searched without success for signs of growth. Certainly he was a man
closer in character to the Sisyphean aspects of golf than the great scien-
tist. Darwin, who gave up a law practice he despised for golf, was an
excellent player himself (he reached the quarter-finals of the British
Amateur), and his ABC's of golf as described in his books are
marvelous—as candid as the remarks of a hellfire preacher. He says of
faults for example:

*There are certain faults which can only be cured in the most obvious
way, namely by trying to avoid them. For example, if a man be
conscious of leaping, figuratively speaking, into the air at the top of
his swing, and so being far too much on his toes, I know of no
remedy, save that he must try not to jump; he must peg his feet down
by dint of sheer determination.*

Darwin has his successors in golf literature—Henry Longhurst,
Charles Price, and Herbert Warren Wind, among others. What is interesting is that the great golfers themselves, with an occasional helping

hand from a ghost writer, have a considerable flair for the written word: Harry Vardon, Bobby Jones, Sam Snead, Tony Lema, Ben Hogan. Though their work may not be honed to such a fine degree as the professional writer's (with the exception of the Jones books, which are at Darwin's level), still there is a finesse and distinction which is a refreshing departure from the usual sports literature and certainly distinct from the "as-told-to" books by contemporary athletes in other sports.

I asked someone about this once, and he reflected and said perhaps a game in which euphoria was so short-lived, the bad shot lurking so surely in the future, was conducive to the state of contained melancholy which produced first-rate literature. Dostoevski, for instance. Conrad. Hardy.

Certainly the literature was contained, and even great moments of triumph were described in muted tones, as if excessive smugness would bring on a lengthy attack of the shanks from on high. Always there was great respect for the fellow golfer, however confused his game. Harry Vardon's book *The Complete Golfer* is absolutely fine (he had help from a superb anonymous ghost writer) — written in as easy and effective a style as his golf stroke, which was so effortless that he often hit a ball with a pipe in his mouth. Yet he shows a considerable compassion for the lower echelons of golfers — such compassion, indeed, that he seems one of them in a common struggle against adversity. Here are his subheadings to Chapter III of *The Complete Golfer,* which tell something of his concern: "The Mistakes of a Beginner"; "Too Eager to Play a Round"; "Despair that Follows"; "A Settling Down to Mediocrity"; "The Sorrows of a Foozler"; "All Men May Excel," etc.

This last seemed, as I settled into my book-bag reading that night, an idiom common to all the books: there was hope. Of course, some writers were of a gloomy turn of mind. Particularly, Sir W. A. Simpson, author of *The Art of Golf,* one of the great classics of the 1880's. In writing of the drawbacks of golf he pointed out that "winds cease to be east, south, west, or north. They are head, behind, sideways, and the sky is bright according to the state of the game." Why, it was even possible, he wrote, "by too much of it [golf] to destroy the mind; a man with a Roman nose and a high forehead may play away his profile."

But then, shot through the golf books I read were gentle suggestions that everything was going to work out all right. Even Simpson, the melancholy peer, writes: "All those who drive thirty yards suppose themselves to be great *putters*.... The duffer is a duffer merely because every second shot is missed. Time and care will eliminate the misses and then!"

The message of one of the books I looked into called *The Happy Golfer*, for example, was "that the major force of all life is *hope*. The golfer should have 'Spero Meliora' as his coat of arms—and he should strain for 'the faintest note that comes from the one long string that remains on the almost dismantled harp.'" I particularly liked the last image—the analogy of the dismayed golfer struggling off the last green as an "almost dismantled harp."

Bernard Darwin, with a fine classical bent, also had an occasional Latin phrase to brighten the golfer's day. "Nec Temere, Nec Timide," he suggested for those about to step into a bunker.

Darwin would always vow on New Year's Eve that his next year of golf would be a fortuitous one, and he always believed that "a miracle would occur, and the dash and strength and glory of hitting which are vouchsafed to the few might suddenly one fine morning descend on us, too, so that we should be as creatures transfigured and made splendid for evermore."

Even great golfers could not do without such mental bolstering. Darwin reports that Braid, the Scottish champion, "went to bed a short driver and woke up a long one."

That was a good place to stop my first night's reading, I thought. I turned out the light. I could hear the sea moving at the breakwater across the 18th fairway. I tried to remember Darwin's prayer: "Creatures transfigured and made splendid for evermore...." Was that it? I stared into the darkness. In the recesses of my mind there was a gentle murmuring. I strained to hear. A message from Braid? From Vardon? Someone called, "Smarten up down there!" I groaned gently. The Japanese admirals were with me, smiling, bobbing their heads....

CHAPTER 7

There was time at sunrise to get in a touch of practice. One item I had not thought to bring on the tour was a bag of practice balls. The Del Monte Lodge did not supply the familiar wire pails filled with red-circled practice balls that one is able to rent at almost all country clubs. Abe had told me not to mind. He had said he would scrounge around his house and bring some practice balls with him the next morning so that we could get some "loosening up" before the first round started. He said he had some balls "down cellar," he thought, from his shoreline collecting days, and he would fetch them up.

Early the next morning he banged on the door of my room at the lodge, and I could hear him wheezing and clearing his throat, and he called out, "Don't be keeping too long."

I got ready. Just before coming out I bathed my hands in the hottest water I could stand. I had read and remembered that it was a preparatory device Gene Sarazen had often used in brisk weather to get his finger muscles loose and his hands supple.

It was chilly outside. Abe was wearing a huntsman's cap with flaps that came over his ears. The street lamps were still on.

"Mornin', Abe," I said.

My hands began to smoke from their hot-water bath.

Abe noticed.

I was somewhat surprised myself by the volume of condensation that rose from my hands into the crisp air. I waved them to get them dry.

"Let it go!" Abe said. "You ain't putting it out that way."

He must have thought I was trying to extinguish a runaway ciga-rette, or a cigar, or something that had caught fire in my hands.

"It's all right, it's all right," I said noncommittally. The steam rose. "They're a bit wet, that's all. It's all right."

We started for the practice range. After a few seconds, the hands stopped smoking.

"You bring some balls?" I asked.

"Ten," Abe said.

There was a faint ground mist easing off the grass and a chill in the air that reminded one of duck-shooting dawns. When we got to the tee it was still so dark that one *heard* rather than saw the few golfers already practicing—the quick swish of the wet-weather gear as a golfer went through his swing, the click of the club head connecting with the ball, and then the hum of the ball as it flew out over the dark field. Far in the dis-tance the caddies, just dark shapes from where we were, could look up and see the ball against the sky, which was light, so they could follow its flight and move accordingly. Pretty soon, with the sun coming quickly, the balls sailing out would, at the top of their trajectory, glow gold suddenly, like planets, then wink off as they dropped into shadow. Down below, where we stood, it was still dark. A tall line of pines close behind us cut the light, and in the grass one could hardly see the tee on which to place the ball.

Abe had a fishnet bag with him; a small clutch of balls bunched in the bottom. We found a place in the line, and he rolled the practice balls out. Even in the gloom I could see their condition—one of the balls rolled erratically, like a pear—and I asked, "Abe, is that a gutta-percha you've got in there? Those seem a mite shopworn."

"Well," Abe said, "I keep things down cellar I can't get rid of easy."

He strolled out across the practice field, his fishnet bag dangling loosely. I hit some eight and nine irons, just to get limber, and the rick-ety balls fluttered out to him noisily, like paper in a windstream. I noticed Abe ranged after them with great agility, and even when I was teeing up a ball he seemed to be moving around out there in the gloom, looking and darting about like a cattle egret.

Paul Christman, the former football star, was down the line from me, also hitting out short irons. He had an eye on Abe.

"That caddy of yours has great range," he called to me, a gentle dig in his voice. "He's moving around like a free safety."

I hit all the balls out to Abe except the one that had rolled like a pear. It had done so, as I now could see in the brightening light, because a portion of its interior protruded like a polyp. I waved for Abe. He trotted in. He gave a glance at the remaining ball.

"I thought it might explode if I hit it," I said.

"No mind," he said. He poured the contents of his fishnet bag out on the grass. There were now about twenty balls, many of them bright and pristine, with not a mark on them except, perhaps, as I imagined suddenly, a small PC for Paul Christman stamped on the cover. Christman was a very serious amateur golfer, the sort who might stamp his practice balls. He was always on the practice tee when I looked out there.

I peered warily down the line toward him. Abe was wheezing loudly with pleasure. "I got us some," he announced.

"Yes," I said, softly. "So I see."

When the sun pulled up over the pines and the practice field shone in its light, Abe had to cut down on his activities. But his fishnet bag was always bulkier when we had finished a morning's practice. I suspected that he thinned out the crop when he got home, picking out the best ones, because each morning he would arrive with his "down-cellar" balls, the original ten, the ball with the polyp among them.

"I thought we had more of these," I said one morning.

"I found ten balls down cellar. You lost one when you hooked it that time. Now there are nine," he said to me, reproachfully.

CHAPTER 8

Just before setting out for the Monterey course, we checked the bag and took out two clubs—the four wood and the three iron—to get down to the fourteen-club limit. I told Abe I felt more comfortable with the woods, even though I knew a wood shot off the fairway was riskier than a long iron. The pros usually carry only two woods in their bag—the driver and the brassie—and they supplement the irons with a one iron. In the old days, until the fourteen-club restriction, pros carried many more clubs, one for every conceivable situation, including such oddities as left-handed clubs for lies where a right-handed swing was impossible. Harry Cooper carried twenty-six clubs and Lawson Little's caddy had to struggle through a round carrying *thirty* clubs. Leo Diegel had four drivers in his bag—one that had a hook built into it, another with a slice, and then he had a pair of drivers especially tailored for wind conditions, one with a high loft for taking advantage of a prevailing wind, and the other with an almost flat face so the ball would bore low into an oncoming wind.

Abe shook his head over the number of woods we kept. I said I believed in them. The irons seemed dinky to me—I never could believe the thin blade could drive the ball very far, and I was apt to press, whereas the wood club seemed so much more of a weapon.

I had on a pair of green golfing slacks. The Pro-Shu shoes were shined. I didn't wear a golf glove, though I should have. It had been my impression that a golf glove was to keep the hands from getting sore and blistering, and since my hands were relatively tough from pre-tournament practice I had not bothered to buy a glove. I learned later that the glove is used mainly to improve the grip.

As for the golf hat I had at hand, I looked carefully at it. It was one of the items that came in the gift kit amateurs received when they checked in at the headquarters. I don't usually wear hats, but it was gray with red piping that read Bing-Crosby-Pro-Am and there was a tab in the back for adjusting the head size so the wearer could either have it sit up jauntily on top of the head, or pull it low and shield the face in brooding shadow. I decided against it finally. Afterward I noticed that the golf professional rarely wore the golfing cap that came with his kit. He would almost invariably wear the golf hat received in the kit from the previous tournament which would indicate that he was an established figure on the circuit and a regular tour performer. Many of the golfers at the Crosby wore Los Angeles and San Diego Open hats, which were the two tournaments that preceded the Crosby.

We drove out to Monterey. It was easy to find Bob Bruno. He was on the practice putting green, a very tall man bending in mournful, prayerful study over a putter that seemed undersized, a child's toy. We chatted a while. He seemed serious and well-meaning, a big-featured man with a slightly pock-marked face. He was wearing a black golfer's glove. He wore a San Diego Open cap. He said he had gone to bed quite early the night before. He was very difficult to get up in the morning, he went on. People really had to work on him, pummel and pull him, and sometimes they just gave up. He didn't want that to happen, so he had had a long night's rest. And there he was, he said smiling, ready to tear the course apart.

The first hole at Monterey was a par 5, an easy one, perhaps the easiest hole in the tournament, downhill off an elevated tee, onto a wide fairway through the pines, mottled with the slants of the early-morning sun flickering through, and the shadows blue-green.

The pro shop is set right behind the first tee. A small crowd was on hand. It was cold, and many of them were in the pro shop looking out through the plate-glass window. I avoided looking at their faces.

There were a number of foursomes in front of us. Bob Tuthill, an assistant PGA tournament director, was standing by the first tee. I fell into nervous conversation with him. He had the comforting opinion that an amateur's shots off the first tee were likely to be good, whatever the pressure: having done nothing wrong or right, and yet to indulge in a streak of bad habit, the second-rate golfer had an excellent chance of stroking a decent shot.

"That reminds me," said Tuthill. "There was this important occasion, opening this European golf course, when the officials prevailed on a German prince, big corpulent fellow, to tee off and hit the first ball. He stepped up, with all these witnesses and newspaper people standing around, and a caddy way down the fairway to retrieve that first ceremonial ball, easing in a bit, perhaps, guessing what was to come, and the prince took a lunge at the ball and missed it completely. Very embarrassing. But there was an old British professional who found the exact words to say: "And now," he said, "if your Royal Highness is ready, I think the opening stroke should now be made.""

"Great tact," I said. "I trust you'll produce the same line if by chance I imitate his Royal Highness. It's quite likely."

"For a small price," Tuthill said.

Maurie Luxford was at the starter's table. He held a bullhorn, and announced each foursome as the players approached the tee and prepared to drive. "And now, about to drive, playing out of Burning Tree Golf Club, the very personable..."

Luxford's introductions were famous on the tour, especially for their hyperbole, which was as flamboyant as a prize-fight announcer's. Over the years many contestants found that their stature bloomed at Luxford's hands. Pandel Savic, for example, who usually played with Jack Nicklaus in the pro-ams, was the Ohio State quarterback, quite a good one, who took his team to the Rose Bowl in 1950. That was his highest honor. In his first Crosby, he was introduced by Luxford as being chosen

All-Big Ten. Then through the years he rose to Honorable Mention All-America, then All-America, and finally he reached a pinnacle of sorts when Luxford announced him as 1950's Heisman Trophy winner.

Luxford was particularly famous for his gift of embroidering the reputations of obscure amateur golfers. He would announce a contestant: "The world's greatest Dodge dealer in San Bernardino!" Or of an obscure stock company actor: "And now, as Bing Crosby himself would surely say, an actor's actor! A *great* actor's actor. Ted Bong."

The crowd would stir and crane forward.

"Who?"

"I think he said Ted Bong. Or Wong. Something like that."

"Oh yes."

My own introduction was short. Luxford announced my name and he added that I was playing out of the Piping Rock Golf Club of Long Island. "He is a...*the* writer from Long Island," he stuck on as an embellishment. "His playing partner is Bob Bruno, the very personable long-ball hitter from San Diego, playing partner of Andy Williams last year, nearly *seven* feet tall, ladies and gentlemen..." etc., etc.

Bruno and I won the honor. I drove first. "Keep it easy," I kept telling myself. The shot boomed down the fairway, long and straight, and behind the bay window a few spectators clicked their rings and knuckles against the glass in appreciation.

Bruno was delighted. "Holy smoke!" he said.

I took an apple from the bowl on the starter's table, and our foursome set off down the course.

I had a good lie, and my second shot was nearly as long as the first, and straight, rolling up to within 40 yards of the green.

"We're moving," said Abe.

As we walked along, I began to feel guilty about my 18 handicap. Would the golf committee complain? Would fingers be pointed and voices lowered when I entered the Del Monte Lodge with six natural birdies on my score card—our team score some 17 or 18 strokes ahead of the nearest competitor?

Bruno came up and walked alongside to encourage me. "You're in great shape," he said. "A good approach, and you've got a chance at a birdie. With your handicap stroke, that'll start us off great—two under par."

I studied the next shot with care. I took out a pitching wedge, a club I felt easy with; but as I stood over the ball, bringing back the club, my old terror of being an unwieldy machine swept over me, and I *shanked* the shot, dumping it into a trap off to one side of the green. The ball skidded off almost at a diagonal. The silence was absolute until I broke it with a strained cry, as if after the first two superb shots the absurdity of the third was unbelievable—like two graceful ballet steps, and then a splay-legged pratfall, a thump and a high squawk of dismay.

I stalked miserably into the trap, and, not catching enough sand with my wedge, I lifted the ball into a grove of pines on the other side of the green. I was still about 40 yards away, just the distance I'd been two strokes back. The ball was stymied in the pines, and it took me two more strokes to get out.

"Pick it up," Bruno called petulantly. "There's no use." He himself had bogeyed the hole. We had started off the tournament by losing one stroke to par on the easiest hole on the peninsula.

"I'm awful sorry," I said to Bruno.

"I told your caddy to stick that pitching wedge in the bag and leave it there," he said. "You had a clear line. You should've rolled it up there with a four or a five iron—a pitch-and-run shot." He shook his head.

"I'm not so hot on those," I said. "I've always felt comfortable with that wedge."

"We'll get going," he said more cheerfully. "Hell, we've got 53 holes to go."

CHAPTER 9

Just off the tee, we heard someone over in the next fairway, beyond a thick grove of pines, call out "Fore! Fore!" and then we heard the crack of the ball ricocheting in the trees. Bruno looked over. He said, "Well, that must have been some hook." We had all ducked instinctively. We raised up, with sheepish grins, looked at each other to check reactions, and resumed our march down the fairway. My drive had been a good one and I could see the ball sitting up, almost all of it visible, which suggested a good lie. Bruno's ball was beyond it, and he too appeared to have a good lie, and we were striding along together feeling pretty good about things. I said, "Every time I hear the word 'fore' I think of a cartoon of a friend of mine, Fred Gwynne, who was a well-known television actor for a while. He drew it when we were both at college together and working on the Harvard *Lampoon,* the humor magazine. He came in one day with this cartoon of a man standing on a golf tee about to drive off. Gwynne's style was patterned after Charles Addams', and maybe Virgil Partch's, a touch macabre, one would say, and in his cartoon the golfer had four heads, four sets of arms holding four golf clubs, which were about to hit four golf balls set up on four golf tees. He's looking down the fairway and he's yelling 'Four!', spelled f-o-u-r."

Bruno nodded gravely.

"Well, we never published that cartoon," I said, "because someone suggested that it would be funnier if instead of 'Four!' the caption read 'Fore!'"

I spelled it. "The twist would be, y'see," I said as we strode along, "that this man dominated by fours would be yelling not 'Four!' but 'Fore!'—f-o-r-e."

"Oh yes," said Bruno.

"The *Lampoon* staff argued about it, back and forth, and the vote was just about even. Besides, Gwynne, though he was a fair draftsman, well, he'd had some trouble doing all those arms, and the four heads and all, coming out of that one torso. So the golfer had a sort of centipede look about him that made it hard to get a laugh going which*ever* caption was used."

"Yah. I can see that."

We were getting up to my ball.

"How would you have voted, Bob—'Fore' or 'Four'?"

He began sloughing his spikes through the grass as we walked along.

"Four sets of arms this guy had?" he asked. "Four *heads*?"

It occurred to me quickly that I had suggested something that might stick uncomfortably in his mind, like the burr of an insult, or the Japanese admirals that I carried around in *my* head, and that his concentration on golf would suffer.

"Forget it, Bob," I said hastily.

"No, no," he said. "I see the problem."

"It's not worth thinking about," I said. "No one's ever going to publish the thing—either way."

"No, it's interesting."

We had reached the ball. Abe handed me a three wood. I tried to concentrate on the shot. Immediately, the four-headed golfer began tramping around in my own mind, along with the Japanese admirals. I had the feeling that the golfer was trying to get in the wheelhouse. The Japanese were looking nervously over their shoulders; they could hear him standing out in the corridor beating on the steel companionway door in a quick tattoo of fists, eight of them, and he was shouting through that thick door: "Four!" (Or was it "Fore"?)

I topped the shot and sent it in a quick hissing thrust through the grass.

"It's straight," Bruno said. He was often solicitous, if his mood was right.

He walked on and hit his own shot—a fine one that ended up on the edge of the green. We did not speak of the four-headed golfer again. He had apparently dismissed it from his mind. But I had three or four bad shots in succession. My concentration was still off. The banging on the steel door continued. Abe said to me, "I don't know what you and your partner were carrying on about back there—what it is he said to ail you and make you worried and put-out. Whatever, forget it. So we can get *moving*."

"Abe, I was telling *him* something."

"You quit worrying about him," he said huskily. "You got plenty about yourself to worry about."

CHAPTER 10

We ended the first day's play discouraged. Bruno's score was 77, and our team score of 74 would be perhaps 14 strokes behind the leaders. I was unnerved by my own game. I never could put together more than three good shots in a row. The fourth, which would invariably have stripped a stroke from par for our team, would go askew.

I could not decide what was wrong. My hope had been that the professional with me, Bruno, would offer advice. He would take a glance at my swing and say, "Well now, look here, you've got to bring the left hand around jes' a mite on the shaft, and maybe you got to open up your stance some. Try that." And then I would do what had been suggested. I would move the left hand around and open the stance, and the ball would take off into the distance with a quality and verve about it that had not been there before.

In fact, the professionals have enough to worry about with their own game, and their advice to amateurs is usually limited to the choice of a club, or often, if requested, they will read the green for their partner. Bob Bruno rarely had anything to say. He cared terribly, but very often he looked away as I addressed the ball, turning his body and staring moodily off into the pines. I was reminded of Ben Hogan's caddy at Carnoustie when Hogan won the British Open. The caddy had the disconcerting habit of dropping his head in his hands just as Hogan was about to putt. It was not the most assuring of reactions.

I went back to my room after the round. A lesson, I thought. But from whom? It seemed so odd to be veritably engulfed by professional golfers—everywhere you looked, there they were—and yet unable to bring oneself to ask any of them for advice. It was no more appropriate to ask the tour professionals than it would be if I were a dentist at a convention wandering around with my mouth ajar asking for an opinion. What made it almost impossible to seek advice was my 18 handicap. If an amateur played to a 2, say, he could with impunity strike up a conversation with the professional just down the line on the practice range, who would turn and see that the amateur was smoking out his shots with authority. After some easy talk the amateur could say, "Charlie, take a peek and see if you don't find a *hitch* or something in my right side as I come into the ball."

And he would swing, and the pro, standing alongside, leaning on his club, nonchalantly, with the toe of one golf shoe set behind the heel of the other, would say, "Well, yes. Try moving that thumb around just a mite."

And that would be that.

There are so many stories about the key. Tommy Armour was supposed to chop strokes off his pupils' scores simply by the way he conducted his lessons—sitting under an umbrella at Boca Raton. "Educated languor—that's the example I want to set my golfers," he used to say. Or the tips that Archie Compton of Bermuda's Mid-Ocean Club used to give. He was a big, rugged and furious man (it was often said that an 82 in the 1930 British Open at Hoylake when he led the field with a 68 had left its mark on him) and a teacher who bullied and shamed his pupils into improvement—a man of such lack of tact that on one occasion he exasperated the Marchioness of Northampton to such an extent that she slugged him on the shin with an eight iron. He is supposed to have yelped sharply and told her to hit a golf ball in just the same style. "You've got it!" he said. "You've got it!"

One of the famous stories about the key concerns Stewart Maiden, a dour Scottish pro at East Lake in Atlanta, Bobby Jones' home course, who was called by Jones just before the 1925 National Open at Worcester Country Club in Worcester, Massachusetts. Jones was having his troubles and Maiden arrived by train and went out to watch him on the practice tee. In the middle of a batch of balls, after squinting at Jones' swing, Maiden suddenly said, "Why don't you try hittin' the ball with your *backswing*?" With this, he turned away and took the next train home. Jones slowed his swing down, and while he didn't win that year (he tied and lost to Willie Macfarlane in a play-off which went two 18-hole rounds) he had rid his game of a major fault.

But that was Bobby Jones. It would take great courage, if not gall, to turn from a series of hooks and slices on the practice range, and even a topped shot or two, as an 18-handicap golfer, and ask the professional alongside, someone like Jack Nicklaus, for a tip. The professional would glance over and his face would compress slightly as if a sudden slag heap had materialized on his lawn; he would sigh and out of politeness he would step over and try to find something to say, which would probably be as follows:

"Well, I think we'd better start with the grip."

I doubt if lessons would have been of much use. During the few lessons I have taken I have often been puzzled by the instructor's phrases. "A bit fat," he'll say. "You hit it just a bit fat." What does that mean? Or he'll say: "Don't come off the ball!" What does *that* mean? "Well," they tell you, looking at you sadly, "That's to say you hit through without moving your left side out of the way *too fast* or moving the right side *in* too fast."

"Oh yes."

My only refuge was to peer into the book bag back in the room for some of the underlined phrases and aphorisms.

Some of them I had selected for solace, such as the fine lines of compensation P. G. Wodehouse puts in Wallace Chesney's mind as that poor duffer considers his miserable game: "It is better to travel hopefully than to arrive. He realized now why pros were all grave, silent men who seemed to struggle manfully against some secret sorrow. It was because they were all too darned good." Or Rex Beach's solace on the same subject of the ills that beset the superior golfer: "Gone were the days when he could top a ball and say something funny."

That afternoon, just in from the round, I picked up a book by Henry Cotton and found myself concentrating on a passage in which he was discussing hands: "A golfer is only as good as his hands." He described the value of having a long left thumb which bends back easily—that such an attribute makes a golf swing, a good one, much easier. Sam Snead, I read, can bend his thumb to touch his forearm, and some people consider this the secret of his great swing: supposedly it's very hard not to swing a club properly and with grooved ease if you have this long pliable thumb.

I considered my own thumb. It moves up off the plane of my hand ninety degrees, with a certain slant back to the first joint—a normal thumb I would have thought. But not a golfer's thumb, apparently. Ah, well—as Vardon had warned: "A golfer must never be morbid."

I left the cottage and dropped into the Del Monte cocktail lounge to have a beer. Andy Williams, the singer, was sitting at a table and he waved me over.

"How did your round go?" he asked.

"Not so hot," I said. "I'm feeling morbid. We're a long way off the pace—probably 14, 15 strokes. My game fell apart. I'm trying to figure what went wrong with it. Maybe something to do with my hands. A golfer is only as good as his hands," I said grandiosely.

I told him about Sam Snead's thumb.

"I've got a notion about putting," Williams said. "Are you in the market for advice?"

I told him that I certainly was. My putting had gone badly. "Well," he said, "listen to this." He leaned forward and suggested that one's putting might be improved by executing the stroke, assuming that it was a short putt, with one's eyes shut tight.

"What's that again?" I asked.

"You hit the putt with the eyes closed," Williams said. "What you do is look at the ball, and then at the cup, concentrating on both, so that when you close your eyes the scene is still right there in your mind—like

"An example of body English—which to judge from the gloomy set of expression did little to assist the shot. Note Abe's expression; he is the caddy holding the flag marked '7.'" (*Russ Halford*)

when you look at a bright light bulb and close your eyes, the light's still there, just the outline of it, right?"

"Sure."

"Well, then you putt," Williams said. "The beauty of it is that if you putt with your eyes closed, there are no distractions, no newspapers blowing to complicate things, no sudden movement in the gallery, and you don't have the idea that your caddy is scowling at you. The trouble with putting with your eyes open is that there is too much to notice, too much for the mind to grasp. With the eyes closed, all the extraneous matter is wiped out, even the color, and what you have left in your mind's eye are the essentials — the ball and the cup."

"Do you actually do this?" I asked, fascinated. "Are you seriously telling me that you putt with your eyes closed?"

He looked at me. "Hell, no," he said laughing, "who'd have enough courage to close his eyes? Can you imagine what would happen if such a thing got around the country club, and just as you were about to putt with your eyes closed some practical joker bent down and snatched the ball away? There you'd be, your mind just tight with concentration, and you move the putter for that little putt and hit nothing, nothing at all! Can you imagine what that would do to the sanity of a golfer?"

"Well, that's a thought," I said.

I tried it, though, when I had finished the beer, out on the practice putting green in front of the lodge, just to make sure it wasn't a revelation of great value. The evening was coming. Abe was in front of the caddy shop. He came over. I told him about it. He was scornful. "I got enough troubles," he said, "to be worrying about leading some golfer around the course who keeps his eyes closed."

"It's just for putting."

"Well," said Abe, "it might get to be a habit." He shook his head and refused to talk about it further. "If you're getting advice," he said, "why not get yourself some *good* advice so that we can get ourselves *moving* in this tournament?"

CHAPTER 11

The easiest book to turn to in the book bag, when I had an hour or so to loll around in my room or out on the terrace that overlooked the 18th fairway and the ocean beyond, was a volume called *The Golfer's Handbook*. It is a British publication, thick as an almanac, and in it is every conceivable golfing record. You can find out who won the Isle of Wight Ladies' Championship in 1929 (Mrs. P. Snelling).

The book, for all its statistics, rules, and tables, has an odd and refreshing individuality and, indeed, an irreverence about golf which in my difficulties with the game I found very comforting. Most of the character of the book turns up in the section entitled "Miscellaneous," which includes such topics, identified by subheadings, as "Freak Matches"; "Birds and Animals Interfering with Golf Balls and Attacking Players"; Dark, Playing In"; "Golf Links on Fire"; "Longest Holes"; "Legless Golfers"; "Balls Hit to and from Great Heights"; etc., etc. The paragraphs under such headings are sprightly and often, typical of British journals such as *Country Life*, are the ultimate in minutiae. For example, the following item of absolutely no consequence, with a bit of ethnic editorializing, appears under the heading "Miscellaneous Incidents and Strange Golfing Facts": "In a competition at Craigentinny, Edinburgh, 13th May 1939, a player, when looking for his ball in the rough, found seven others. This incident of golfing treasure-trove is all the more remarkable as it happened in Scotland."

The editors may be interested in little harmless digs of this sort, but there is also a somewhat more satanic edge to be found—especially under the odd heading "Hit by Ball—Distance of Rebound." A number of cases are given. The following is representative: "Mr. R. J. Barton...was approaching the green of a blind hole 354 yards long, when his ball struck a caddy, named John M'Niven, on the head as he was replacing the flag in the hole. The ball rebounded 42 yards 2 feet 10 inches, which distance was measured twice in the presence of three people." Thus ends the item, without a word about the caddy, whom I've always imagined sitting dolefully on the edge of a bunker, holding his head between his hands while the measuring tapes are being stretched out and one fellow is calling, "...and two feet ten inches. Got that, Tom?" And the other, holding the tape, is saying, "What's that again?"

"Two feet ten!"

"Right. Got it."

This record took place on September 1, 1913, at Machrie on the Isle of Arran, Scotland. The former record was a rebound of 34 yards off a caddy's noggin conked in August, 1908, on the Blairgowrie Golf Course. The *world's record,* which still stands, happened on September 28, 1913, at the 7th hole of the Premier Mine Golf Course in South Africa. A 150-yard drive by Edward W. Sladward hit a native caddy on the forehead just above the right eye, and the ball, which was a "Colonel," bounded back on a direct line 75 yards. The tapes were brought out and the distance, as in the case of the John M'Niven affair, was measured. The native's name was not recorded (a sign of those times and perhaps the locale) but it was reported that he suffered no more than a slight abrasion of the skin and was able to continue. The ball's name, though, the Colonel, got into the records, and so does a description of the drive which produced the record: "...one so dear to the heart of a golfer—a hard, raking shot."

I have often thought about the scene, just as I have about the John M'Niven rebound—particularly about the Colonel golf ball.

"Charlie, what's that distance again?"

"It's seventy-*five,* seventy-five *yards.*"

"Good Lord. That has it all over the Islay record."

"What? I can hardly hear you."

"It beats the Machrie record."

"I've got the tape absolutely stretched out. Are you holding it at your end?"

"Right! Oh Lord, Charlie, I've got the record!"

"Bully! Edward! Bully for you."

"A hard, raking shot, Charlie."

"What?"

"It was a Colonel I hit. A Colonel."

(A side glance at the caddy.) "A what?"

"A Colonel."

"Oh, a Colonel *ball.* Bully for the Colonel. Oh bully," etc.

Violence quite evidently fascinates golf editors. In *The Golfer's Handbook* they have chosen to immortalize the following: "At Texas [the editors are often vague as to exact place names] Mr. Moody Weaver in a practice swing used such force that he broke his leg in two places." Or this: "At Darwin, Australia, in 1951, a lady, so excited by a successful shot, threw up her hands, stepped back and stumbled over her golf bag. She fell and broke her arms above the wrists."

By chance, I actually received further news from the Moody Weaver people. His daughter wrote, in fact, that *The Golfer's Handbook* information was not completely accurate. The father had fallen and broken *both* legs rather than one leg in two places. The event, which she wished cleared up, took place in Wichita Falls.

The *Handbook* editors are quick to chronicle the hazards of nature on the golf course: "At Rose Bay, New South Wales, D. J. Bayly MacArthur, on stepping into a bunker, began to sink. He shrieked for help and was rescued when up to the armpits." Or: "A magnificent beech tree with a trunk five feet in diameter, at Killermont Golf Club, Glasgow, collapsed when hit by a ball driven by a member."

Since the editors are often scanty with details about items that beg for amplification, one of the particular pleasures of browsing through the *Handbook* is the flow it can give one's imagination, as in the case of those rebound records. For example, the first item under the heading "Freak Matches" reads: "In 1912, the late Harry Dearth, an eminent vocalist, attired in a complete suit of heavy armor, played a match at Bushey Hall. He was beaten by 2 and 1." One can only lean back and speculate. "2 and 1" means that in match play—competing for each hole rather than for overall score, which is medal play—the armor-suited golfer was beaten when he was down 2 holes with only 1 to play. What sort of a golfer must his opponent have been to allow the armor-clad gent to stay in contention until the 17th hole? Was he somehow equivalently handicapped—playing out of a potato sack, for example? Perhaps his game suffered from the embarrassment of playing with someone who creaked and swayed in armor down the fairways. Did Dearth do any sudden singing? That could explain it. Just at the backswing to have that singer's voice boom out, muffled by the visor but still concussive, with an added timbre by dint of coming from the great voice box of iron.

Sometimes there is an item that is pleasant to visualize, like a cartoon: "At Dungannon Golf Links, Country Tyrone, October 1936, a ram attacked two players on the 7th green. They tried to beat it off with their clubs but were unsuccessful..."

Typically, the *Handbook* does not specify what it means by "unsuccessful," whether, indeed, the players survived the assault by the ram, and got back to the clubhouse to have a shaky whiskey, or whether the ram prevailed completely, and did them in, so that their lifeless forms had to be removed when discovered the next morning by the greenskeepers:

"...Charlie, put in a call for a wheelbarrow. Have a couple of them sent down from the toolshed so we can get these two members carted away before the first foursome comes through."

"Right."

"Nasty business cluttering up the course like this. A matter for the Greens Committee…" etc.

I could always count on the *Handbook.* It was a fine relief from the realities of my travails out on the golf course.

CHAPTER 12

The trouble with *The Golfer's Handbook* was that it was not a practical solution to my golfing woes. That evening, after supper, I came back to my room and looked at the notes I had kept of my day's play at Monterey. I found that one bad shot was almost invariably followed by another, and then another, until there was a whole stretch of them to assault one's poise.

> *5th: Fair drive. Long iron to right of green, ball lodging under tire of Cushman pickup truck. Truck carefully moved. Poked ball on green with six iron. Three-putted, missing two-footer.*
> *6th: Feeling low about two-footer. Apologized to Bruno. Hit drive out of bounds. Hit another drive out of bounds. Apologized again. Picked up and left Bruno responsible for the hole.*
> *7th: Hit drive 15 feet into gully. In appalling mental condition. Apologized...*

It is one of the precepts of golf that a bad shot is best dismissed from mind immediately. It is not easy to do. Perhaps the one who could do it best was Walter Hagen, who was famous for his bad shots, particularly off his woods, the weakest department of his game. He accepted the fact that a wild shot would come from time to time, and rather than fretting and being nervous and wondering when it would come, he allowed it to, and then did not let it disturb him when it did. I could not emulate him. My fingers twitched nervously as I thought back on those long strings of flubs.

I spent some time that evening going over my notebooks to see if there wasn't a phrase I had copied which would be helpful. I had written down a number of aphorisms—the golf books were absolutely chock-full of them—and my notion was that if studied they might have the same effect that slogans and such commands as THINK pinned on the office walls are supposed to have on company employees.

I turned the pages and stared at a Harry Vardon suggestion: "Perfect confidence and a calm mind are necessary for the success of every stroke."

I began shifting uneasily in the armchair as I reflected on the cluttered state of my own mind. Perhaps, it occurred to me, I could try the next day to let my mind go *absolutely blank* as I stood over the ball—that I could produce a vacuum rid of Japanese admirals, the paraphernalia of that battleship control room, voices and commands stilled—*that* might be the "calm mind" to which Vardon referred. There was a school of golf instruction, I knew, whose precepts were simply to forget everything and get up and sock the ball. But I had my doubts. Is there not the famous children's wager: "Hey, I'll bet you a dollar you can't stop thinking of the word 'rhinoceros' for two minutes, that's all, two minutes, starting *now*"? Well, it's impossible, of course, because no matter how hard you think of tulips or maiden aunts who died tragically in auto crashes, the rhinoceros nibbles at the edges of your mind, stomping around out there, and then suddenly he is *inside,* and if you are honest you pay up and admit that not only is he in your mind but he's crowding its borders with his bulk.

I had sensed that the same thing would happen with my Japanese— I might get them out of the control room for a while—the area suddenly vacant and vast like an empty silo—but soon enough a steel door would creak, and there they would be, smiling and bowing, reaching for the voice trumpets...

I skimmed the pages and came across another suggestion by Harry Vardon, this one a recommendation that the golfer wear suspenders and a coat. His notion was that it helped "hold the shoulders together."

I hurried to the next; culled from Henry Cotten's book, it read: "Imagine the ball has little legs, and chop them off."

Then I came to a sheaf of notes under a paper clip which seemed more worthy of study. I had put them together some months before. They dealt with the "waggle"—namely, the movement of the club head before beginning the swing. Could my trouble lie here? It seemed farfetched, but then I had collected the waggle material because many golf authorities believe that a very specific type of waggle is not only helpful but essential to the execution of a great golf swing. Bernard Darwin, in an essay engagingly entitled "Some Reflections on Waggling," felt that a change in waggle, if things were going badly, was a definite help.

The purpose of the waggle, of course, is to see that everything is perfectly adjusted for the stroke. It is simply impossible to hit a golf shot without some sort of preliminary physical action. In his chapter Darwin speaks of two schools of wagglers. In the first, there are those who indulge in the quickest action possible (three examples of his time were Taylor, Duncan, and Ray). Doug Sanders would be a contemporary example of this school. There is a slight jiggle that moves the material of his golfing trousers as he sets himself, but his club stays right behind the ball until the actual process of his shot begins. In the second school are those who rely very heavily on the waggle to get started, who simply cannot begin without it—"...like the toy animals," Darwin writes, "who have to have a key inserted in their stomachs before they will walk around the floor." Baird and Herd and Hilton were representatives of this latter school. Darwin wrote of Herd's waggle as being a cumulative preliminary, and that, gradually, with his waggles, he lashed himself into a "sort of divine fury before hitting the ball."

In more recent times Tommy Armour was noted for his waggle—maneuvering as many as fifty times before getting his shot off. He also thought of it as an exercise which "accumulated" power.

Perhaps the oddest waggle notion was that suggested by Eddie Loos. He was the author of the famous theory "Let the club swing you," in which he urged golfers to forget about balance and arms and forward press and where the elbows are, and so forth—just forget all that doctrinaire advice and concentrate instead on getting the "feel of the club." To do this he suggested waggling one's name in the air, writing it out as if the club were a gigantic pen, the longer the name the better, and doing it as often as one could, not only as a waggle but while walking down the fairway or waiting for one's partner to hit. "Feel the club head and let it swing you." That was what Loos kept telling people. He evolved his theory from watching the golf game of a one-legged player who shot consistent rounds in the low seventies—Ernest Jones (a relatively short name to waggle in the air), a flier who had lost a leg in the war, and who could sit in a chair and hit the ball 200 yards. There were many golfers who subscribed to the theory. Leo Diegel, just as an experiment, shot a round in the 70's standing on one foot. The father of Manuel de la Torre of our foursome—Angel, his name was—was employed as a professional at the Lake Shore Country Club in Glencoe, Illinois, where the experiment started. I had asked Manuel if he was a proponent of the system. He said that he had been started off in the system, willy-nilly, because he was only eighteen months old when he was given his first club, cut down to a foot and a half, and since he couldn't talk or understand very much, certainly not the arcane instructive phrases of golf, at the beginning he was surely a natural student of the "Let the club swing you" school.

I set my notes aside and left the room for the lodge and a nightcap. I sat down at a small iron garden table in the bar and ordered a drink. The place was crowded.

"Mind if I sit down?"

I looked up. A long-faced man was standing by the table. He had a drink in his hand.

"Not at all," I said. "Have a chair."

He sat down and put his legs straight out.

"Had a good round today?" he asked. "I take it you're in the tournament."

"Yes," I said. "But I had a rotten round."

"Too bad." He had a very sunburned face, too pink for the almost leathery copper color of the pros. So I took him for an amateur. Probably a very good one. He had said "Too bad" with a certain superior sense of pity.

"I've just been sitting in my room reading about the waggle," I told him.

"The waggle?"

"Some people think it's important. You can see I'm reaching for straws. You're supposed to write your name in the air with your club."

"I'll say," he said. "The waggle? Hell, a waggle's a waggle."

"Darwin says..."

"Darwin? That old guy." He held up a hand. "Hold on," he said. He turned and gulped down his drink and ordered another. "I'll tell you what my philosophy is. What you need is confidence. Pure and simple. That's what the game is. Confidence. Concentration. Control. The three C's. That's all that the game is about."

"I see," I said.

"That's all you need to quote to yourself—those three C's."

"I know a Vardon quote," I said. "Just been reading it. Let's see: 'A golfer must never be morbid. Perfect confidence and a calm mind are necessary for the success of every stroke.'"

"Yes, yes," he said impatiently. "Boy, you certainly know some old fogies."

"Well, he agrees with you, it turns out," I said.

"Confidence *is* the thing," the golfer went on. "You got to have that. That's the first C. Very important. Byron Nelson used to say that at the height of his career when things were going good for him he could actually *tell* during a practice round whether he was going to win a tournament. He'd let his wife in on the secret. He'd say, 'Hey, stick that chicken in the oven 'cause we're going to celebrate!' Or take Ken Venturi. Before he got the shakes and that circulatory trouble in his hands, he could do it. His wife once admired a Ford Thunderbird they were giving away as a bonus to the tournament winner, and he said, 'Don't worry, honey, I'll get it for you.' Well, he did, and he said, 'I told you so.'"

"Well, I understand all that," I said. "I *want* to have confidence. But it isn't the sort of thing…"

"The most confident player I ever heard of was Max Faulkner. What confidence he had. In the Open Championship at Portrush, Northern Ireland, in 1951, he autographed a fan's book 'Open Champion'—and there were still two rounds to go. He made it too."

"I've read quite a bit about him," I said. "He used to have those old caddies. He had one called Turner, who had a great red flowing beard…"

The golfer looked at me and said: "You certainly pick up strange pieces of information. A reader, eh? Let me give you something that might be more helpful to your game."

"Yes," I said, "a redheaded caddy is not—"

"Take concentration—the second of those three C's. Let me tell you a story about Claude Harmon and concentration. Claude Harmon once told me that Hogan comes to him the year the Open was played at Winged Foot, which is Harmon's home course in New York and thus duck soup for him—every curl and swoop of it known—and Hogan says, 'You can win this. You should. But you won't. Because you play "jolly golf."'

"That riles the hell out of Harmon.

"'I'm telling you absolutely honest,' Hogan says. 'You can't play your own course half-decent. You haven't got a game plan. I could give you one, but you won't accept it, because you're stuck on "jolly golf."'

"Harmon stomps around and that phrase 'jolly golf' upsets him so much that he says he'll put himself entirely at Hogan's disposal— y'know, he would accept whatever directions Hogan gives him.

" 'All right,' Hogan says. He lays down a number of directives. They were: 'Don't answer any phones, not for a day or so before the tournament; you being a home pro, people are going to be telephoning for tickets, parking stickers, God knows what all, and Winged Foot's got a good staff to handle all that; so no phones. Then, get to the tournament exactly one half-hour before tee-off time; practice, but don't talk to anyone. On the way to the 1st tee, don't lift your eyes off the ground; don't lift your eyes off the ground for the *entire round*—it'll save you having to talk or listen to anyone; no one's likely to start a conversation unless you're looking him in the eye; just plod around staring at the ground, and keep your mind on the game. Don't say anything to anyone—don't say "good shot"; don't say a damn word. On the 18th, after you hole out, clear off of the course; don't stay around; go home.'

"That's tough on Harmon," the golfer continued. "He says, 'Can't I say anything to anyone then?' Very petulant. He's a very gregarious sort, big jowls, a howling loud voice, full of stories and he loves to talk.

" 'No,' says Hogan. 'You go home, and you think about the next day.'

"Harmon tells me that was the hardest thing," the golfer explained. "You see, you walk by the front terrace at Winged Foot with all the members sitting there, and they call out your name and they know how you've done and you know they got a big grin working, waiting for you to look up, and if you don't, if you don't recognize them, you don't last long as a club pro."

"What happened?" I asked.

"Well, Claude told me he resisted it. But he sneaks out the back way."

"Did it work?" I asked. "Claude Harmon's game plan?"

"Damn right," he said. "He didn't cop it all—but he got a 284 to Billy Casper's 282, just two strokes off the pudding."

"I wonder if Hogan lives up to his own directives?" I asked. "Does he ever talk during a round?"

"Harmon tells me never," said the golfer. "Never says a damn word. He told me that the last day of the Masters at Augusta in 1947, he was paired with Ben. Harmon made a hole-in-one on the twelfth hole. Hogan never said a thing. The people were screaming, of course, when they went down the fairway, and they got to the green, and there was the ball wedged in the hole against the flag. The first words Harmon hears Hogan say are to his caddy. He says, 'Get that flag out of there.' Hogan had a long putt for a two and he made it for his par. On the way to the next tee he said something about Claude's hole-in-one shot but he waited until then—until he'd got his own ball down."

"That's quite a story," I said when he had done. "Did you try the Hogan plan yourself today?"

"Damn right," the golfer said. "Didn't say anything to anyone. Just plodded around looking at the ground. Maybe that's why I'm talking so much now. Got a whole 18 holes of gab to get off my chest."

"Well, how did it work?"

"Didn't work at all!" he said. He gave a short burst of laughter and he took a swallow of his drink. "I shot a ninety-five on my own ball—didn't help the team a damn. I think we're lying ninety-second in the field. I tell you, trudging along looking at the ground through those last holes, I felt like a mourner following a coffin. I found a dime just off the twelfth green. Only positive thing I can say about the whole day."

"That's too bad," I said.

"Ah well. Now the third of those C's is Control," he said, moving on blithely. "What I mean by that is control of both the physical and mental. How are your nerves out there? Not so good, eh? Well, that's natural. And proper. Bobby Jones said that the worst symptom he could find in himself in a tournament was the absence of nervousness. But nerves must be kept under control. Sam Snead had a great word for it: 'cool-mad'—controlled tension, that's what he was talking about... You ever hear that phrase? Good one, isn't it? I think about it all the time. So there you have the three C's. Confidence. Concentration. Control. That's all the game is about."

"I know an interesting thing about Jones," I said.

The golfer looked at me across the brim of his drink.

"Well, he used to relax those nerves of his by lying in a tub of hot water after a round of golf and drinking a stiff highball. He said that was the finest relaxing combination he knew. Then he would get into bed and read. At Flossmoor, the year he was competing in the National Amateur Championship, he was reading Papini's *Life of Christ*."

"No kidding?"

He put his glass on the table.

"Where do you get all this information?"

"I have this book bag," I said. "I browse through it. You get a lot of interesting stuff. I don't know how *valuable* it is. It's confusing sometimes. You read about Jones and his relaxing and reading, and *then* you find out that Hagen had three hours of sleep and a hangover when he won the National Open in 1919. Sometimes the stuff is pretty esoteric. I mean last night I read a long paragraph by Henry Cotten on how to tee up the ball—you'd think *that* would be easy enough, but no, he has a special way of using the back of the hand so you get the tee the same height each time."

"What else?" asked the golfer.

"Well, a little while ago I read that Vardon thought a golfer's game would be improved if he wore suspenders and a coat. He felt it kept the swing more compact."

"Oh, yes," said the golfer. "Well, he may have a point. I mean the game's crazy enough anyway. Maybe a guy *should* get himself dolled up in a suit—hell, an *overcoat*. Why not? And he should get himself a red-bearded caddy, like that guy you were talking about, and what's that book...?"

"Papini's *Life of Christ*?"

"...Papini's *Life of Christ,* and walk around the course with it under his arm. He might have a helluva round."

I couldn't tell if he was being cynical or not. He was turning his drink rapidly in his hand.

He shook his head. "Jesus, after today I tell you I'm willing to try anything."

"How about those three C's?" I said. "That seems an awfully solid base right there."

"Jesus, I don't know," he said.

CHAPTER 13

There was a great deal of discussion about handicaps in the lodge. I was surprised to hear of the number of golfers who would willingly increase their handicaps to give them a better chance at the prizes. I could appreciate the chicanery, but I thought what a great wrench it must be to the system to look someone in the eye and announce an 18 handicap if in fact one played to a 10. It seemed more plausible to somehow *lower* one's handicap—to suggest being a better golfer than one actually was. Surely one of the grandest phrases in the language of pride is as follows: "My handicap? I play to a 2." I have on occasion announced my handicap as 15—a dismaying example of peacock pride because I was subsequently taken to the cleaners out on the course.

I had entered the tournament very late and there had been some confusion about my handicap. The information from my golf club had not arrived in time to be tabulated. The form sheets and the official scorecards passed out by the thousands had a blank opposite my name, as did the official scoreboard out on the Del Monte Lodge front lawn. People would remember my name opposite the blank, and if we were introduced they would say, "Oh, yes, you are the mysterious fellow whose handicap isn't posted."

"Yes," I would say.

"Well, what is it?" they would ask. Perhaps they thought they would be privy to information they could wager on.

"Well, I play to an 18."

"Oh."

One of the troubles with a very high handicap is that the owner is either looked upon as a poor golfer or a possible cheat. Some years back, in the days of the great Calcutta pools, two men (A and B) got themselves into a $45,000 Calcutta pool tournament at Deepdale professing handicaps of 17 and 18 respectively. Together A and B turned in a net score of 58 and 57, a total of 115 for the 36-hole, two-day tournament, and they walked off with a considerable percentage of the Calcutta betting pool. And well they might have, since it turned out that A's handicap was actually 3, and B was not even B but an impostor called C, a young player whose handicap was also 3.

If the handicaps are honest, golf is a great gambling game — one of the few where the handicap system works to perfection. Claude Harmon once told me how odd it always struck him that golfers would struggle through an afternoon of correctly handicapped golf, a perfectly equalized test of performance under pressure, and then, flushed with pleasure, sit down with their tall drinks to games of backgammon in the club rooms where the better players, because there was no handicapping system, must invariably destroy the opposition: "A guy wins forty dollars, say, a lot more, maybe," Harmon said, "on a clutch putt or so, and then loses ten times that at a game which has no method of equalizing ability."

I had heard about gambling among the professionals — rumors that Nicklaus and Palmer played for enormous wagers when they played together. The players scoffed at such stories. Perhaps a small wager would be set up during a practice round, but then once the tournament was on, the golf course itself became the common enemy. It would be a lunatic act for the golfers to set up anything that would deflect their concentration. If they gambled, it was off the course. One heard the flick of cards behind the doors in the motels, and the murmur of voices. In the older days of the tour, quite a lot of money was made on the physical attributes of Sam Snead. He was the best natural athlete among the pros—double-jointed everywhere: legs, arms, toes, fingers. The players would bet the locals that Snead, "That ol' boy sittin' in the corner over there," could leap up and touch the ceiling with his toe.

"You're joshing," the local would say in scorn.

The bets would be placed and Snead would unhook a leg from his chair and step into the middle of the room where he would gaze aloft just momentarily, and then he would fling himself up with a little squeak of effort, his leg would fly, as if a puppeteer had jerked the appropriate string, and his foot would fetch the ceiling a clout.

"That's plumb unnatural," the local would say in awe, as he reached for his pocketbook. "The guy's a *geek*—belongs in a road show, I'm telling you."

Bob Rosburg, the golfer who gripped his club with a baseball grip, had a trick of flipping playing cards great heights and distances. He would bet he could flip a card over the clubhouse roof, and he would do it, too. A quick, strong flip of the wrist and the card would soar out like a skipped stone. It was a trick you could learn, like juggling or spinning a yoyo, and he won handsome amounts doing it.

In golf, the amateurs were the heavy bettors. They were very confident about their game. A number of them who played scratch golf—the betting kind who made fortunes hustling suckers—felt they could even take a pro given the right day and circumstances. That was so much balderdash, at least according to the pros. Frank Gifford, the football player, told me about a dinner at P. J. Clarke's restaurant in New York, a big pleasant hangout which many athletes frequent. He was sitting with Arnold Palmer and their wives, and behind them, at another table, a man kept leaning across and touching Palmer on the shoulder, pushing a question or two, perhaps a comment, trying to insinuate himself into their circle. Gifford was more annoyed, he said, than Palmer. It was a farewell dinner for Palmer, who was leaving for a trip abroad—Cairo, or some such place—early the next morning. The man's efforts seemed impertinent. Then to Gifford's astonishment he realized the man was trying to hustle Palmer. He was trying to *goad* him into a match. "I'd seen the guy around before," Gifford said. "I knew he was a damn good golfer—a country-club player—but it was hard to *believe:* I mean, he was telling Palmer that he didn't think that there was that much difference between a crack amateur and a pro, and he was willing to prove it."

He wanted to tee off the next morning; he offered Palmer his choice of golf courses in the vicinity; the only concession he wanted was a handicap of one stroke a side. The two would play $500 Nassau—that is to say, a bet of five hundred a side and five hundred more on the final outcome of the match. Palmer was very polite in refusing. He half-turned in his chair and said that he was flying for the Middle East the next morning, it really wasn't something he could fit in.

The amateur put on a smug expression and he hitched his chair around to turn back to the people at his table. His voice rose as he explained how the great golfer, the pro-*fess*-ion-al, had backed down. He was pretty exuberant. He clicked his fingers and ordered a beer.

Suddenly Palmer swung his chair around. He tapped the man on the shoulder. He said: "All right. I'll tell you what I'll do. I'll postpone my trip to Cairo. We'll tee off at Winged Foot at nine o'clock tomorrow morning. O.K.?" The man was staring at him, astonished. "Except I'm not giving you one stroke a side; I'm giving you *two* strokes. And we're not playing $500 Nassau. We'll play $5000 Nassau."

Gifford said you could hear the man gulp. He looked down at the table top, and he never said another word. Palmer looked at him a bit, and then swung back to his table, disgusted. Palmer really would have stayed, Gifford felt. He wasn't trying to scare the man off by increasing the size of the bet; he had just been trying to make it worth his own while to postpone the trip. As a competitor he was interested in the challenge, perhaps even in the man who had made it. But then he had swung the chair around and leaned half out of his chair and confronted him, so that the man was suddenly looking into that familiar face with the eyes full-blast on him, and that had folded the amateur up: he had gulped and felt foolish.

The fact is that in golf there is a fantastic disparity between professional and amateur. Much more so than in tennis where the open tournaments almost invariably have their quota of upsets. In the 1968 Open, for example, Lee Trevino finished 25 strokes ahead of the nearest amateur—which means that according to that tournament the professional could afford to give the finest amateur a handicap of 3 strokes a side in match play.

The Crosby was not a haven for hustlers, because the tournament itself rather than a side wager was what was on everybody's mind. But occasionally someone passing through the lobby, or leaning up against the bar, the fingers of his golf glove sticking out of his back pocket, would be pointed out as a big money player. Claude Harmon told me one harrowing story of a member at Winged Foot who was fleeced steadily by such big-money people—a tragic case because the victim was not only a compulsive gambler but he was seemingly unable to arrange the odds in his favor, or even to where he had an equal chance. A foursome would be arranged and the handicaps and bets (enormous ones) would be settled beforehand—and if the victim protested, the others would argue at him collectively; if the victim persisted, they would threaten to dissolve the game. They would sit and unlace their golf shoes and rattle open the locker doors to stow their stuff, and finally, on their way out, looking back over their shoulders, they would see him knuckle under, calling after them: "Stick around, fellows, O.K., we'll do it your way." Harmon told me that the member had been taken for three and a half *million* dollars over the course of years. I asked someone else who said well, he thought that was *pushing* it a bit, but it was certainly a rock pile of cash, probably more likely in the neighborhood of $750,000.

The golf stories about gambling were doubtless exaggerated, but I never could tire of listening to them, perhaps because I have great awe of people who put substantial portions of the gains of their livelihood on the line. I go vaguely askew, myself, when more than five dollars of mine is up to support a contention I've made, and when I fork the money over it takes me an evening or so, often more, before I can accept the other fellow's company with equanimity.

One of the best hustler stories I heard was about a man called Ted Lacey. I was told he was a figure of great reputation in Las Vegas. On one occasion he arranged a golf match with Bobby Riggs, the former tennis champion, and he won with such clever conviction that Riggs, realizing he had been taken by an expert, stormed around the locker room after the match and announced that while he was quite willing to pay what he owed, he wanted Lacey to know that he was *aware* he had been victimized, that he knew a hustler when he saw one. Lacey seemed very contrite. Oh Lord, Bobby, he kept saying, You've got me wrong. I don't want to give the wrong impression. Riggs did some snorting, and finally Lacey said, Well, Bobby, I'll tell you what we'll do, just to show you my heart's in the best place, and all that—we'll play off the bet double or nothing at *your* sport.

Of course Riggs took him up on it and the two had a tennis match the next day. Some sort of handicap was arranged. Before he could get himself settled down and onto his touch, Riggs found himself in such great difficulty with his younger opponent that he was unable to extricate himself. He had very little to say at the conclusion of the match— suddenly aware that the golf match had been simply a step to set him up for the big kill at tennis.

The story seemed improbable, but I had heard that Riggs often told the story on himself. Once, I called Las Vegas, just on impulse, to check on it, wanting to hear from him, and about this fellow Lacey. At the other end—I had called a hotel number there—I heard someone say, "Hold on, you want Riggs? I'll get him."

I could hear the clatter of the receiver being put down on the table top, and then in the background I could hear the murmur of voices, and the wrench and clack of what I took to be slot machines in the hotel lobby. A pair of voices became more distinct—one of them a woman's. I strained to hear.

"The best mulch has got corncobs in it," she was saying. "Ground-up corncobs." The other voice was inaudible.

"What you do is use your thumbs," she continued. "Alongside the root."

The phone was picked up and a third party in a man's voice said piercingly: "Sam! It won't work."

"I'm sorry..." I said. "I'm waiting..."

"You Sam?" the voice asked.

I explained I was waiting for Riggs.

The phone was replaced on the table top. I could no longer hear the conversation about gardening. The pair must have moved down the counter, or perhaps they had gone to dinner. I looked at my watch to calculate if it was dinnertime out in Las Vegas. Then in the distance I overheard: "Sam! It won't work. What? No, I tell you it won't work."

Someone came along and I heard the receiver being picked up and replaced in the cradle. The line went dead.

I did not bother calling Riggs back. The story was too fine to be refuted, and I would have been pressing my luck to have reached him, and too disappointed if he had said, "Lacey? Lacey? What the hell are you talking about? Who *is* this?"

There was another gambling story that I *did* check, reaching the man involved by phone, and explaining what I had heard, and then I said damn damn damn in absolute delight because the story was true and it was about the tables being turned on the hustler, which was the best kind of story.

The golfer involved was T. Suffern Tailer, a man of considerable charm who was a fixture at the grander watering spots, a fine amateur player, an expert at cards and backgammon, and a man with a considerable zest for the wager. A number of years ago he had a fallow period — a long series of expensive set-backs — and to recoup his losses and regain a sense of stability he took a temporary job with Louis Marx, the toy manufacturer. His job at Christmas time was to demonstrate a Swedish-made game called The Labyrinth, which was a box with a top perforated with sixty-four holes that could be tilted by manipulating a set of handles at the side. The purpose of the game was a simple one — to start a lead ball on an intricate path between the holes, which were numbered, and coax it along to the finish without losing the ball and having it drop through a hole to the bottom of the box with a dismaying clunk. It was a game which required dexterity, a very careful touch, and considerable practice to get the ball more than halfway to the end. Tailer got very good at it, from hours a day demonstrating the game in the toy department at Macy's.

When he left the job, financially refurbished, he went down to Miami and in his first golf match at the Indian Creek Club he put his new bankroll on the line and lost it—hustled for over two thousand dollars.

A normally ebullient man, Tailer came off the 18th green subdued, and somewhat uncertain of his immediate future. But as he wandered into the locker room with the others he noticed with a start a Labyrinth standing on a table in the corner. He swallowed and thought it was too perfect—the lead ball was probably missing.

He said, very easily, and perfectly contained:

"What is that thing over there?"

I have always envied Tailer that grand line—the timing of it, and the opportunity to make it. Of course, he capitalized on the situation. The golfers took him over and showed him how the Labyrinth worked. Would he consider a game?

"I was worried about that particular model," Tailer told me. "It was wood—an expensive Swedish original. The ones I had been demonstrating at Macy's were plastic and slicker and easier to move a ball on. Well, it worked out. They were awfully eager. I dropped a ball in the four hole and then the nine hole just to sweeten the action and then when the big bets were down I ran the ball all the way to the finish, past sixty-four holes, and *back,* just to show them that they were being taken. I mean you have to take that satisfaction every once in a while. I got my stake back, and a bit more."

The largest amount of money I ever heard of being involved in a golf match was one million dollars, perhaps even more. The story involved Charles B. Macdonald, a financial titan and autocrat of the boom period, and his nephew, Peter Grace, later of the Grace Line, who used to tell this story on himself. His uncle was the founder of the National Golf Links of Southampton, Long Island, which has a succession of some of the truly great golf holes of the world. A number of the holes are patterned after those Macdonald had played abroad and admired — the Redan from North Berwick, and then the famous Road Hole of St. Andrews, with the deep potholes, and along the right fairway a line of trees to substitute for the railroad tracks. Macdonald loved his course so much that his private home was not placed to take advantage of the best possible views but was faced, instead, to look down on his golf links. He ran his club with an iron hand. He was famous for listening to criticisms, rectifying them, and then sending the bill to whoever had complained. A member would say, "Lord, there ought to be a place in the clubhouse where a fellow could play a spot of bridge" — and if Macdonald was within earshot, soon enough a room would be tacked onto the clubhouse, and then charged to the bridge enthusiast. On one occasion a club member had mumbled about the mosquito swarms rising off a pond on the 14th hole. Macdonald had the pond drained and sent the bill to the member. Members either paid up or were dropped from the membership lists. Fortunately, the membership was extremely affluent. But I have always imagined members of the National in Macdonald's time wandering around the course with fixed grins trying to remember not to say anything.

Peter Grace would have done well to be so advised. One afternoon he was sitting in the National clubhouse with his uncle after having played the course for the first time. He said rather boldly that he thought the course was too easy. "Nonsense," his uncle had replied.

"Well, not so," Peter Grace had said. "Take the first hole. Par 4. But a good drive can reach the green."

"Nonsense," his uncle had bristled. "No one has *ever* reached the green."

"It can be done," said Grace. "I'll show you."

So the two walked to the first tee, where Peter Grace hit a tremendous drive which sailed in a prevailing wind and bounced and rolled and just barely got across the apron to the green itself. Macdonald watched, absolutely speechless, and turned on his heel. When he got home that night he wrote Peter Grace out of his will—an amount denied him, Grace used to say in later years, of well over a million dollars.

I played the National once. I remember that of our foursome I was the first to hit. The hole is appropriately named—the Valley—a long slope down to a trap and then a rise, curving up to the lift, almost 300 yards, to an elevated green. I hit a high angry slice that ended up on the edge of the forest to the right—a miserable beginning. I banged my club down, but then I suddenly remembered the Macdonald-Grace story. "Hey," I shouted happily. "You know what? I just made a million-dollar shot! Maybe a million and a *half*, truly!"

The other members of our foursome stared dully after my drive.

I was going to explain it to them, but then the next fellow stepped up to his ball, beginning his waggle, and it was too late then, and somehow we never got around to it again.

CHAPTER 14

———

Our starting time at Cypress Point, the second of the three courses, was set for midmorning. The course, while one of the Del Monte Properties, was some distance off. Abe said he would come around to the cottage an hour or so beforehand and we would drive to Cypress from the lodge and arrive there in time for some practice on the range before tee-off time.

I awoke quite early. I had time to look into my book bag and dig amongst the inspirational prose before breakfast. I turned up an interesting notion of Walter Hagen's: To get into the proper mood of controlled languor for his golf round he tried relaxing as soon as he got up in the morning. He would shave very slowly, work his toothbrush up and down with careful patience, his breakfast would be a lengthy affair...all of this an exercise to get accustomed to taking his time so he would be unlikely to hurry his golf swing on the day's round.

The idea made considerable sense. In my mind's eye I had an image of my form of the previous day: a quick snatch at the ball, the swing hurried and spastic, with none of the easy flow that would come with relaxation and confidence. I put the Hagen notes aside and I rose from the chair with the slow torpor of a man whose foot has gone asleep. I continued the Sarazen hot-water routine. This time I soaked my hands longer, flexing the fingers carefully.

I stepped outside and ambled very slowly down to the lodge dining room. My hands smoked. I looked carefully at the flower beds and the shrubbery. My head moved as slowly as a turret. It was Hagen, after all, who had given the memorable piece of advice about going down a fairway, which was applicable not only to golf but to just about anything: "Along the way," he had said, "be sure to take the time to smell the flowers."

By coincidence, a single long-stemmed rose stood in the vases at every table in the dining room. A number of players were there. Jack Nicklaus was seated at a corner table with his wife. I looked over and saw that he was dipping into a dish of dry cereal topped with strawberries. I lowered myself slowly into a chair.

A waiter came by.

"Yes?"

"A grapefruit," I said painstakingly.

"Yes?"

"Corn flakes and strawberries." The speed of my delivery was that of group recitation in class.

"Scrambled..." I went on.

"Yes?"

"...eggs..."

"Yes?"

"...toast."

He made a mark on his order blank.

"Coffee?"

I considered. "Yes," I said.

I took my time when the meal arrived. I am a rough-and-tumble eater, and it was interesting to indulge in a regimen so markedly different. I spent a long time arranging the napkin in my lap. Should I tuck it under my chin? I thought not. My mind just barely ticked over as it considered what to do with the napkin. The meal arrived. The waiter seemed to move with the speed of a dervish. A plate with the grapefruit on it slammed down. The grapefruit rocked back and forth. A platter of eggs came down with the pop and clatter of its cover. A plate of toast appeared. Smells rose slowly. I exhaled carefully, and bent forward with the dignity of an earl to inhale.

"Ah-hah," I said in appreciation. I raised my hands to rub them slowly in anticipation of the meal. The waiter had disappeared.

I dawdled over the grapefruit. I raised the spoon. I felt my teeth pop slowly into the skin of the fruit and I felt the spray of the juice hit against the roof of my mouth. The sensation was astonishing: taste considered in such reflection was almost overpowering. The mind boiled. I turned to the toast. Slowly I scraped a knife with some butter on it across the toast—spreading it evenly. Then came the honey. Ho-hum. It was in a tiny container with a paper top with a tab for removing. I peered at it. I felt the process of my eyes focusing. A NAPA VALLEY HONEY! That was what the writing said. There was a picture of a bee with a crown on its head. I turned the container upside down. The bottom was blank. I opened the container carefully and dipped the knife into the honey and spread it on the toast. The eating was interesting—the juxtaposition of butter and honey, the difference in consistency, just the slightest, so that one could lose oneself in contemplation. My jaws barely moved. I moved on to the scrambled eggs. They were cold. So was the coffee.

I brought my arm up slowly and looked at my watch. My blood jumped. It was later than I thought possible.

I rose abruptly from my chair, which almost went over behind me.

"Check! Check!" I shouted.

Some heads turned from neighboring tables.

The waiter arrived, startled at the sudden shift of behavior in the near-somnambulist he had been serving.

I paid the check and hurried from the room.

But out on the walk, I began to slow down. "Hold on," I said to myself. Hagen's precept returned. "Take it easy." I slowed down my pace. It wasn't that late, I told myself. Plenty of time. Smell the flowers.

I could see Abe waiting by the door of my cottage.

I sauntered up to him.

"Good...morning...Abe."

He looked at me uneasily.

"Stiff from yesterday?" he asked.

He already had the golf bag in the car, he said. Everything was set.

We strolled out to the parking lot. I eased into the front seat. I put the car in gear, and we moved out of the parking lot as slow as a boat maneuvering in a harbor. I felt my nerves settling.

We drove along for a while. Abe told me something about his furniture-moving business. Occasionally, he would lift an arm and point when we came to an intersection. I felt the anticipation of the golf round coming up, the keenness and excitement of it, but I was relaxed. Some cars passed us, one of them a Tortilla Flat truck piled high with crates of chickens. We drove behind that for a while, the chickens inspecting us with pale cyclopean intensity.

Then suddenly Abe announced that he thought we had taken a wrong turn.

"What?"

My heart began to pound.

"Mebbe you should turn back."

"Lord, what time is it?"

Abe consulted his watch. "We got a good half-hour," he said.

"But we're miles out into the country."

"You ain't been pushing the speed limit much," Abe said. "You been...well, you been moseying along awful easy."

I spun the car in a whirl of gravel, pumped it in reverse, got it straightened out, and pushed the accelerator hard. The wind began to sweep in the side window.

"Where are we supposed to go?" I asked frantically. "Where'd we go wrong?"

My heart pumped hard.

"There should've been some signs," Abe said. He lit a cigarette. The front of the car billowed with cigarette smoke, shredded away quickly, and he coughed.

"God...Abe, where are we?"

He was taking swift drags at his cigarette, somewhat unnerved by the speed at which we were traveling.

"I don't rightly know."

"What?"

"Cypress is not my club," he said. "I caddy at Pebble Beach and Monterey."

"But you must know where it is."

"Mebbe not."

We were really ripping along. My throat was dry and I swallowed rapidly.

Abe said: "Try a right here."

We spun around a corner. I was sure we were hopelessly lost. Bruno would have to start the round alone, I assumed, without me, because the starting times were absolutely inflexible. What would I do? I would have to set out across the golf course after Bruno and try to intercept him on some tee, the third or fourth, perhaps, depending on how late we arrived, with Abe trailing along far behind with the heavy oxblood bag. I would take a driver along with me on that long run, with the Titleist 2 ball I had decided to use that day, and I would arrive on the tee, puffing, and apologize ("Sorry, Bob!") and then hit a boomer down the fairway. But it wouldn't be a boomer. I'd be tuckered out, rib cage heaving from the run: it would be surprising if I hit the ball at all.

We stopped to ask someone directions. He turned out to be a tourist in the area. He didn't know, he said, staring at our anguished faces. We drove on. We went past a long grove of high pines. The sun's shadows flicked over the car.

"Damn! Damn!" I beat at the steering wheel with my fist.

"There's a sign!" Abe shouted. My nervousness had affected him. I saw the sign with an arrow pointing to Cypress Point.

"That's it!" I yelled.

We turned off. A few miles along the road we ran into the end of a long line of cars turning up a long slope into the public parking lot. I could see the clubhouse roof above the trees on the hill.

"We've got to get by, Abe," I shouted. I began to pass the line on the left, moving slowly, and I could sense the drivers' heads turning and the stares. "Tell them 'contestant,' Abe."

He cranked down the window. "Contestant, contestant," I heard him announcing in his wheezing voice, clearing it from time to time. "Contestant, contestant."

At the head of the line a policeman stopped us. I put my head out the window as he came over. "Contestant, contestant. We're due on the first tee."

"You got a contestant's badge? Parking badge?"

"We're late," I said.

"Badge?"

"The badge is on the golf bag in the trunk," I said. "The parking badge came off the windshield. It was on there yesterday. Must have blown off. Look, there's the outline of it." I pointed. "Look in here," I said. "Here's my caddy."

The policeman bent down and looked in at Abe. "Well," he said, "I don't know. Where's your parking badge?"

"It blew off," I said. "It's lying back on the road somewhere."

He stepped back and scratched his ear. He looked in at Abe again. He let us through, finally, pointing out the turn that led to the contestants' parking area.

We had about ten minutes to spare. I could see Bob Bruno and his big caddy up on the first tee, and Manuel de la Torre with his partner, Bill Henley.

I rushed up. "Hello, hello, hello," I said. "Hello, hello, hello."

Everybody looked very relaxed, Bruno swinging a club easily in his black-gloved grip. The foursome ahead of us was getting ready to tee off.

I sat down on a bench and laced my golf shoes. My hands were shaking. Bruno ambled over. He said, "We're really going to mop up the course today."

"Sure," I said.

"Get right back up there in the running."

"Absolutely."

"It's just a question of taking it easy and not pressing or getting flustered."

"Right," I said. I cleared my throat. I had come at quite a clip up from the parking lot.

"Just being relaxed. That's the key."

"Right," I said again. I could barely get the word out. I was still breathing hard.

CHAPTER 15

O n the 4th at Cypress Point I made one of my best shots of the
Crosby, a 40-foot putt. It dropped in the back of the hole, true all
the way, with a grand rattle, and I let out a whoop, and everybody stood
around grinning. But Bruno missed his putt, and suddenly his calm left
him — it just sidled off — and the rage came in and settled. It was not
evident at first. He putted out with dispatch, handed the club to his
caddy and accepted his driver in return. But on the way to the next tee,
striding along, he suddenly swerved off the path into the woods. He
disappeared. We could hear him moving through the underbrush. I
thought perhaps he had gone in there to take a pee. Then we heard an
odd bopping sound.

Someone looked and said, "My God, he's in there beating his driver
against a stump!"

I peered around a tree to look, and it was true. I saw him in there, a
tall figure with his golf hat a startling white in the dark shadows of the
eucalyptus forest, flailing away, the club swinging in the air like a wil-
low switch. There was an echoing *bop* as it hit, as if he were trying to
drive the stump and its network of roots down into the earth.

We stood around on the path uneasily, wearing the cow-like expressions of children when one of their group collapses into tears. The bopping continued. The caddies moved restlessly, the irons clinking in the
golf bags. I wondered vaguely if I should wander into the woods and try

to fetch him out—sidle up to him as he toiled at the stump, and say something easy, calming, like: "Anything I can do to *help*, Bob?" I was, after all, his partner.

The clubbing stopped abruptly. After a while we heard Bruno's footsteps again. He came out on the path. He still held the driver, its shaft down near the club head bent in a grotesque curve. He saw us staring at him. He seemed aghast. He was purged and controlled again, but he didn't know how to put it right with us. His caddy, who was a florid-faced youngster, very stout, perhaps still in high school, looked petrified. "Bob...er...ah," he mumbled, "you want me to try to *straighten that club?*"

"I'll have to use the three wood," Bruno said. He turned the driver in his hand and stared at it miserably. "This thing's done with. I got another driver in the back of the car, but this is the one I liked."

We started along for the tee. "I'm sorry, everybody," he said. "My game is just so damn terrible."

Our compassion for him was immense. On the tee our team had the honor due to my great putt that had given Bruno and me a birdie on the hole, the exhilaration of which still ticked in me despite the drama in the forest.

"We're on our way, Bob," I called.

Bruno stepped up first. Due to the loft of the three wood, his drive, despite teeing the ball down low, soared up until the ball almost lost itself against the sky before beginning its downward flight, which was nearly vertical from the apex and was completely so as it hit the fairway, so that the ball bounced straight up and came to rest, it seemed to us watching from the tee, not more than a foot or so from where it had landed. There was an obvious loss of yardage due to the trajectory of the ball, but one would not have known this from the chorus of approbation that rose from our little group.

"Sweet shot, Bob!"

"Bob, you really popped it!"

"Great poke, Bob!"

Bruno knew better, and he slumped down on the bench by the side of the tee and stared between his feet.

Then I stepped up to the ball, meaning to do my best for him, my concern for him really quite palpable in some corner of my mind. After a quick check down the alley of pines that opened up into the wide fairway beyond, I looked sharply at the Titleist 2 on its tee and then drove it 50 yards in a low, hard trajectory into one of the pines just at the end of the alley. It hit with a bopping sound, and then another as it ricocheted through the quiet pine groves, and I was struck suddenly with the thought that the sound was exactly what we'd heard when Bruno was whacking at the stump with his driver—perhaps more hollow and a bit sharper but about the same—so that sitting on the bench, his head down (I'm certain that he never looked up to see me hit my drive), he heard once again the mournful sound of his own rage, an audible reflection of his despairing moments back up the path.

Then he heard me calling out cheerily, more concerned for his melancholy than my own: "Sorry, Bob, I'm truly sorry. But you'll pull us through."

He rose off the bench. He said tightly, "It's all right! It's all right!"

When our foursome moved off the tee, Bruno's caddy took the bent driver and matter-of-factly worked the woolen cover with the red pompon down over the club head and the curved shaft and set the club back in the bag. The club was bent at its end in a curve so pronounced that it seemed as if what was under the woolen cover was a shepherd's crook. I was surprised Bruno didn't fling it away somewhere, into the sea, perhaps, on the ocean holes; but it stayed the day with us, palpable evidence to remind us of the melancholy crisis in the woods.

CHAPTER 16

P oor Bruno. Golf is one of the few games (along with croquet, perhaps, which is also famous for lost tempers) in which there is no outlet for pent-up emotions. In contact sports one can usually purge one's frustrations by smacking into the other fellow, or biting at the turf with one's teeth (a common habit of soccer players), or one can let off steam simply by running hard. I have seen Alex Karras, the great Detroit football tackle, drain himself of frustration by running very hard in one place with little, short choppy steps, like the tantrum of a schoolboy refused a favor, and as he does so he emits a tiny high whinnying sound. Even the calmer, more decorous sports have outlets. In tennis one can stomp around and slam one or two balls angrily straight up, or into the fence, and while there may be some pursed lips around the court, one can get away with this without materially affecting the game score. At the very least, in almost all sports one can purge oneself by letting off a furious bellow of frustration. Not so in golf. Decorum is demanded. Yelling is frowned on. Throwing a club or cussing can cost a professional golfer a fine and suspension. Lack of emotional control costs the professional in his golf score as well. Golf cannot be played in anger, or in any mood of emotional excess. Half the golf balls struck by amateurs are hit if not in rage surely in bewilderment, or gloom, or in cynicism, or even hysterically—all of those emotional excesses which must be contained by the professional. Which is why, because emotional balance is one of the essential ingredients of golf, professionals invariably trudge phlegmatically around the course—whatever emotions are seething within—with the grim yet placid and bored look of cowpokes, slack-bodied in their saddles, who have been tending the same herd for two months.

There was a golf pro, once, Harry Stephens, from the Druid Hills course in Atlanta, who perhaps had these frustrations in mind when he held a club-throwing contest—an event recorded by O. B. Keeler, Bobby Jones's biographer. Some sixty-odd eager contestants turned up, including a number of professionals. Apparently much of the pre-contest discussion was devoted to which club was best to throw. Most of the contestants picked the putter, one of which was thrown 61 yards to win the contest. The altitude record went to a golfer who tossed a pitching wedge 20 feet over the top of an 80-foot pine tree. As for the pro, Harry Stephens, he entered the contest with a driver, but revolving rapidly in the style of a hammer-thrower, with the club singing in the quick turns, he let go at the wrong second and the driver whirled up into the veranda, scattering a group of people who were sitting in big wicker armchairs drinking lemonade, and cracked up against the clubhouse wall.

The contest was held in the days before the heavy-headed sand-blaster, and one of the pros I talked to about it in the Del Monte Lodge said that he reckoned that with good timing and no wind he could rip a sand-blaster out maybe 70 or 80 yards. "Damned if I wouldn't like to try that," he said. We were sitting in the cocktail lounge. I thought I might mention it to him the next day—but I resisted it.

The professionals talked about temper tantrums with an odd rueful reticence, as if they were quite aware that such excesses ticked quietly in themselves. If they were going to talk about golfers losing a grip on themselves, they preferred reminiscing about amateurs. Jim Ferree remembered one who missed a putt and hit himself in the face with his putter much harder, in the reflex of his disappointment, than he intended to, and his knees buckled and he fell to the green. His embarrassment was intense despite his semiconscious state, and he made an effort to get to his feet and pass it off, as if he'd just stumbled, but his head was still too addled and, halfway up, his legs wobbled and he fell down with a big thump, flat out this time, as if he'd been dropped with a bullfighter's *puntilla*.

"We all looked away," Ferree said. "Way off at the horizon, with these big grins, while that guy pulled himself together. He really busted himself one."

"All that's gone now," Dave Marr said. "At least among the pros. I've never seen a great golfer who didn't have a temper of sorts. But you control it. There's too much at stake. So you never see much more than a guy maybe whacking his club down once, digging the club head in a bit in the grass. Or, maybe, after a bad shot, he'll whip the club back in the bag awful quick."

"Of course it's colorful," one of the golfers said. "The public is all for it. Ralph Guldahl said he'd throw his clubs in the lake if he didn't win the Jersey Open this one time. Well, he didn't win the tournament, and he didn't throw his clubs and they criticized the hell out of him."

Of the old-time professionals mentioned who were especially susceptible to rage, there were four I took a fancy to: Ivan Gantz; a part-Indian named Ky Laffoon; the Texan, Lefty Stackhouse; and Clayton Heafner. Gantz, who played through the 50s, was particularly noted for cracking himself with a club or, preferably, a rock, if one happened to be at hand, in self-deprecation. Don January said that once during a tournament he looked across onto the adjoining fairway to see Gantz tottering along bleeding at the nose—as if a bear had got him in the rough and mauled him. It turned out, as January expected, that Gantz had missed a putt on the preceding hole and bopped himself.

Lefty Stackhouse, who played during the two decades before Gantz, was also famous for taking it out on himself—hitting himself with his fist, rearing back with one foot and kicking himself in the shin with it, and so forth. On one occasion he knocked himself cold, according to a story Dave Marr had heard. Dave went on to say in awe, "Joe *Louis* couldn't have done a thing like that—I mean, he'd've pulled his punch."

If Stackhouse hit a bad hook he would take his right hand, which had come too powerfully into the shot and caused the fault, and he would look at it as if it were disembodied, and then carry it over to a tree and whack it against the trunk. He'd shout things at it such as: "Take that...that'll teach you."

I never could hear enough about him. Dave Marr said that on one occasion Stackhouse had shot an 80 in a tournament at Memorial Park in Houston and on his way back into the clubhouse he ran into a big arbor of rosebushes and thrashed around in there, lacerating himself as he beat at the plants, until he calmed down and came out looking as if (Marr described it) he had "fought a bunch of wildcats in a small room."

Stackhouse's golf clubs were the most available targets of his rage. On occasion he would break the entire set, one after another, and then he would go after his golf bag, clawing and ripping at it. And one day, after a frustrating round, he demolished the Model-T Ford in which he traveled to and from tournaments, scaling the windshield off in one direction, a car door in another, the seats, and then he opened up the hood and went to work on the engine, shouting imprecations as he did so.

"Come on," I said.

"Absolutely," I was told.

Old-time players would describe how out on the golf course they often heard Stackhouse across the fairways — usually directing a voluble commentary to his clubs or the ball. Preparing to tee off, he would look his driver in the face and admonish it, and then warn the ball down on its tee that if it didn't behave and fly true he was going to drop it in a pot and boil it. When he left tournament golf, the strain being what it was, and became a teaching professional, his temperament remained the same. His patience with pupils was short. If too many bad shots were hit in succession, he would rear up from placing balls on the tee for them and advance on his pupils, pushing at them and shouting.

Claude Harmon told me Stackhouse's rage was interesting because sometimes it would arrive completely unexpectedly, just suddenly well-ing over. He would finish a poor round in control, to everyone's surprise, remove his golf glove slowly, give his putter and the ball to his caddy, tote up his score, all very calmly, and then pay off his caddy and compliment him on his work—at which point, just as abruptly as if he were stuck with a fork, his rage would strike him.

"What about off the course?" I asked.

"Very calm...though he drank like a fish," Harmon said. "Why sometimes he'd start in with his drinking Sunday and keep going through Monday, Tuesday, Wednesday, Thursday, right *through* his tee-time, and then he'd get up out of his chair, weaving a bit, and head on for the next tournament without ever having gripped a club. He had these long fingernails, always remember that about him, like a Chinaman's. He was a pretty good golfer, too, though he took things awful easy, except for an occasional temper bout. I remember there was this tournament during the war in Knoxville—which was really more of an exhibition because there were prizes, which were U.S. war bonds, for everyone entered. All you had to do to win something was hang on to the golf club and haul yourself around the course. I remember they brought Sergeant Alvin York, the Medal of Honor winner who was the state's celebrity, out to dole out the prizes. He didn't want to come, it being Sunday and all, and York a religious man, but they finally persuaded him on account of the war bond prizes. Besides, he'd never seen a game of golf, and they got his curiosity going pretty good. Well, he chose to follow a foursome that had Lefty Stackhouse in it. Stackhouse wasn't tending strictly to business with all those prizes available and not too much to worry about, so he was nipping whiskey from a Coke bottle from time to time. They got to one of the late holes and Stackhouse had been doing so much nipping that when he leaned over to sight this putt, he fell flat out on the green. He had to be carried off to the clubhouse where they laid him out on a locker-room bench. Sergeant York was fit to be tied. He watched Stackhouse topple over and he said, 'The poor man *exhausted* himself. I had no idea golf was such a strenuous game.' As for Stackhouse, when he came to and realized where he was, he bolted out of the locker room to get back on the course so he could finish out and collect his prize. But the sun was long down and the moon up and he never did fetch a bean out of that tournament."

The Indian, Ky Laffoon, like Stackhouse, had the same personal relationship with his golfing equipment—just as a child has for a stuffed pet—cajoling, praising, admonishing, and very often simply brutalizing.

At a tournament in Jacksonville, Florida, he tried to choke a putter that had let him down, squeezing it at the neck of the shaft, and then, frustrated by the implacable nature of his victim, he took it down to a water hazard and tried to drown it. "Drown, you son-of-a-bitch, drown!" he is supposed to have shrieked at it.

He was a man of melancholy moods. Driving from one tournament to the next in his car, he would begin to brood about his play and the clubs which he felt had let him down in recent rounds—that putter of his, for instance—and if his disenchantment with the club got the best of him, he would stop the car, pull the offending putter from the bag, and attach it to a length of string. Then he would drop the putter out on the road, the string attached to the car-door handle, and he'd start up his car, leaning out the window from time to time to watch his putter bouncing along back there, flailing at the end of its tether and fetching up sparks from the macadam.

A passenger riding with Laffoon would say, "Well, Ky . . . ah."

Laffoon would explain—with difficulty because it was a private matter between him and his club—that if a putter behaved the way *that* putter had, well, it deserved to be humiliated. That was what was going on: it was being "punished."

"Oh, yes," the passenger would say.

At one stage Laffoon owned a yellow Cadillac. It had a brown streak that ran down its flank from the driver's side window. Laffoon was a tobacco chewer and not a consistent spitter, the speed of his driving markedly affecting the trajectory of his efforts. He was a very fast driver in the days when all the traveling between tour stops—very often enormous distances—was done by car, and it was the talk of the tour if you could beat Laffoon to the next tournament. Not many golfers enjoyed driving with him, though, because of the tobacco habit for one thing (the backseat was also stained), and then, for another, because of Laffoon's madcap speeds, and the racing turns he took as quick as if he were on a pony. Laffoon's wife used to drive occasionally, but that wasn't much better, because she was almost as fast. And besides, Laffoon would often open the car door to "punish" his clubs or just to grind the weight down, not "punishing" a club in this case, but honing an edge, using the macadam at seventy miles an hour as one might use a lathe, holding the club down hard so that a big rooster-tail of sparks kicked up behind.

He carried a gun in the car, just at hand, so he could wing a shot at anything moving on the road. Guns were his great hobby. Claude Harmon, who worked as an assistant under him, told me that Laffoon would tour the course at 5:30 every afternoon shooting at gophers.

"It was one of the hazards of the course late in the afternoon," Harmon said. "At those gunshots I've seen people leap right up off a putt like Laffoon plugged *them* 'stead of a gopher!"

In his early days Laffoon performed as Titanic Thompson's caddy, and he was involved in some of the famous hustler's more lucrative hauls. Thompson would say, "For Chrissakes, my *caddy* can beat you," and Laffoon would grin just slightly and begin to slide the bag off his shoulder.

The fourth golfer of the genre whose name cropped up as we talked about rage was perhaps the ultimate sufferer from the frustrations of golf. His name was Clayton Heafner, a top-flight golfer of the late forties. Sam Snead is supposed to have said of him: "Heafner's the most even-tempered player on the tour: he's *always* angry." He was a big bearlike man who, on occasion, lunged into the crowd and berated those in the gallery he thought were being critical of him.

Usually the golf course itself was the object of Heafner's rage. On the way to a tournament his resentment would begin to build up in him before he ever got to the clubhouse headquarters to check in, and as he drove into the outskirts of the tournament town he would think of the indignities to which the golf course would subject him—the putts missed because of worm holes, the unraked sand traps, the bad lies in the sun-baked fairways; in his mind he would hear the clout of balls hitting tree trunks—such a variety of disturbing images and sounds that sometimes when he'd get to the door of the headquarters room and look in and see the country-club ladies behind the long plywood tables waiting with room assignments for the golfers, dinner invitations, information sheets, starting times, and so forth, he'd call out to them: "Your golf course is a goddamn pasture!" He would glare at them briefly, then turn, and out in the parking lot he'd ease himself into his car and drive mournfully out of town.

Almost anything would upset Heafner. On one occasion at Oakland, on the first tee the announcer pronounced his name "Heefner" through the megaphone, "from Linnville, North Carolina," and he went on to say that he hoped "Heefner" wasn't going to have the same trouble with Oakland's *trees* that he'd had the year before. The crowd around the first tee grinned and carried on hearing this gentle quip. Many of them remembered Heafner hauling his 260-pound bulk up into a tree the previous year to punch a ball out of the fork of a tree where it had perched like a bird's wayward egg. Heafner listened to the announcer, and when he had finished he walked over and said: "My name's *Heafner,* not Heefner. I come from Charlotte, North Carolina, not Linnville. And as for staying out of your goddam trees, I'm not allowing myself the chance to get *into* them." He motioned to his caddy. "Come on, boy, stick that stuff in the car." He changed his shoes and drove to San Francisco.

Bobby Jones, it should be mentioned, had a tremendous temper as a young player. His father once asked Long Jim Barnes, an excellent player who had won the British Open, and the PGA twice, about his son's temper, concerned about it, and Barnes said, "Come now, that spirit'll help him. He'll control it one day."

That day came on the 11th hole at St. Andrew's in the 1921 Open.

Jones had a series of poor holes and in the 11th in a fit of pique he tore up his score card, symbolically removing himself from competition. He was aghast at his behavior—and vowed that from that point on he would make his temperament work for him. He was nineteen at the time. He kept to his vow, but he never pretended to forget the club-throwing impulse. "It's gone forever—" he once wrote about a bad shot, "—an irrevocable crime, that stroke...and when you feel a fool, and a bad golfer to boot, what can you do except to throw the club away."

Tommy Bolt is the contemporary golfer spoken of when temper tantrums are the topic, particularly fits of club-throwing, though he has kept them under control in recent years. I have always liked the following exchange:

> **Caddy:** Mr. Bolt, you'll be using either a two or a three iron for this shot.
>
> **Bolt** (*incredulously*): Hell, man, that's 350 yards out there. Ol' Tom can't begin to reach the green with a two, much less a *three*, iron.
>
> **Caddy:** Mr. Bolt, all you got left in your bag are those two clubs. Unless you want to use your putter.
>
> **Bolt:** Oh.
>
> **Caddy:** And your putter's missin' its handle. You snapped it off on the first nine.
>
> **Bolt:** Oh.

One of Bolt's most famous outbursts occurred on the Cherry Hills course in Denver during the 1960 Open. He was playing well until the 12th hole when he suddenly got himself in trouble by dropping a shot into a pond. He had a heated argument with a USGA official as to exactly where he should drop his ball for the penalty shot. His concentration upset, what he refers to as his "tempo" gone askew, he proceeded to three-putt the next hole, bogey the next, and then, on the 18th hole he hooked two drives into the lake. He strode down off the tee up to the edge of the lake, peered in, abruptly reared back, and then, with his left foot far advanced and planted to get leverage and power, he sailed his driver into the water. What happened next surprised everyone, Bolt included. A small boy, marking the splash, waded into the lake, belly-flopped down, and disappeared. He surfaced with the club. The crowd, a considerable one around that last green, which had given an odd grunt of dismay and surprise at Bolt's temper, now cheered as the boy worked his way to the bank. Bolt himself stepped forward, his rage eclipsed quite completely by the ferocity of his club throw, a smile, if a somewhat grim one, working at his lips as if he had in mind to say, "Ol' Tom sure appreciates this, son...thanks," some such pleasantry since the driver was a favorite. The boy hauled himself up the bank and, giving a startled look at Bolt advancing on him, took a few quick steps this way, then that, dodging him, and then lit out across the fairway, the club still in hand, and the crowd roaring. Someone in the gallery, which was not particularly sensitive to Bolt's dismay after watching his display of temper, gave the kid a leg up over the fence, and he was gone.

Bolt kept his sense of humor about this incident, as he generally does about his rages. I have always liked his dictum about club throwing: "If you are going to throw a club, it is important to throw it ahead of you, down the fairway, so you don't waste energy going back to pick it up."

Of course, club throwing and club snapping often occurred when rage was not a factor at all. There was a young pro, Chuck Matlack, who "wrung" his putter, trying to give body English to a putt he had stroked in the Azalea Open. He broke the shaft and had to continue using his driver to putt with, and occasionally a two iron. He was six under par in the tournament when he broke his putter—and by the time he had finished he had lost all six of his shots, and more, and finished out of the money.

As for an odd example of club throwing in glee, Bobby Cruickshank once told me that in 1934, leading by two strokes at Merion, with seven holes to go, he had played a weak second shot on the 11th, letting up on a nine iron, and he was convinced the ball was going to drop in the creek that fronts the green. When, instead, the ball bounded on the green and kicked near the pin, he let out a shout of relief and in a quick, spontaneous gesture of exuberance he flipped his club up into the air and strode on for the green. When he'd gone about six paces, a bright smile fixed on his face, the club came down and hit him on the head. His reaction was that someone had come up from behind and put the slug on him; his wife crossed his mind; he had completely forgotten about the club spinning above him. The corner of the blade hit him directly; there was a substantial amount of blood, but his playing partner, Wiffy Cox, could hardly play his next shot for laughing. He would stand up to address his shot and then back away, emitting a high-pitched *snee-snee-snee* sound. "A fine golfer," Cruickshank said. "But I wasn't so sure about his laugh."

I asked so many questions about rage that by and by someone asked: "Well, what do you want to know about that for? I mean, you seem obsessed."

"Well, golf is supposedly such a controlled game," I said. "It's interesting to know about excesses—when something gets out of hand."

They took me up as an expert on the subject, and they asked me to tell them about some examples of rage I had seen in other professions.

I thought a bit, turning my glass on the table top, and I said that what came quickly to mind was an example of rage I had seen in an unexpected place in Paris some years before—on the big pond in the Jardin du Luxembourg where on weekends old men in wading boots come out with their lovely ship's models and long thin bamboo poles to guide them with.

I had just happened by. The children were there, kneeling on the long curved edge of the pond, and occasionally they would lean to the water to tend the bathtub craft they took there, or what they had turned out on the school lathes—the flat boards with the single masts—but they did this rather perfunctorily, just a quick push, because their attention was committed to the graceful models the old men brought.

They came in the afternoon. They had wooden stands to set the boats on, and a toolbox alongside. They would prepare the boats for the water, working a tiny screwdriver the size of a thumb at the innards, while the children clustered around wordlessly and enthralled to see the work being done.

On this particular afternoon there were two great models on the pond. One was a schooner with a foremast that rose above the water to the height of its owner who was a thin, melancholy man, very tall, standing in oversized rubber boots that his legs seemed too thin to move, like a stork's, and he trod very gingerly through the water as if in slow motion. His bamboo pole was very long and had a little ivory button on the tip. His schooner's topsides were a fine maze of lines which he would bend over and adjust before giving the craft a small shove; then, standing upright, his pole over his shoulder, he would watch as her sails filled and she moved away through the flotsam fleet.

The other boat was a steam yacht of turn-of-the-century lines, lean and graceful, with a raked red funnel and little lifeboats in davits on either side. The topsides lifted up on hinges and there was a little motor inside the hull—a steam boiler that made a pumping sound as the craft moved, with little spurts of steam jumping out of the funnel. Its owner had a pair of large mustaches. He set the yacht's rudder to take the model on a long curve around the circumference of the pond and back to him—adjusting it so perfectly that often at the end of her turn he would reach out just an arm's length to stop her and lift up the topsides to peer within and to do a bit more tinkering.

The trouble started when the steam yacht passed by and struck the schooner the slightest blow—a glance, no more—enough to shudder the sails and spill some wind, just temporarily, before she filled again and heeled.

The schooner's owner, the thin man, shouted at the other in a thin, high querulous whine. He reached for the steam yacht and pushed its stern under—a quick impetuous move—bobbing it under and letting it go so that the yacht slid up like a surfacing submarine, rocking furiously and getting underway in a ruffle of water.

Across the pond the gentleman with the mustaches looked on. It just happened that the schooner, after a moment or so, coasted by within reach of his pole. He reached out and fished her in, carefully but swiftly, and he held her steady in the water with his forefinger on the top of the mainmast. Then he did the most extraordinary thing. He bent down and snapped off a little cloth flag that was flying at the stern of the schooner—a French *tricolore,* I think it was—and with infinite finesse, like a gourmet sampling a fine pâté, he popped the flag between thumb and forefinger into his mouth and *ate* it. Or chewed on it, rather. I could see his jaw working. Then, after a while, he leaned forward and spit the flag out on the water and stared evenly across at the other fellow. Challenging him obviously. The thin man let out a high shout and set out after the steam yacht, a long haul for him because of his frailty, his pole with the ivory tip quivering, but he caught up to the yacht finally and fetched her to him. His own act of retribution was not especially inspired: he scooped up some water in his palm and poured it into the steam yacht's funnel. A puff of steam came out. But then he unlatched a miniature lifeboat from its davits and, holding it so the stoutish man with the mustaches on the other side of the pond could see, he held it under water and sank it.

The stout man seemed unshaken. He continued to hold the schooner steady with a forefinger on the top of the mast. He let it go just long enough to extract a Gauloises cigarette from a breast pocket and light it. He blew a thick puff past his mustaches. Then, with as fastidious a gesture as he had used to bring the flag to his lips, he first flourished the cigarette, puffing on it to get its end glowing nicely, and then bent and burnt a hole in the schooner's mainsail, just below a design that looked like a fleur-de-lis.

The schooner's owner was again enraged. He let off some brisk shouts and his whole body moved in agitation as he shimmied over the steam yacht, his fingers twitching in speculation. His first reaction was again uninspired and crude. He pushed the bow of the yacht down with the palm of his hand so that the stern came out of the water, a propeller whirring suddenly. But then he let the bow up, and he reached into the stern of the motor yacht and with hideous, demoniacal care removed a family of lead figures sitting around the after-cockpit—a boating party, two of them women in turn-of-the-century yachting clothes with little red sun parasols tilted back over their shoulders. He scooped them up hefting them in his palm—there were about four or five in the family it seemed to me—and then he threw them out into the pond. Four or five separate little splashes.

For the first time the stout man across the way reacted. His hands started up in astonishment. He took two heavy strides toward the other, shipping water over the tops of his boots, before he stopped to turn back to the schooner. He reached down and snapped the bowsprit. Out of the corner of his eye he must have seen the enraged man across the pond wrenching another lifeboat from its davits, squeezing it between his fingers, and stuffing it down the funnel of the steam yacht.

By now the violence of the efforts of the two men had begun to kick up considerable turbulence in the pond. The small toy boats bucked and swayed in the wash. The children on the parapet of the pond knelt and looked on solemnly. One of them bent and set a soap dish with a stick for a mast on the water.

"Of course, finally," I said, "the two men started for each other across the pond—"

"What happened then?" the golfers wanted to know.

"Well, a gendarme turned up and watched for a while, rocking back and forth on the balls of his feet, y'know, the way they always do, and he called out something across the water, and they stopped just as they were about to get to each other. Quite calmly, they started collecting what was left of their boats. They were purged. The stout one, with his face just above the surface of the pond, began trying to spot his parasol family on the bottom."

"What a guy *that* fellow was—the one that threw the family into the water!" one of the golfers said.

"There was a man next to me," I said, "who reported that these two had these rages regularly—every two months or so."

Another of the golfers stirred. "Well, I'll tell you one thing about those two. They may build model boats in their spare time, but I know where you'll find them when they're not doing that."

"Where is that?"

"On a golf course. Those two have got to be golfers. Particularly that fellow who threw that little family in the water. That's a golfer if I ever heard of one."

"How about the flag-eater?" someone asked.

"Sure," he said. "Both of those guys are golfers. Got to be."

CHAPTER 17

The 16th at Cypress Point is one of the famous golf holes of the world, certainly one of the most difficult and demanding par 3's. In the 1952 Crosby the average score of the entire field on the hole was 5, an average bolstered by Lawson Little getting a 14 and Henry Ransom an 11. Ben Hogan got a 7. The golfer stands on a small elevated tee facing the Pacific Ocean that boils in below on the rocks, its swells laced with long strands of kelp. Occasionally, a sea lion can be seen lolling about, turning lazily, a flipper up, like a log in a slow current. It would be a clear shot to the horizon if it weren't for a promontory that hooks around from the golfer's left. On the end of the promontory, circled by ice plant, is the green, a 210-yard carry across the water.

The green is shallow, with some traps behind, and then the ice plant, and beyond that, ready to receive a shot hit a touch too powerfully, the Pacific Ocean. There is a relatively safe approach to the 16th, which is to aim to the left of the green and carry a shot 125 yards or so across the water onto the wide saddle of the promontory. A lonely storm-bent tree stands in the fairway, and it is in its vicinity that one drops one's first shot. From there the golfer must chip to the green and sink his putt to make his par.

Many players are critical of the 16th at Cypress. Gardner Dickinson told me that he thought it was no sort of golf hole at all. His point was that risking a direct carry to the green, particularly if any sort of wind was blowing in the golfer's face, was ill-advised and "cotton-pickin' stu-

"Here is the famous 16th par-3 hole at Pebble Beach. The green, a 200-yard carry, is in the center of the picture with the three traps around it. Prudent golfers, including many of the great professionals, hit an iron toward the wind-blasted tree to the left and then pitch to the green." (*Russ Halford*)

pid," and the sensible golfer was penalized for the shot he *should* make — that is to say, to the fairway on the saddle of the promontory, from where he must get down in two for his par. The chances of birdieing the hole playing it that way are, of course, almost nil. Dickinson himself would not try the long shot. (One's whole daily score could be affected; Jerry Barber got a 10 on the hole the year that he was PGA champion.) He always chose the safer route, cutting across as much ocean as he dared with an iron, aiming for the promontory saddle, all the while mumbling and carrying on and pinching up his face in disgust as if the kelp surging back and forth below him in the sea were exuding a strong odor.

The spectators loved the hole, though. They gathered on the wooded bluff above the tee, some perched on the wide cypress branches, squat-shaped, like night herons. When a player motioned—somewhat theatrically, one always felt—to his caddy for a wood, and the caddy, warming to the drama, removed the woolen cover with a flourish, there would be a stirring in the trees, like a rookery at dawn, and a stretching forward, since the spectators up there knew the golfer was going to "go for it."

And it was a wonderful thing to hear the click of the club and see the ball soar off over the ocean—as senseless an act, at first glance, as watching someone drive a ball off the stern of a transatlantic liner—the ball rising up against the wind currents and high above the line of the horizon beyond. Then, with its descent, one realized the distant green had become available, until it was a question of *distance*—whether the ball would flash briefly against the cliffs that fronted the green and plummet into the ocean, or whether the green itself would suddenly be pocked by the whiteness of the ball, the feat done, accented by a roar and clatter rising out of the trees behind the tee.

Here was the distinction of this ocean hole at Cypress: it epitomized the feat of golf—excessively, Dickinson would say—namely, the hitting of a distant target with accuracy, a shot so demanding that it was either successful or, with the ocean circling the hole on three sides, emphatically a disaster.

When our foursome reached the 16th tee the wind was slight. Amid a stir of excitement, Bob Bruno went for the green with a wood. He made one of his best shots of the day, it seemed to me, and behind us the cries came out of the treetops. Bruno wasn't so sure. The ball had landed on an area of the green that we couldn't see from the tee. He thought he had "come off" the ball somewhat, a bit "fat," he thought, and that as a result the shot might have caught the ice plant. Not being at all convinced that the hole was secure for our team, he suggested that I play my shot safe and short for the promontory and, done with his advice, he walked away and stood looking moodily out at the sea. I think I would have played it that way in any case. A 210-yard carry into that slight wind would have created sufficient pressure that I would have missed the shot in some way.

I motioned for a wood, a three wood, a club I had been feeling comfortable with that day, and again there was a hum of expectation and interest among the spectators. Abe, my caddy, coming forward with the golf bag, said, "You going for it? You'll be needing a driver. Maybe *two* drivers."

He was speaking loudly enough for some of the spectators to overhear.

"I'll take the wood, Abe," I insisted.

I reached for the wood and handed him back the woolen cover.

"You're up," Bruno said from the edge of the tee, still staring out to sea. He was impatient to check the lie of his ball.

I set the ball on the tee and did what I had been intending to do all along—I hit a good easy wood across the short neck of water to the saddle, just what Dickinson would have done, except he would have used a five iron, possibly a six, but if it took me a wood to feel comfortable and get the ball there, well, that was wise golf, too.

There was an odd stir and fidget in the trees and in the crowd around the tee. I could imagine an elderly man, sitting on a golfing stick, saying impetuously and sharply: "You see that? That big fellow takes out a wood. He's going for it. So what does he do but hit a tiny little wood over yonder...Shortest wood I ever saw without it being topped."

The thing to do was hurry off the tee as quickly as one could.

CHAPTER 18

After a round almost all the golfers would go and peer at the big scoreboard set off to one side of the clubhouse lawn and watch the official PGA scorekeeper—I was told his name was Dom Mirandi— post the scores; they could look to see how well they were doing against the field. After the Cypress round I went down to see how Bruno and I had fared. Mirandi was posting our score, his pen squeaking as he put down the 4's that looked like sailboats, and too many 5's, and the one ugly 6. I remembered the 6—which we took on the Cypress 14th when Bruno got himself in trouble and I fluffed a chance to help him out. I had had an easy approach but I had ended up just off the green in a heavy patch of trees and bushes. I had gone in there and found the ball, intending to punch it through the thick screen of vegetation to the green. I called out: "Keep an eye out. Here it comes." I choked up on the club and swung. The ball disappeared. Above me there was a sudden puzzling rush and flutter, and a slight rain of pine needles. "Did it come out?" I called.

I heard Abe wheezing out on the green.

"Did it come out?" I repeated. I tried to peer through.

"Not the ball," I heard Abe say. "But a *bird* come out."

"A bird?"

We never did find the ball. I may have driven it down into the pine humus. Abe said he thought the bird that was frightened out by the

George slips his scorecard into the pile while the scorers look away. Note Abe's pursed lips. (*Russ Halford*)

shatter of my swing was an owl. "Big fluttery type of bird," he said. "We heard you swing in there, and all those bushes shook, and y'know we was all ready for a golf ball to come through, out on the green, and then what come over the bushes and fly right over us, maybe thirty feet up, was this damn big bird. Owl, or maybe a hawk. Great big thing. Eagle, maybe."

"I don't suppose anyone was amused," I said. "I don't suppose Bruno was."

"I don't reckon you heard much laughing?"

"No," I said truthfully.

"'Course that bird was so big, maybe everyone was a little surprised. I gave quite a start myself."

"Here is a golf ball which remained up in a tree during the Crosby. At the execution of the shot a large bird flew out from the upper portions of the tree." (*Russ Halford*)

On the scoreboard I watched the numerical evidence of this discomfiting occurrence posted as Mirandi finished in the spaces and added up the total, which was 70. Our two-day total was a long distance off the pace. I leaned across the restraining rope and introduced myself. He had a moment to spare and I asked him what was the highest score he could remember posting for a single hole. He thought a minute and said he recalled putting an 108 down for Dave Hill's 18th hole in some tournament. Hill had shot a bad round and scribbled down the number quixotically, and then signed his card, which made it official. Of course, there were the more unfortunate cases, quite unintentional. Jerry Barber had once added up his total for the back nine and by mistake he inserted it in the space reserved for the 18th hole score. He signed his card, thus giving himself 36 strokes for the 18th and a horrendous total that dropped him from high in the field plumb to the bottom.

As might be expected from someone who spends his entire day mounting numbers on a scoreboard, Mirandi was of a very methodical turn, and he talked almost entirely in statistics. He had a three-tray tool chest with him, and he showed me what he had in it with the delight of a fisherman showing a kid through his tackle box.

"First tray I keep the pens," he said. He took one out and revolved it between two fingers. "About two dozen of them, dry-ink pens they are. Different colors, as you can see: one color for posting the morning scores, another for the afternoon. In the course of a year I wrote over one million figures with these pens. Now here in the second tray we have spare parts for the pens, cans of ink in these compartments, crayons here, rubber bands, clips, and so forth, benzine cleaner fluid, clean rags for erasing, everything right here where I can get to it. And then in the third tier here, well, as you can see, we have the *Rules of Golf* (never can tell when you're going to need them), the PGA constitution, by-laws, maps, scissors, clips, more crayons, and a few other tools of the trade. I carry this kit sixty thousand miles across the country on the tour each year. Been doing this since July of '63. Before that I was sixteen years with the New England PGA."

"How about the scoreboards themselves," I asked. "How long does it take you to prepare them?"

"Yes," Mirandi said. He looked at the big board behind him. "Well, it used to take me eight hours to get a scoreboard prepared for a tournament. I've narrowed that time down to about six hours. What I do is set out these big cards on the motel floor and work on them, lying on my stomach, working the lines and setting in the names from six in the evening until after midnight. When I assemble the cards the next morning and set them up out on the course, you'll have yourself a scoreboard forty feet long, eight feet high. That's with an average field of 144 professionals. The biggest field I ever had to prepare was 347 names for the PGA National Golf Club Championship in 1962 at Dunedin. It took me eighteen hours to copy down the draw and get that scoreboard prepared."

"Is there any way electronic gear is going to replace this?" I asked.

"Nonsense," Mirandi said. "Not a chance."

A professional came by and peered over Mirandi's head at the board. He said, "Dom, what do you think?"

Mirandi looked back at the board. "Can't tell, Harry. Too early yet. Hang around, that's what I'd advise. You're right on the edge."

When the golfer had wandered off, Mirandi explained that the pro had been asking what his chances were of making the cut. It is usually at the end of the second day's play that a cut-off point is established, a 36-hole total which lops out of the tournament those players with higher scores — a level which cannot be determined until the last foursome is in and the score tabulated. But Mirandi, posting scores, kept in his mind's eye a fairly accurate overall picture of the tournament, and he was able to make a reasonable prognosis for players on the borderline who had no wish to stick around the course any longer than necessary if they hadn't made it — those who wanted to rid themselves of the place and get on as quickly as possible to the next tournament for the refreshment of new surroundings and a new challenge. So they would hang around the scoreboard area, ducking under the ropes from time to time to confer with Mirandi as the afternoon wore on.

Finally he might say: "Well, no chance, Toby. You might as well pack up, and maybe we'll see you in Tucson."

"Hell," Mirandi told me. "I've seen players hang around these ropes for years, ducking under and coming in and asking me, tournament after tournament, and they never make the cut. Think of that. And people play this game for fun. Oh my!"

CHAPTER 19

After the second day's round it was quite clear that the Bruno-Plimpton team was not going to make the cut. The cut came after the third day's play and we would be required, we reckoned, to pick up almost a stroke a hole to continue as a team for the fourth and final day. On his individual ball Bruno was in better shape. He had a chance to survive the cut and go into the last day's play—on his own, of course, our team being dissolved. I left him working on his putting in the semi-darkness of the practice green and I went into the lodge. Dave Marr saw me wandering by, and he called out cheerfully: "They tell me you were doing a lot of chilly-dipping out there today."

Not knowing what the term meant, I did not feel it was an assessment that I could agree to readily, so I said, "Well...ah."

"You were hitting some shots out there that weren't making any *noise*," Marr said.

It seemed safe to say, "That's so." So I did.

"You had those divots coming up and just curling over the ball."

"That's right," I said, surer of myself. "Absolutely."

We went down to the bar and joined some of the other golfers. I asked about "chilly-dipping," just to be certain, and they said it meant a flub, the same as not putting any "noise" on the ball. They weren't sure where the expression came from. A Texas phrase, most likely. Many of them came out of Texas, and almost surely they originated in the dirt yards under the pines behind the caddy houses. "Those caddies come up with the great ones," one of the golfers said. They began talking about golf expressions, and how they had changed through the years.

In the present-day idiom a player with a bad round that day, such as the one I'd had, was described as having "crashed and burned." He had not stuck to the "track," which was how golfers referred to the course. He would complain that his game had been troubled by "snipes" or "blue darters" (hooks). He would say that he had hit too many shots into the "tall and uncut," "the asparagus," "the cabbage," the "zucchini," "the lettuce," or "Marlboro Country"—all expressions for being in the rough. "Man, I just put it in jail," he might say.

If he wasn't in the rough, he was in the sand traps, which were referred to as "cat boxes," "silicone," "on the beach," or "in the bogey dust." Actually, "bogey dust" could be used for any shot out of the fairway, as in, "Man, I never saw that shot, but she sure blew up the bogey dust." Another variation was: "Baby, that duck hook's moving those field mice for *real*."

As for expressions describing shots well hit, they had also changed considerably. A few years ago a professional golfer would say, "I was hitting it a ton today." Now he says, "The Fat Man [Nicklaus] really shot the lights out today." Or he'd say, of a good strong shot hit by his partner, "Man, you put some *hurtin'* on that one." Or perhaps, "Partner, you really got some *swift* on that shot." A long, low drive would be "a frozen rope," and a long putt successfully sunk is referred to as a "field goal" or a "gobbler" or a "snake," as in "on the 12th I got me a snake." A short putt is a "knee-knocker" and would be stroked from an area called "the throw-up zone." A fine approach shot would be described by a pro as having been knocked "stony," or perhaps his partner would say, "Man, you hit that one *adjacent*." A great shot, if hit at the right time, was always a "career shot."

It was odd how quickly descriptive words fell into disuse and disappeared. Good ones, too, that had fine euphonious effect, a surprising number of them utilizing "s" sounds. Scottish, I suppose. In the last century "scaffing" or "scafling" was the word for a flubbed shot, more specifically for digging a club into the ground before hitting the ball. To "scuffle" was to top a shot. "Socketing" was the old word for shanking the ball. A complete miss was called an "aerial swat"—what we now call an air shot or a "silent shot," or what Gary Player, the South African, refers to as "fresh air." A longer phrase of interest might be, "He snodded his man on the seventeenth with a long steal," which is to say, the golfer won the match on the seventeenth against his opponent by holing a long putt. Some of the expressions were perhaps a mite precious. The rough was occasionally referred to as "Mrs. Wiggs and her Cabbage Patch."

In those days the clubs went by such names as "cleek," "lobbing iron," "niblick," and so forth. Nowadays, clubs have almost entirely lost names other than the numerical—only the sandblaster, the pitching wedge, and the driver remain as descriptive appellations. Brassie and spoon for the two and three woods are fast disappearing. In the old days some golfers actually had alliterative female names for their clubs. A spoon might be "June." Darwin's mashie, which would be the equivalent of a five iron, was "Maud." ("Just pass me along Maud," he might say to his caddy.) Some irons had first names—"Sammies" and "Bennies." One of the odd names for a club, in the early days of American golf, was the word "arm." The usage was apparently home-grown, because when Vardon, the great English player, paid his first visit to America he was startled to have people come up and ask him what "arm" he had used on such-and-such a hole. It took a time for Vardon to realize what they were asking him.

Vardon seems to have had a number of bewildering experiences on his tour. In Boston it was arranged, without his being aware, that he give an exhibition in a Boston hotel, hitting shots into a net in front of an audience of some 200, for a half-hour, and then getting an hour's rest before doing it again before a fresh house. Vardon started at 9:30 in the morning and went on until 5 in the afternoon—going almost crazy with boredom. He whiled away the time trying to slap a shot through the netting and hit what looked like a knob up near the ceiling. The manager, who'd been watching idly from the wings, started suddenly and rushed out on the stage and whispered that the knob was the tap of a fire-extinguishing apparatus, and that if Vardon happened to hit it, the hall and the audience would be bathed in a heavy shower. Vardon was tempted to say such a diversion might help his act: he didn't see what enjoyment an audience could get watching him drive balls into a net just a few yards from his stance.

The mosquitoes in the United States made a big impression on Vardon. His ankles were bitten so badly that he could barely get his shoes on. The heat was memorable, as was the fact that golfers played in shirt-sleeves, and so did the cries that came out of the gallery. He described one fat gentleman under a very large umbrella calling out: "Lordy, lordy, child, some approach."

One golfing expression that was very common in Vardon's time, a marvelously apt word, absolutely connotative in sound, seems sadly to have dropped utterly from circulation. It peppered the old golfing books I skimmed through, particularly Darwin, namely, the word "foozle." It was a favorite word of P. G. Wodehouse in his great golfing stories. It meant to mis-hit a shot. But nowadays if one announced loudly in the country-club locker room that one had "foozled" one's drive on the 5th, meaning one had topped it, or messed it up somehow, the heads would turn at that word, and maybe someone would lean around the corner of the locker and look and withdraw, and in the corridors the murmured conversation would start up, "...who's that guy...foozle!...what sort of antique cat is *that* in the next aisle...?"

"What about that word," I asked my golfing friends at the table. "Foozle."

"We don't hear that one any more," one of them said. "They come and they go, these expressions, and it doesn't take a week for them to fall out of fashion."

Golfing expressions, those in vogue, were often shifted to suit every-day observation. For example, sipping at his beer, a golfer might say about the girl across the bar room:

"An unraked sand trap."

Or perhaps, which was the ultimate in disparagement: "She's 18 off the reds," using the term for a handicap of 18 off the women's tees to indicate their low opinion.

"She's 2 off the blues," would suggest a girl ranked very high in the general estimation.

The handicap system could be applied to anything. A golfer, looking out the window at the weather in the morning, could call back over his shoulder to his roomie and indicate its state to a nicety—from "scratch off the blues" to describe a perfect day to "18 off the reds," this last meaning, very likely, a blizzard, or that the golfer was suffering a terrible hangover and had a bad day to face.

Some of the transitions were involved and took some work to understand. For example, seeing a girl of questionable reputation leaning against the bar, a golfer would say, "George, see that bird. Well, you'd say about her that she's got a real strong right hand, wouldn't you?"

I leaned forward, puzzled. "I don't get it."

"What happens if your right hand comes in with too much power? What is produced by a person who has that problem?"

"A hook," I'd say. "Oh, yes," I said, looking at the girl. "That's pretty damn clever. Hooker. Yes. Yes." And they would all sit back, pleased, sipping at their beer.

"Nicknames?" I asked. I supposed these must be colorful, considering the lively patois of the game. The players looked at each other. Well, there were the familiar ones. Arnold was, of course, the "Bull," Nicklaus the "Golden Bear," or more familiarly, "The Fat Man." "The Buffalo" was Billy Casper, for his odd habit of dieting on buffalo meat. Mike Souchak was called "Smokey the Bear," because he looked like the original article—the Prevent Forest Fires symbol. Ken Venturi was known as "Silks," though no one was quite sure why. Usually a player who wore fancy golfing trousers of a special material was known as "Silks." Rex Baxter, for example. But that wasn't particularly true of Venturi. Don Massengale, for the set of his mouth and teeth, was "Bugs Bunny."

Julius Boros, for his bulk and his dark potato face, was the "Moose." Mason Rudolph was known as "Spy" for the round glasses he wore. Gay Brewer was jokingly called the "Fag Winemaker," although in polite company he was referred to as "Hounddog" for looking slightly like one. Many of the names came with the player onto the tour. Charles Sifford had always been "The Horse," Harold Kneece "The Catfish," Gene Littler "The Machine," Paul Harney "Boston Blackie." Kermit Zarley, for his somewhat extraterrestrial name, was called "The Pro from the Moon." Lionel Hebert, the Louisianan, was known as "Lionel from Montreal" from the tag line of a Cajun song he sang. Gardner Dickinson, for being Ben (The Hawk) Hogan's imitator, with an identical golf style and for affecting the same clothes, in particular the famous white cloth cap, was called "The Chicken Hawk," though never within his hearing. If golfers sitting around caught Dickinson in a cough, or even clearing his throat, they would say to each other behind half-cupped hands, "Oh-oh, Ben's come down with a bad cold, sure *enough*."

One of the best nicknames (for its derivation) that I was told was Jack McGowan's. "Deadman" they called him, a name not derived from his personal appearance, but from caddies, who hung it on him for his habit of calling out rapidly after a poor shot, "Man, I'm dead. I'm dead, I'm dead over there, just dead over there, just *dead*."

"You have a name yet?" they asked me.

"Not yet," I said, thinking back on the calamities of the day. "First, I got to put some noise on my shots," I said, trying out the phrase. "Some swift."

"Yes, you try that," they said.

CHAPTER 20

In each tournament I played in California, as our team approached a tee on the back nine somewhere, a man wearing an enormous cast on one foot, the size of a full-grown watermelon, would rise painfully out of a canvas chair and, flipping open a large notebook, stagger a step or so forward, teeter, steady himself, and ask us individually about our golf equipment and apparel. Eddie Darrell, I was told his name was, and he represented golfing manufacturers interested in finding out what equipment golfers, both professional and amateur, were using in the tournaments. Even more important, he was supposed to check to see that players were using the equipment that they were paid to endorse. He and I always had an odd exchange, and after a while a wary look would enter his eye when he saw me. He was never quite sure what my participation meant, why I should turn up, with my poor brand of golf, in a succession of big tournaments. Our exchange during the first round at the Crosby had gone as follows:

"Golf hat?" He was looking down at a checklist in his hand.

"Well, I'm not wearing a hat."

"Golf gloves," he said impatiently. "What make?"

"None. Don't wear one."

He looked at me and sighed. "Well, you got a sweater and shirt?"

"The shirt has an alligator on it. I don't know what the sweater is. I'm sorry."

I didn't tell Darrell that my eclectic choice was conscious—since I had wondered vaguely about the awkwardness of, say, outfitting myself in an Arnold Palmer line of clothes and then, by the luck of the draw, having to spend the tournament in the company of Jack Nicklaus. It seemed more sensible to outfit oneself in nondenominational clothes.

"How about your shoes?"

"I happen to know what they're called," I said. "They're Pro-Shu, that's spelled s-h-u."

He made a mark. "All right. Clubs, then."

"Those...ah...I have. Wilson Staff."

"Golf bag?"

"That bag of mine's a Dunlop, I'm pretty sure," I said. The both of us stared moodily at the bag. "It's a big one, isn't it?"

Darrell always wanted to know what sort of ball I was using.

"I started with a Wilson Staff," I told him one day.

"Yes, a Wilson Staff." He began writing.

"But then I switched to a Titleist 2."

"Something wrong with the...?"

"I lost the Wilson Staff. In the rough on the third hole," I said.

"That a Titleist 2?" he asked, pointing to the ball I was revolving in my hand.

"The fact is," I said, "it's a Maxfli 3." I looked at it to make sure. "The Titleist 2 is in a pond."

"You must have had a helluva first nine," Darrell said.

After one of the Crosby rounds I saw Darrell hobbling painfully across the clubhouse lawn and I asked him if he'd like to ease his limb over a drink. He said he would be delighted. We reached two camp chairs under a table with a beach parasol running up through the middle, and he set himself down with a sigh of pleasure. He told me that his foot problem had first been diagnosed as gout, and he had been taking the appropriate medicine for some time now, over a year, and laying off the liquor, but then quite by chance it had been discovered that he was actually suffering from three broken toes.

"You got the worst diagnosis I ever heard of," I said.

"Well," he said. "I've still got the gout pills in case I ever *get* the gout. I was going to hit the doctor with a chair when he told me," he went on. "But then I thought, oh well, it's good to hear I *don't* have the gout. At least you can clear up broken toes. Boy, the gout had me worried about my job . . . being on my feet all the time, and on the go . . ."

Darrell had been surveying for golf equipment companies since 1927, he told me, nearly forty years. His usual stand during a tournament was on the short par-3 holes where the field would jam up and he could get a chance to talk to the players.

When I looked surprised at his mentioning all those years, he said defensively that it was an interesting job. Things had changed, of course. He had come in at the time of the hickory shafts, and the players wore white caps back then and silk shirts, cuff links, and ties. Tommy Armour, Harry Cooper, and Walter Hagen — they were the best-dressed.

"You know something interesting about Harry Cooper?"

"What was that?" I asked.

"Well, he couldn't hit a Spalding Green Dot." Darrell said. "The balls had colors then — the Spalding Blue, Black, Green, Red, and so forth, and you put a Green Dot down in front of Harry Cooper and he could not hit it. Don't ask me why."

"When did the fancy dressers appear?" I asked. "The forerunners of Doug Sanders?"

"Demaret was the first," Darrell said. "Pink shoes and violet pants. He had five hundred hats. They came along pretty fast after that. But I couldn't believe it when I first saw those painted shoes of Tommy Bolt. Damn near fell down. Nine and a half C's they were."

"What's the widest shoe you've seen come along?"

"Porky Oliver's. A pair of nine triple E's. Speaking of shoes and Porky Oliver," Darrell said, "he had a caddy, this crazy nut, who kept his money in his shoe. You could always tell if Porky was going well, and his caddy was in the chips, because this guy would peg along pretty lopsided on the course, like he had a wooden leg."

I asked him: "Has anything really ever surprised you — I mean in those forty years of standing on those par-3 holes around the country?" I was beginning to get depressed thinking about his job, particularly seeing him sitting on the canvas chair with his leg stuck out at an angle, with the big cast on the foot.

"Well," he said, "the other day this guy, Cameron Mitchell, came by with a twelve-pound putter in his bag."

"No," I said.

"Never seen anything like that before. I suppose he thought it gave him a better sense of touch on the greens—damnedest looking thing."

"What did his caddy look like? How did he take it—that great extra weight in his bag?"

Darrell looked at me. "Well, I don't know. I didn't look at the guy. But he couldn't have looked very happy—I mean, that's quite a weight to be carrying...twelve extra pounds."

We ordered drinks. "It's been a good life," he said. "The travel is great, tournament to tournament, and golf has its great characters. For example," he began, "Carl Lohren, not a bad golfer—when he was on the road, well, he used to jump out of his car and practice his swing when they'd pull up at a red light. There was this one time when he stepped out of his car in some little hick town when he and his partner was waiting at a railroad crossing. His driving partner never heard him get out because of the noise of the freight going by—thought he was lying in the back seat asleep. Well, he went on without Lohren...just driving straight on for the Jacksonville Open, whatever it was..."

"What about...ah...?"

"Lohren? Well, he was left in the dust, looking off at the back of his car disappearing down the road, and then the noise of the train dying away, and it got awful quiet and then he was in this little hick town with his golf club—and that was *all* he had, not a dime, just a pair of house keys in his pocket, and this golf club."

"Lord, what did he do?"

"Well, he survived. I don't know the exact details. I suppose he went into a diner, y'know, and explained it to them..."

"God, what do you suppose he could have said? Was he wearing golf shoes and a golf hat?" I asked illogically.

Darrell said, "I suppose he showed them the golf club, y'know, and he said, y'know, my *car* drove away"—he suddenly sounded peeved—"why should I know *that*. I didn't ask nobody. Everyone wants to know the damnedest things. I wasn't there, after all." He moved and his leg must have twinged him slightly. "God Almighty!"

"No, no," I said. "It's just a fine little scene—a golfer with his club just dropped down there in the middle of nowhere, maybe some red-dirt town in Louisiana just hundreds of miles from the nearest golf course, and the hillbillies in the diner looking up when he comes in...it's such a fine scene for *speculation*."

"Yes," he said. He thought for a moment, and then he said again: "Well, he survived. I mean he got out of there."

The drinks arrived.

"You ever see a hole-in-one from one of those par-3's?"

"No," he said.

We sat for a while. The drink began to cheer him.

"It's interesting," he said suddenly, "the individualities of the different players. Bruce Crampton doesn't wear a glove. Neither does Ben Hogan. You know, of course, that they all have very distinct preferences about golf balls, even the numbers on them. Balls are numbered for identification up to eight or so, but you find very few touring pros who'll ever play a round with a high-numbered ball."

"I wonder why that's so?" I asked.

"I can give you one explanation," Darrell said. "Marty Furgol used to say, 'Now you tell me how you can shoot a 3 with a number 6 ball!'" Darrell grinned. "So you think maybe a lot of pros use a number 3? Not necessarily. Johnny Pott and Jim Ferree, you wouldn't ever find them with a number 3. They feel it might tend to make them 3-putt."

"I'll tell you something not many people know," Darrell went on. "When golfers replace the ball on the green, they do it with great care to have the trade name facing the putter blade running vertically. It gives the golfer an angle to help him on his line for the hole. Catch?"

"Well, vaguely," I said.

"Gay Brewer places the red dot of his Maxfli so he hits it with his putter."

"What about Hogan?" I asked. "What number ball does he use?"

"Ben Hogan, until he founded his own line of equipment, liked to use a Titleist 4. Sam Snead uses a ball with a zero on it. But how about you?" Darrell asked. "You don't seem to have made a habit of using a particular ball." He moved himself painfully in the canvas chair. "You settled on anything yet?"

"Not yet," I said.

"I've seen you with just about every make of ball they've got — short of the old gutta-percha."

"I'm still experimenting," I said cheerfully.

"That figures," Darrell said.

CHAPTER 21

———

I had a dream that afternoon about Lohren, the man Eddie Darrell had told me about, the fellow who got out of the car at the railroad crossing outside of the Louisiana red-dirt town with his golf club to practice his swing and got himself left there by mistake without a bean in his pocket, and his partner driving on unaware toward the next town on the tour. I guess the lonely figure standing at the railroad crossing with a golf club in his hand had stuck in my mind.

I had taken a drive that afternoon down toward Big Sur along the Pacific. The whales were moving again. From as high as you get on the road, way up, I suppose 1,000 feet, perhaps more, the Pacific below stretches to the horizon as gray and flat as sheet iron, but as you descend, the car slow and wheeling on the corners, the vague corrugations become more evident, and the ocean *moves,* the lines of surf just infinitesimally attacking the shoreline, and it's then, from that height, the whales can be seen—just the touch of plume, and a pock in the water as they surface on their way north.

I got back to the lodge before dark. I thought I'd try some putting on the carpet, but I flopped down on the bed instead. The room was very quiet. The breakwater, and the quiet sea beyond, was a couple hundred yards across the fairway, deserted now, with all the players through with their rounds. I thought about the whales, and then about Eddie Darrell's man at the railroad crossing.

He was wearing a baby-blue turtleneck sweater, blue golfing slacks, and sky-blue golfing shoes with big flaps down over the laces. He was getting his feet acclimated to the shoes, which were new and needed to be broken in. He wore a blue golfing glove which he removed and put in his pocket when the car disappeared down the road. His golfing hat, also blue, had a decal on the front with crossed golf clubs and a red tee, and letters identifying the country club around the border. It was a very long Indian name which I could not quite make out—the Chippequa National Links Club, something on that order. The hat was very jaunty. His golf club was a Spalding Executive driver, which he lifted and gestured with as the dust cloud settled in the distance behind his car.

When the train had gone, and nothing was left of it but the faint moan of its whistle through the pine trees, the noise of the frogs started up from the railroad ditches. The golfer looked around. He took a despairing swing with his Spalding. It kicked up a fine puff of white dust which settled back on his blue golfing shoes. How many miles, he wondered, before his golfing partner would look back over his shoulder and see that he was missing from the back seat. Perhaps not until the car pulled into the outskirts of Jacksonville. His partner was a very laconic sort of bloke, slow-thinking, and golfers called him "Sleep" because that seemed his condition as he stood over his putts. He loved to drive cars on those long stretches between the stops on the tour, perfectly content to hunch over the steering wheel with little murmurations escaping his lips—snatches of songs, little dialogues, jokes, small ho-hums of laughter, like the gentle indistinct sounds of occupancy drifting from the house next door. He was alive with inner voices.

The golfer had overheard these dialogues on the fairways—so soft that he was never sure that he had them straight, hardly sure that anything had been said at all. But he would see Sleep's lips moving, a thin little dialogue going on, and he could catch just suggestions of it: "My, look at that lie, just perched up there." "Yes, yes, excellent." "No, no, Priscilla—it's a six, a six iron would be nifty—"

"Priscilla!" the golfer thought. "What a great break—*that* guy at the wheel," he said aloud.

He turned and started back up the road toward a filling station with a clapboard lean-to structure alongside that had a sign above it reading EATS. It stood out from the pine forests, a lonely place, white in the sun, as quiet as a vulture's perch. He walked toward it rather halfheartedly, not expecting to find anyone about. He stepped up on a small porch that creaked alarmingly underfoot and he pushed open the screen door to step inside. It was darker within, like stepping under the lip of an overhanging rock, and there was a sudden strong country smell of ripe apples. The wood on the floor was old and soft and he felt his golf cleats sink in. A woman in a straw hat stood behind a scarred counter next to a tall old-fashioned cash register. Her eyes widened.

"Claude!" she called.

There was an abrupt movement off to his right, a chair leg slamming down, and he perceived in the gloom three men sitting around a table, all of whom had apparently been asleep.

It took some time for everyone to adjust their senses: the three of them had been sleeping with their legs on the table, their chairs tilted back, and to get themselves seated properly and attentive required a certain amount of shifting and settling. One of them, the one called Claude apparently, wore a tall hillbilly hat.

"What in tarnation!" he said finally.

The golfer took a clumsy step forward, the pleasant smile on his face frozen as his spikes popped noisily out of the wood. "Ahem," he said. He lifted his golf club. "I'm a golfer," he announced, shaking the club, and trying to speak as matter-of-factly as he could. "Just got left behind there at the railroad crossing. Fellow with me just drove off. Stepped out, you see, to practice my swing..."

"Not so fast, young man," said the man sitting next to Claude. He had come half out of his chair to look at the golfer.

"Don't quite know what to do," the golfer was going on. "Haven't got a dime, but maybe I could put in a telephone call collect to *some-one*...if I could borrow..."

"*What crossing you talking about?*" the man insisted.

"The crossing? Well, the railroad crossing just up the street."

The man looked at his watch. "Hopped off the 5:15 freight—that your story?" He looked slyly at the other two.

"No," the golfer said. "I came by car. The car drove off by mistake. We're on our way—or we *were* on our way—to the Jacksonville Open."

The third man at the table made a quick expansive gesture to quiet the other two. He was older, with a sun-creased face, black suspenders crossed at his chest, and he had taken longer to awaken than the others; he now had the sly questing look of a turtle about to go to feed. "Martha," he said to the woman in the straw hat, "go on out back and fetch Mark Tanner." When she had gone, scuttling quickly behind the counter through a screen door in the back that slammed loudly in the gloom, the older man reached into his coveralls and set a large pistol on the table.

"Now, stranger." He cleared his throat. "What you got them shoes painted blue for? And what about them spikes? And what does that scribblin' on your hat say?"

"I'm a golfer, I'm the home pro at the Chippequa National Links Club. That's what it says on the hat," the golfer said. "This is a driver, this club," he said, brandishing it.

"We kin see that," the older man said. He stretched a hand out casually for the pistol.

The golfer brought his club down. "All I'm looking for is a phone," he went on, "and to borrow a dime for a collect call."

The older man raised his hand: "You reckon to hit a ball with that stick—that's the purpose, *kee*rect?"

"Yes, that's right. You hit the ball with this...ah...stick."

"You bring a ball along with you? Mebbe you can show us the ball?"

"Well, no," the golfer said.

The three stared at him. The one with the suspenders said slowly: "What was you fixin' to do with that there *club,* if you please, if not to hit a ball with it?"

"I stepped out to practice my swing," the golfer said, restlessly.

"Any reason 'tall why you pick Mullins, Louisiana—"

"I beg your pardon."

"—Mullins, Louisiana, to do this *practicing*?" The hillbilly leaned on the last word with sarcastic emphasis. "This 'ere town is Mullins—Mullins, Louisiana."

The golfer shrugged hopelessly. The three conferred briefly behind cupped hands. "The name Mark Tanner mean nothing to you?" Claude asked.

"Mark Tanner?"

The one with the black suspenders leaned across the table, his hand on the pistol, and asked: "Dan Reilly? That name don't mean nothing to you neither: Dan Reilly?"

The golfer shook his head.

"Well, I'll tell you somethin' very frank, mister. We're of the notion you come into town, into Mullins, to *kill* Mark Tanner."

"*Mark* Tanner. Kill Mark *Tanner*?"

"We're of the notion that Dan Reilly brought you in from outside. From Memphis, mos' like."

"Memphis!" the golfer said. "Can't you read?" he said, pointing at his golf hat. "I'm from the Chippequa National Links *Club*. That's not far from Fairfield, Connecticut!"

The older man ignored him. He knit his brows and continued: "Everybody in town know that Dan Reilly fixin' to kill Mark Tanner 'cause of the trouble up there at the gin mill at the north forty. Now you tell the folks heah in Mullins that Mark Tanner been kilt with a *golf stick* and they say about sech a thing that it was an outside job. Nobody connect sech a thing with Dan Reilly, 'cause he *don' play golf*. Why, that man's so clever it done want to make an honest man *sick*. What better idee than to get some low-slung animul who swings a golf stick sashaying 'round Mullins pretending to be practicin', but in *fact*, waitin' for the chance to hit Mark Tanner on the noggin!"

"Listen," the golfer said, "I don't know Dan Reilly, and if I had orders to hit Mark Tanner with a golf club, hell, I wouldn't know who to hit. It's jes' ... just ... crazy!"

The screen door slammed in the back. The woman appeared behind the counter. The straw hat wobbled alarmingly over her pinched face. "Claude!" she shouted. "He's *daid*—up in the nawth fawty!"

The three men stood, rising as slowly as smoke. They stared at the golfer.

"Claude! He's daid."

"Shut yo' mouth, woman," Claude said. "How'd they git him?"

"He done been beat to death," she said.

"You're fur it, stranger," said Claude. He checked the charge in his pistol. "You like to recollect any last words afore you go to yo' *ree*-ward?"

"You're just absolutely crazy," said the golfer, backing up slightly. "I mean use your haids…heads. You wouldn't beat someone to daith—death—with a *driver*. I don't think you could *kill* a man with a driver—it's wood, very light wood, a type of very light maple. I think you'd have to use a wedge, for Godsake, or a mallet putter—hell, I'd as soon swing a *golf bag* at a man…" He was speaking more quickly now, the words rushing out of him. "A wood's too damn *whippy* for such a thing, too much length in the swing of it for accuracy—that is, against a moving target—too tough, absolutely. And if I were going to knock off Mark Tanner you'd find me stepping around town with a wedge or a sandblaster…Besides, this is a Spalding Executive with a relatively small head. I mean if I *had* to use a driver, I'd use an Arnold Palmer model with a big head…at the very least."

"The guy's loco in the bargain," Claude was saying. "Listen to all that insane caterwauling. He's well out of his misery." He raised the pistol and fired. The golfer sagged flat out on the floor, and going down he sensed the bullet going over his shoulder with the rush and force of an artillery shell.

"Holy mackerel!"

A gust of acrid smoke boiled across the room. Behind him the wall seemed to explode. A shelf collapsed and its contents rolled out around him. A can of Pappy's Peach Preserves spun easily just off his nose.

"You wung him," someone was shouting.

"Claude!" It was the woman in the sunbonnet shouting. "Lookit, Claude, you're not doing the right thang. It's Dan *Reilly* lying daid up there in the nawth fawty. Mark Tanner's healthy as a mule."

"Well, that's the bestest news," said the man in the suspenders. The three of them stepped out from behind the table. The golfer began to pick himself up. The three surrounded him, pulling him upright, and cuffing him happily. They barked at him.

"You really done fool us."

"Who'd a thought!"

"Why didn't y'all *tell* us?"

"You done in a *varmint* in that Dan Reilly."

They lifted his club and admired it.

"To cotch a man jes' right with a stick liken this!"

"Boy, they teach a man things in Memphis!"

The woman in the sunbonnet kept clearing her throat, trying to say something more. "Claude!" she finally said. "Them Reilly brothers— Hugh, Eugene, Hoss, Timothy, and the one that ain't got no name— they all riled up and fixin' on gettin' the killer." She lifted a gnarled hand. "Y'all better clear the stranger out o' heah afore the Reillys git to him."

The three quieted down.

The golfer nodded his head. "Yes," he said. He was thinking about the Reilly who didn't have a name.

One of the hillbillies took out a watch and inspected it. "The local's goin' through," he said. "Mebbe we can flag her down."

They hurried down the dusty street toward the railroad crossing. They could hear the whistle, thin and sifting through the pine woods, and they reached the crossing in time for Claude to pull a tattered flag from a turpentine bucket by the railroad track and wave it for the engineer to see. The train pulled up. It had a mail car and one coach.

"Yo'all come on back when you have half a chance!" they were shouting at him.

"Mullins thinks a *peck* of you!"

He hurried on up into the car without a word. The train began to slip ahead almost immediately. The hillbilly hats were moving along beneath the windows as the three men trotted to keep up to wave good-bye and call up, "Come on back to Mullins, you heah? Welcome any time!"

George chows down between holes. (*Russ Halford*)

As he went down the aisle his golf cleats made a sharp sucking sound as they went in and out of the corridor matting. The car was almost empty and he eased himself into the nearest seat. He set his golf club down next to him. The window was open and he took big draughts of the thick summer air blowing in. "Mullins," he said to himself. The pine woods were moving by very slowly.

He felt a hand on his shoulder. He looked up. The conductor was eyeing him, taking in the baby-blue golfing outfit and the shoes with the blue flaps over the laces. "Ticket, please."

He reached for his wallet instinctively, knowing it wouldn't be there, and feeling instead his golf glove, the fingers sticking out, empty and spooky against his touch.

"Ticket. Ticket, please."

CHAPTER 22

I woke up to the phone ringing beside the bed. The golfer on the train blinked off. I had a quick sense of dismay at his disappearance, but I suspected he would return — that he was stuck in my mind for a while. I reached for the phone.

It was Bruno. He had called to say that he hoped I wasn't being put off by his "intensity," as he expressed it. He was just so hung up on doing well that he felt perhaps some of the pressure he felt was getting onto *me,* and that my play was suffering because of it.

I assured him that my difficulties with golf were largely a personal matter (I resisted a description of the Japanese naval personnel), and that nothing *external,* short of a sonic boom, or an earth tremor, could materially affect my game.

Well, that was good, he said, because he had been worried. He felt he had been too hard on me. He went on to say that he felt we were a good team and that with just a bit of luck with "ham 'n' egging" — that is to say, combining our scores to maximum efficacy — we would do very well, just "mop up the course," as he put it. That was a favorite phrase of his. We still had a chance.

We chatted for a while, and then he said he was going to turn in. I looked at my watch. It was getting on toward eight. He was the earliest and heaviest sleeper I could remember coming across.

I hung up, and thought what a decent thing it was of him to have

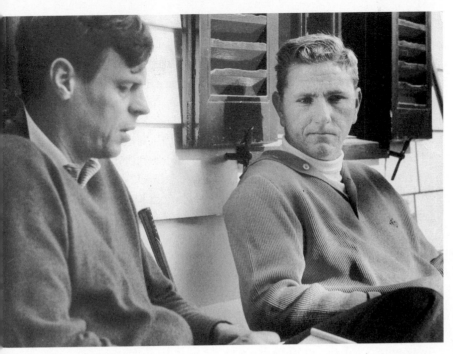

George conducts an informal interview with his playing partner in the Crosby, Bob Bruno. (*Russ Halford*)

done. A partnership in golf was obviously not as demanding on team-work as, say, tennis, since the individual score was still what counted, but there were such intangibles as morale and state of mind, and Bruno knew this.

A little later that evening I had a drink with Mark McCormack, whose partnership with Arnold Palmer is one of the most enduring of the pro-am teams. McCormack is Palmer's business manager—an agreeable and astute financial adviser whose golf is also impressive: a big man with a football player's build, he has played in four U.S. Amateurs and one U.S. Open. He is a scratch player, though one year the Crosby Committee, which is lenient with handicaps because the amateurs play off the back tees with the professionals, awarded him two strokes. I asked him if there was any exchange of professional advice between him and Palmer. He said that on occasion Palmer would ask his advice, perhaps more to make conversation and for assurance than out of indecision. McCormack remembered one year at the 8th hole at Pebble Beach when Palmer, pacing around his drive and looking down toward the green, asked both his caddy and McCormack what club they might suggest. The two disagreed hotly. The caddy, whose name was Tony, a tough-minded and irreverent character of Italian extraction, as McCormack remembers him, finally protested to Palmer loudly: "Hey, who's caddying for you — that guy over there or me?" The question was put with such acerbity that Palmer felt he had to find a provident answer or lose the caddy's services entirely.

"You," he said to the caddy.

Palmer often gives McCormack advice, but it is not always accepted. The usual point of dissension in their partnership is McCormack's prudence in certain situations: he is uncomfortable hitting out of the fairway with a wood, and invariably he'll select an iron and play a pair of comfortable shots rather than pressing and trying the spectacular approach. Palmer, who knows no golfing philosophy other than to attack a course, will wince and shuffle his feet, and he'll say, "Mack, if I played a golf course the way you do, we'd both be broke." On a hole like the difficult 16th at Cypress, where if power isn't applied perfectly the attacking golfer will put his ball in the ocean, McCormack, as he reaches for his irons, knows that Palmer, looking over, will call out: "Try it, Mack. Take a three wood and *hit* it. If it doesn't fly right, and falls in the drink, don't worry." And he'll add with an abiding self-assurance which is not cockiness but simply confidence: "I'm sure to be birdieing the hole anyway."

On the 16th at Cypress the strategy had always been for Palmer to hit first, and if he made the green, then McCormack would try the long over-water carry. His handicap allowed him a stroke on the hole, so that if his drive were successful, their partnership had a good chance for a birdie. Both in the 1964 and 1965 Crosby, Palmer made the back edge of the green, and both those years McCormack followed by dropping his drives in the sea. Palmer then proceeded (both years) to confound the strategy by 3-putting, giving their team a bogey 4.

McCormack told me that in the morning round at the 16th the two had a stiff argument which McCormack finally won on the insistence that a powerful onshore breeze simply denied him of any chance to reach the green. Palmer, grumbling, finally acquiesced. McCormack hit a safe five iron across to the promontory leading to the green, and then pitched onto the green and sank a 6-foot putt for a par 3, net 2. He said he wasn't going to let Palmer forget about *that* hole for a while.

I asked McCormack about playing as an amateur in the great crowd—Arnie's Army—if that was disturbing, not being used to it, and he said that he wasn't much put out by it. Not *too* much, at any rate. He said that if there was any reaction, it was that one was likely to play the shot more quickly—to get it over with so that the attention was off him and onto Arnie, where it belonged. The crowds were more of a problem while moving from one shot to the next—hemming in close behind them, the kids particularly, so that one's heels got trod on. Palmer didn't like that at all. There was only one thing worse, and that was to have the marshals in close behind, and the kids shoving them, so that *they* stumbled forward and clipped one in the heels. If it *had* to happen, it was better to have the kids, who were light and limber, at least, than the marshals or the guards, who were good heavy locker-room types wearing heavy brogans so that if they clipped you and caught you right they inflicted a bone bruise that could linger on throughout a tournament.

"Who is your partner?" McCormack asked.

"Bruno. Bob Bruno's been my partner," I said. "We didn't exactly have people running up the backs of our heels. It's peaceful out there when we play—it's like hunting in the North Woods sometimes, particularly when you've gone out early, and the ground mist hasn't lifted yet."

"Well, I'm sure there are times when I envy you," McCormack said. "You can get...well, pretty anxious playing in Arnie's Army—I can tell you."

CHAPTER 23

The last hole of play for me in the Crosby was the famous finishing 18th hole at Pebble Beach. On one side of the fairway, to the golfer's left, the ocean boils in against the long curve of a sea wall. Dan Jenkins, the sports writer, once described the 18th: "For those who believe that man came from the sea and faces a deep-hidden necessity to return to it some day, there would be no better route than to get a golf club and go to the 18th at Pebble Beach." With the sea so tempting, a number of wags have recommended that in the play of the hole the left eye be kept tightly shut.

The other side of the fairway, the inland side, was usually packed thick with spectators. The temptation under their gaze was to press and to attempt the spectacular shot. I kept telling myself to play the normal shot, but the presence of the gallery was unsettling. I really wanted to smite the ball.

I started by topping my drive badly. It skittered forward a short way. I too rushed forward — as if in an effort to hit my second shot before the enormity of my muffed drive attracted the attention of the distant crowd. The second shot hooked to the left, hitting on top of the sea wall and fortunately kicking back in toward the fairway. It took one high, long bounce and landed in the sand next to the wall. I could hear a faint sigh go up from the gallery as it watched the sand spurt into the air.

When I reached the ball I could see that the prudent shot was to

George tees off on the famous 18th hole at Pebble Beach, his last hole of the Crosby. (*Russ Halford*)

play safe with an iron and get the ball back out onto the fairway. But I had an idea that I could flick the ball off the sand with a wood—its lie was fair—and drive directly for the green. The shot was complicated, however, by the ball lying so close to the sea wall that I was forced to stand on the wall to address the shot—my golfing posture not unlike that of someone standing on a stool and trying to hit a ball off a rug. I could hear the sea sucking at the sea wall below.

Abe said, "How can you hit it that way?" He began snorting loudly.

I didn't answer him. It would have taken too long to explain that I hoped with one last dramatic shot to undo all the endless iniquities of the previous rounds—to finish with a shot that would restore my confidence.

Abe, seeing I was going to try the shot, said, "Well, don't fall off the wall. That's the ocean behind you."

I swooped at the ball with a nervous quick swing and topped it, pushing it a few feet onto the fairway. I stepped after it quickly, and before the chagrin could settle in, I addressed the ball again, swung, and caught it with power. The ball rose in a titanic slice, soaring diagonally across the fairway, and landed far up in the crowds on the clubhouse lawn. There were distant cries of alarm.

"You're ending up just grand," said Abe.

"See how Bruno's doing, will you, Abe?" I asked. "I'll meet you where it landed."

I set off across the fairway. The line of spectators watched me come. They divided and let me through.

"Your ball's back up in there," someone said. "Damn near hit a marshal."

The ball lay on the lawn that stretched from the green up to the clubhouse. Tea tables had been set out, with chairs placed around, and groups were sitting sipping summer drinks—tall orangeades with fruit slices on the lips of the glasses, gin-and-tonics that shone metallic blue in the sun. People strolled to and fro in that warm and unseasonable weather, many men in club blazers, the girls in bright Italian prints, so that I had the sense of intruding into a wedding reception. My ball, lying starkly on the lawn, seemed an object quite out of place, rather obscene, and the temptation was to stand away from it and pretend that it was none of my concern, not my doing at all. The strollers looked at it curiously. Abe came up, wheezing, a cigarette stuck on his lower lip. He was bent far forward under the weight of my bag, as he always was, as if perpetually climbing the slope of a hill.

"How's Bruno doing?" I asked nervously.

If my shot was necessary for the team score, the marshals would have had to clear an alley down to the green, and divide the big ring of spectators to give me a view of the flag. The dramatic possibilities of the shot were considerable. I wanted none of it.

"Your partner's putting for a birdie," Abe said. "He's going to make the cut. The guy's working up a smile, I think."

"I can pick up, then?"

"No reason not to," said Abe.

I bent and picked up the ball with a scooping, nonchalant, relieved gesture. Immediately a tug came at my sleeve. "Ball, mister? Can I have your ball?" A youngster was standing there. It was the custom on the 18th green for children to cluster around the players holing out to try to cadge golf balls. The more important the golfer, the larger the crowd around him and the more imploring the pleas. Often, to show no favoritism, the golfer backed up and threw the ball, the kids scurrying after it like a pack of terriers after a stick. It was the golfer's grand gesture, particularly if he had holed a long putt or made a fine score or especially if he had taken the championship, to bestow the ball, which he had endowed with such magic properties, to the throng.

"Please, mister, please."

"It's all yours," I said. I palmed it to him surreptitiously, as if it were contraband.

CHAPTER 24

One of the professionals, Johnny Pott, had seen me play the 18th hole. I had wished Bruno good luck on his round the next day, and I had said good-bye to Abe. We were sitting at one of the garden tables on the lawn. Pott said, "That was a pretty risky shot you took— standing on the sea wall and swiping at it that way."

"Lunatic," I agreed. "What a way to finish the tournament. I think the crowds had something to do with it."

"Why?" he asked.

"Well, I felt rather obligated to try the spectacular. They seem to have an effect—at least on the amateurs."

I told him from my observations as I went wandering on the course that the golfers who had greatest difficulty with the crowds were the celebrities. After the first delight of seeing a celebrity, and nudging each other, and saying, look, there's So-and-so, the crowds would begin to cool down, the awe would go, and the galleries would begin to take a critical look at the celebrity's *golf*—which invariably was second-rate, or at least not comparable to the skills which had given him his fame. The gallery's mood would change to irreverence, and then their comments would begin, just a few erupting to begin with, and then a chorus. When Lawrence Welk, the orchestra leader, stood over his drive about to swing, his gallery would chant a nasal "one an'...two an'...three an'..." in imitation of his practice of vocalizing the beat for his orchestra. The baseball stars—DiMaggio, Drysdale, Koufax, and others—were offered a chorus of "Foul!" or "Strike two coming up" or "You got a piece of it, Joe!" or if the ball was bounced off the tee down the fairway, someone would shout, "Right up the middle, Don, great clutch hit!" and everyone in the vicinity would grin and carry on.

Dean Martin, the actor, whose imbibing was a trademark, had a gallery of quipsters who followed him down the fairway making "drunk" jokes, and if Martin so much as stumbled—which he often did on purpose just to set them off—they would smack their thighs and hee-haw with delight.

The celebrity with the most awkward golf game was Sandy Koufax, the great pitcher, who had a handicap of 18, the same as mine. He had a quick lashing left-handed style and the ball rose in towering trajectories at alarming angles. His galleries stood in small nervous knots and at right angles to his stance and slightly back. His game was so erratic that the crowds never could quite settle down to a barrage of quips.

A group of golfers came by and joined us at the table—among them Dave Marr and Mason Rudolph.

Pott said that we had been talking about crowds and their effect on golfers.

"You get used to the idea of a big crowd watching you," someone said. "It's the noises that really get you. Hogan hated cameras so much that he had an official carrying a NO CAMERAS PLEASE sign in big letters, you know. They used to say that the whir of a movie camera was what really upset him—because it sounded like the rattlesnakes he remembered from growing up in Texas...and the temptation was to jump."

The golfers said that the crowds changed markedly in personality—from the well-mannered armies at the Masters to the less knowledgeable and thus unruly crowds at the big metropolitan classics, such as the Speedway Open in Indianapolis, with the one-dollar admission fees. Rudolph compared competing in the Buick Open to stroking the ball down Atlantic City's Boardwalk at high noon on a summer day. Johnny Pott concurred and said that everyone at the Buick Open brings a picnic lunch and invariably you find yourself playing your ball off the remains of a chicken.

"The craziest guy I remember from tournaments like that," Dave Marr said, "is this guy who came jumping over the ropes when I was walking down the fairway, and he had his hand out and this big grin on his face like he was some long lost cousin. He was just *striding* to meet me. I must have had a grin too, but hell, I was perplexed. I kept trying to place the guy as he came. Well, when he got up to me, just all-fired happy to see me—hell, I thought he was going to *embrace* me—he said, 'You're not going to remember me, because you've never *met* me.' Man, what do you do with some cat like that?"

The golfers laughed. "Another time," Marr went on, "this guy came rushing up with his hand out. I shook it and brought my hand away covered with some sort of slippery sun-tan oil. Couldn't play a shot for three holes."

"How about playing with Arnold Palmer?" I asked. "Do you get used to those people all pulling for him? Is there any special procedure?"

"The Army moves with the play of his ball," Johnny Pott said. "So everybody tries to putt out before he does. He's certainly understanding about it, Arnie is, and he'll wait up so you don't get spooked trying to putt against a background of people moving by."

Mason Rudolph, sitting across the table, said: "I'll tell you one advantage of playing with Arnold. The Army defines your targets; it outlines them. It's easy to drive because you're driving down an alley of people. Then down on the fairway you look up toward the green, and with all those people around, it looks like a catcher's mitt. And then again, if you hit a shot that's off line or too hard you got a good chance that it's going to be contained by the crowd—that some poor admirer of Arnold's is going to get a painful shock and hit, but that your ball's going to stay in good position as a result of the ricochet."

"Where are the best galleries?" I asked. "You were saying the Masters..."

Dave Marr said he thought the best galleries were to be found in

England and Scotland. "In those two countries," he said, "they don't clap unless you lay it dead to the stick. Any sort of a miss when you should make the shot, or a mediocre shot, or even a fair shot, and man, some silence. Next case! On the other hand, if you come out of a difficult lie and you're still some way from the hole, and you've made a shot you're proud of yourself while it may not look so good, you'll get applause, a fine round of it. Here in the U.S., if you knock it stiff, no matter how you do it, skulking it, the crowd will always give you a big hand. At the Buick Open, hell, they'll applaud a big duck hook, give you a hand for five minutes. It's very good for the ego, but not much else."

"How about pandering to the galleries?"

"You mean hot-dogging it?"

"I mean trying a shot you wouldn't if it weren't for the gallery looking on."

The golfers thought about that, and said it wouldn't be much of a golfer who played his shots, or formed a style just to interest the crowds. Someone at the table told the story of John de Forest at the Masters. A good player, he was a former British amateur champion. Coming down the back 9, he knocked a shot into the creek that fronts the 13th green at Augusta. A groan went up from the considerable crowd collected there to watch such disasters—a groan from them, and then a low hum, half of sympathy, half of delight, with everyone craning forward to see what de Forest would do, to see how he would "take it."

When he walked up, he could see the ball just a foot or so out from the bank in the water. He had an option—to drop another ball and take the one-stroke penalty or to try to explode the ball from where it lay, two or three inches below the surface in the mud. With the big crowd watching, the inclination was to try the extravagant shot, to offer the multitude the spectacle of the golfer with one leg on the slope, the other deep in the water, the trouser leg rolled up, then the flash of the club, the resulting tower of water, with the ball rising out of it and lofting onto the green, and then the yells and applause of the great semicircle of onlookers as he pulled himself up on the bank, the water glistening on his bare leg, his foot muddied, his head modestly lowered.

It was a scene de Forest could not resist. Deciding on the explosion shot, he sat down and amid a murmur of expectation removed a shoe, stripped off his sock and rolled the trouser leg up above his knee, doing all this with fastidious care. Then he took his club and dramatically stepped down with one foot into the water. It was the foot with the shoe on it. With the crowd craning to see, he must have thought as he felt the water squish into his shoe and the sock go damp, "Oh good gracious *God*," but he decided to brave it through, as if that had been his intent all along — to immerse the foot with the shoe, his bare foot up on the grass slope. He made the shot that way, almost weeping with embarrassment, and he flubbed it, of course, just barely scraping it out on the grass. He now has a title — Count de Bendern — but it's doubtful that he can ever lace on a pair of shoes in the morning without thinking back to that day on the 13th at Augusta.

CHAPTER 25

Daydreaming at the wheel, driving through the artichoke country south of San Francisco, heading up there for the Lucky tournament. The mice had attacked the fields that year and there were trucks out in those flat plains, the poison being set out. I was back in Mullins, Louisiana, with Carl Lohren.

"Ticket, please!"

The golfer groaned. He was watching the pine woods go by, very slowly, as if the train's engineer was finding it difficult to resist the attractions of Mullins.

He looked up at the conductor.

"I'm a little confused," he said, stalling for time. He reached idly back for his wallet, aware that it wouldn't be there, and feeling instead the empty fingers of his golf glove where he'd stuffed it in his back pocket. "Where does this train go?"

The conductor clicked his ticket clipper impatiently, but he announced: "Pitcairn, Caroline, Jehovah's Junction, The Gulch, Beulah, Plum Flats, Junction City, Parsons, Logan, Bailey, Edwin, Shrake, Loblolly, Mullins, Pitcairn…"

"Mullins!" cried the golfer, "But aren't we just pulling out of Mullins? What was that place back there if not Mullins?"

The conductor clicked his ticket punch again. "Course that was Mullins. You must be a stranger in these parts." He peered closely at the golfer. "What sort of duds you got on there? Ain't seen so much blue on a man since the day they drug in Abe Parsons that time he froze to daith up on Catclaw Mountain." He cackled sharply. "Hell, stranger, they ain't many folk in these parts who travel on this railroad line without knowing it goes in a *circle*. If it's Mullins you're fixin' to go to, I'd be inclined to step off and walk back. Otherwise, that'll be twenty-eight dollars and we'll be getting back into Mullins along about eleven-thirty tonight."

The golfer groaned again. "I'm trying to get to Jacksonville—for the Jacksonville Open."

The conductor looked up at the ceiling. "Well," he said, "they got a trunk line that moves out of Beulah out along the ridge through Persimmon, Courtney, Howard, Cushing, Moore's Bottom, and peters out in Long Fork. But I reckon that's not quite what you're looking for…"

"No, that's not so good for me," said the golfer.

"Course we got buses runnin' in an' out of Junction City goin' just about everywhere. Up to Nash's Falls, places like that."

"What goes on in that town, The Gulch?"

"Well, they got the County Fair comin' on into The Gulch next week."

"Nash's Falls," said the golfer thoughtfully. "Well, how much is a ticket to Junction City?"

"That's fourteen dollars," said the conductor.

The golfer looked mournfully down between the toes of his Pro-Shus with the big blue flaps over the laces. "Listen," he said. "I've had this odd time. Got left behind by my driving partner in Mullins back there. My mistake…without a penny in my jeans, y'know. Left my wallet in the car. I just *got* to get to Junction City and get a bus out of there. Anything goin' southeast, if that's in the direction of Jacksonville, I'll take."

"Junction City is fourteen dollars," the conductor said stubbornly.

"What about barter," said the golfer after a pause. "This club is a Spalding Executive, worth a good eighteen, twenty dollars, and this beaut's scarcely been swung—spanking new!"

The conductor bent over and inspected the club.

"Barter? For a stick like this? Maybe three chickens and a duck might get you to Junction City. But for a piece of stick like this here, why that wouldn't fetch you more than a couple hundred yards down this railroad line. You got anything else. Seegars maybe? A timepiece?"

"How about these Pro-Shu shoes," the golfer said. "These flaps are fancy and they are the new look on the golf courses today...that's just about a direct quote from *Golfing Magazine*."

The conductor shook his head. "Mos' folks aroun' these parts have one pair of boots for plowing the forties, and another set for going to Nash's Falls, places like that. Anybody seen sashayin' aroun' in blue shoes like yourn, well, he'd be in line for a lynching. You're not wearing a watch?"

"No," said the golfer. "It looks like it's back to Mullins."

He watched the conductor reach up and pull an emergency cord that ran the length of the roof.

"I'm right sorry, stranger," said the conductor. "I hope you got no hard feelings."

The train pulled up. The golfer could hear the panting of the engine as he stepped down the long step from the coach to the cinders of the railroad track. The engineer was looking back. They were perfectly polite about it. The engineer made a sort of gesture that seemed a friendly wave. The conductor had a suggestion to make as the train started up: "This railroad runnin' in a circle, we'll be coming back 'round here about eleven-thirty pee-em tonight, which gives you plenty of time to mosey 'round and pick off some livestock. Now a *sheep* would get you jes' 'bout anywhere on this railroad line you'd be fixin' to go. The Fitzhughs got a flock t'other side of Mullins..."

The golfer trotted along with the train, listening politely if idly, and then he pulled up, panting, and the conductor's words were carried off swiftly as the train clicked down the straight track and slowly drew into the distance between the pines.

It took him an hour of walking to get back into Mullins. There was no sign of activity. He stood on the railroad crossing where his driving partner — that crazy coot they called Sleep because his mind just barely seemed to be ticking over — had left him when he stepped out to practice his golf swing.

He waited a half-hour or so to see if anything would come by — a bus, or even a horse cart, but the crossing lay breathless under the heat, and he listened dully to the frogs croaking in the railroad ditches and the dry whir of the insects back in the pines. He started up the road for the EATS establishment where he had last left the Mark Tanner hillbillies.

He walked slowly because of the heat. He stepped up on the rickety porch. From inside came a low murmur of voices. He pushed open the screen door. They can help me, he kept telling himself, they can flag down a car for me, if one should pass by, or lend me a mule, or at least get me pointed in the right direction so I can hike out of here.

At his entrance four heads looked up at the corner table from under tall hillbilly hats. Complete strangers. My God! he thought, the *Reilly* brothers, kinfolk to the Reilly he was supposed to have killed up in the north forty! And here they all were waiting for him…Hugh, Eugene, and my Lord! he thought, there's one of them who doesn't even have a name!

He smiled. "Howdy, folks!"

All of them stood abruptly, with grotesque efforts like puppets being pulled up by strings, and they hauled out long pistols which they leveled at him.

"Whar you from, boy?"

"I come from Fairfield, Connecticut."

The four hillbillies stirred and looked at each other. "There's a mighty big rumor 'round these parts," one of them said, "that you're in from Memphis with that club of yourn and that y'did in our brother Dan Reilly up in the nawth fawty."

"That's crazy," the golfer said loudly.

"The Mark Tanner folk, why they is hee-hawing an' carryin' on an' talkin' 'bout this professional killer all duded up in *blue*, hired from Memphis to per-pet-u-ate this foul deed 'gin our brother Dan."

"Someone's made a perfectly natural mistake. I *am* a professional," the golfer said. "But a professional *golfer*, not a killer. I mean, I'm not even a killer in my own profession." He laughed hollowly. "Hell, I choke. I get these big apples. I'm a rabbit. You want a killer, fetch in someone like Hogan or Snead. I finished tenth in the Cajun Classic. Best I ever did. They call me Four Putts."

"Look at them-air duds he's wearin'," one of the hillbillies was wailing in a thin, high voice. "He's sure-nuff blue." He looked at the golfer in awe.

"That's enuff for us Reillys," the leader of the group said. "Stranger, you're a loco, low-slung animul and you ain't deservin' to draw another bref of good Mullins air."

He leveled his pistol carefully and pulled the trigger. The concussion nearly popped the golfer's ears. A wall of white smoke rolled toward him. The wall behind seemed to buck and a fine spray of peach scent enveloped him.

Went right over my shoulder, and plugged a can of Pappy's Peach Preserves, the golfer thought as he sagged to the floor once again. He thought, Lord, I'm in for it. The smoke will clear and they'll get in a couple of more shots from those cannon . . .

He heard a voice bellowing through the smoke.

"Hold on thar. It's me — Hoss Reilly." A heavy-set man stood in the door. "What's gwan on 'round heah?"

"We *wung* the varmint, Hoss," one of the hillbillies was shouting. "Two or three mo' shots and we gonna have brother Dan Reilly what was beaten to daith up in the nawth fawty all nice and *avenged*."

"Dan's been *done* avenged," Hoss said. "Mark Tanner's lyin' up thar 'n Bull Creek Pasture daider than a skinned mule. This kid from Memphis done his job right smart." He gazed pleasantly at the golfer who was picking himself off the floor.

"*He* done it?"

"Don't that beat *all*?"

"Bull Creek? Oh my, I wish't to been there to see it done."

"He been beat up jes' *grand*," said Hoss Reilly. "I seen it myself." He looked admiringly at the Spalding Executive.

They had moved up and clustered around him, dusting him off and slapping him on the back.

The golfer dodged them. "You mind telling me something?" he asked. "What about those folk that were in here before—the Tanner people, Claude, that woman in the sunbonnet? What about that man in the black suspenders?"

"You're talkin' 'bout Mark Tanner's kinfolk," Hoss Reilly said. "Well, I reckon they're fetchin' up some more kinfolk and mebbe in a few days we'll be havin' a hot time in Mullins. Regular ol' shoot-out. 'Course, it's you they'all be gunnin' fur. After all, you was the one who popped Mark Tanner and got our kin Dan Reilly all nice and avenged. Mebbe you'd be doin' the healthy thing to clear out of Mullins."

The golfer murmured uneasily. His mind lingered briefly on his difficulties with the conductor of the local train. He gripped his golf club. "I got to have me some money," he said sharply.

The hillbillies looked at him.

"Well, how about my *fee*?" the golfer asked. "You ain't reckoning," the golfer said in a voice thick with a variety of tough accents, "that I come down from Memphis and knock off Dan Reilly...I mean t'say *Mark Tanner*...without charging for my *services*. Why, I usually charge ten G's for putting the slug on someone. You got to pay for someone who's so highly skilled. In Memphis we're taught by the very best people. It's a great art to mash a man t' death with a wood golf club—to foozle a guy we call it—it's right up there with learning how to use an ice pick properly, and building cement shoes for a guy you want to drop in a river—very technical skill. Particularly a Spalding" (he brandished the golf club) "with its small head and no aluminum shaft, mind you, like everyone's going to these days, but the *steel shaft*—not your old hickory which is what they did the bludgeoning with in the twenties, but steel, your good one-hundred-percent *steel*. That's what you call *craft*! And mind you," he went on without drawing a breath, listening to the rush of his words with surprise, "take a look at these expensive *shoes* with the spikes for getting a good footing" (he held a Pro-Shu-clad foot aloft) "and creeping up on your man in case he's chopping wood or something on the side of a hill. And look at the blue glove I've got here" (he pulled it dramatically from his back pocket) "just in case the bludgeoning goes badly and you've got to step forward and *strangle* your man...." As he talked, he watched the hillbilly faces opposite— discerning there through the bewilderment a faint tightening of the features: apparently fees were not topics which came easily to them.

"Look," he said. "I'm willing to give you good folks of Mullins a break, considering that you can't be expected to pay big-city fees for having a guy cooled. The fact is, I am willing to waive the fee and charge you just the expenses back to Memphis, or even better to Jacksonville, Florida, where I am scheduled to foozle a bloke with my Spalding the day after tomorrow." He looked at them appealingly. "How about thirty dollars on the barrel head?"

Hoss Reilly was speaking. "Wal, I reckon you get owed *some*thing," he admitted. He dug into his coveralls and the golfer could hear the jingle of change. Then the golfer noticed Reilly's brow furrow and the hand came back out empty. "Hold on heah," he said. "Le's do a bit of figurin'. Now Mark Tanner warn't worth much more than six dollars on the hoof—no 'count rascal! And I ain't sure he could fetch *three* dollars alive, much less'n five. Now the big question is what he might fetch *daid*. I don' reckon very much. Why I don't know any folk hereabouts who'd fork out a *nickel* for him daid." He shook his head. "Now mebbe in the big city Memphis, sort of place you come from, why, daid folk get some value, but aroun' Mullins we jes' don't stock sech things. In these parts you couldn't *give* away a daid person, nor indeed a whole truckload of 'em."

Both parties stared at each other. "Look," the golfer said abruptly, "I'll take barter." What was it the conductor had said? He remembered something about a sheep. He heard a chicken clucking outside the back door. "I'll take a chicken," he said, his eyes staring about wildly. "And a sackful of Pappy's Peach Preserves," he said, pointing. "Otherwise," there was a bright smile to take the edge off his threat, "why Ah'm goin' to have to lay around just a mite with my Spalding. Foozle Mullins up a bit." He had a sudden inspiration. His voice became tougher: "Mebbe some of my Memphis boys—some of those enforcers up there, the Memphis Foozlers—well, they might take a notion to journey on down here to do a bit of practicing on their skills. Some of those cement-feet boys might like to work Bull Creek...."

Hoss Reilly said: "Go on out, boys, and cotch that hen. Fetch up a sack of them peach preserves." The hillbillies moved briskly through the store. Outside, the golfer heard the chicken squawk rapidly, and the beating of its wings. A potato sack was produced. Into it a shelf was swept clear of cans; the hen appeared amid a storm of feathers, its wings working as it hung from a hillbilly's clutch; it was eased into the sack and offered to the golfer.

Just then a car horn sounded loudly out on the street.

Everybody jumped. The golfer's eyes widened. The horn sounded again. A familiar sound. The golfer stepped quickly to the screen door and looked out. There was his Oldsmobile, the old family car he had painted red, and there was Sleep, his driving partner, looking up at him curiously from the wheel.

He took a quick glance behind him in the store, where the hillbillies were lounging nervously in the shadows as if perhaps the horn had announced that the cement-feet boys from Memphis had pulled up and were about to appear upon the porch, darkening the door, stooped from the weight of the paraphernalia on their backs.

The golfer stepped out on the little porch.

"Well, man, *there* you are," Sleep was saying. "Been asking for you in every one-horse town since I turned back hundred miles ago."

"A hundred miles!" said the golfer. "That figures."

He slid the big sack and then himself into the front seat. "Stick her in gear and move," he said. He stared straight ahead.

About two miles across the railroad tracks he turned and hefted the sack over the seat into the back. He kept his golf club between his knees.

"What you got in that thing back there?"

"Pappy's Peach Preserves. About ninety-nine cans. It's handy stuff to have in this part of the country."

That seemed to be the extent of Sleep's interest.

"There's a chicken in the sack too," the golfer said. "Next farmhouse you see, pull up, and we'll let the bird out."

"Anything you say," said Sleep.

Lord, thought the golfer. The *interest* that guy takes in what goes on around him. He listened to Sleep begin to hum, and the gentle dialogues start up. "So, listen, Martha, I think I'll go down and get the paper." "Why all right, that's just fine, tum-te-tum, and, hey, bring me back a pack of Old Golds."

"Hey, Sleep," he said.

"Hmm."

"Listen, thanks for turning around. How far down the road was it when you did?"

"Damn, man, it was a long way — not so far out of Jax."

The golfer groaned.

"Let me see," Sleep said. "Not so far outa Jacksonville I asked you a question, that was it — what club you use on the par-3 water hole there, and I must have driven along ten miles waiting for you to give the answer, thinking, Boy you're really putting your mind to it, and then I looked over the back seat and you wasn't there! Jesus! Damn near drove the car into a tree. Well, I figured, you stepped out somewhere to groove your swing — and I remembered that railroad crossing... where was it?"

"Mullins," the golfer said. "They have another town in that area called The Gulch."

"Yes," Sleep said. "So I drove back. I like driving. You know I like driving."

They drove in silence for a while.

The golfer finally couldn't contain himself. "You know what I did there in that town of Mullins?"

"No, what?"

"Well, not much," he said calmly. "Worked a kink out of my swing. Got my follow-through feeling a bit easier. Beat a man to death up in the north forty. Beat another man to death in Bull Creek Pasture."

Sleep began laughing. "The sun got to you, eh? Man, this country's hot." He pointed to the passing pine forests. "You know something I figured: not much *golf* in these parts. Haven't seen a course, a driving range, pitch 'n' putt, nothing like that for three hundred miles. Must be tennis country."

"Yes, that must be it," said the golfer.

CHAPTER 26

The putter I carried in the big oxblood bag was a mallet-head type that someone had recommended, and I had cast around and bought one just before leaving on the tour. I had left my old putter, one my grandfather had given me years before, at home, and I was sorry I had. I have great affection for certain inanimate objects and cannot bear to throw them away — particularly if associated with memory or performance. My old putter, a very warped object, had not performed well for me, but it was *traditional*. I had always used it; it was designed exactly like Bobby Jones's famous putter Calamity Jane; indeed, it even had the two black bands of whipping around the shaft, essential for the original since Jones had broken it on one occasion, but in the imitation models, of course, absolutely superfluous. As Darwin wryly wrote about these copies when they first appeared: "Did ever imitation pay success more flattery than that!"

Still, I missed my old putter. I was used to its vagaries and it was an easy putter to blame if one putted poorly. It was the sort of putter which in tight matches drove one's partners to distraction. A putt of mine would die 15 feet short and off to the left. "How can you *do* anything with that thing. How can you *hit* the ball," they would say.

My new putter hefted splendidly in the hand, and on the face it had a small gold area the size of a dime where you were supposed to hit the ball. Still, I did not feel comfortable with it. My putting had been a constant source of dismay to both Abe and Bob Bruno at the Crosby. "I wish I had my old putter," I had said. "I'm not used to this one yet."

"Yes, we can see that," they had replied.

It was a question of gaining confidence in the club, being familiar enough with it so that it became an extension of one's body rather than a separate instrument.

On the drive up to San Francisco for the Lucky International, I vowed I would do what Bruno had urged—more practicing with the putter, whenever I had the chance. Why not in one's hotel room?

I had a reservation at the Fairmont Hotel in San Francisco—I had stayed there before—a great ornate building with the trolley tracks running by one side, and then down the hill, but the rooms were quiet with high ceilings and tall unwashed French windows with heavy curtains to draw across. I parked the car in the garage under the hotel, and took the putter from the golf bag in the trunk along with four or five balls and my suitcase. I rode the elevator up to the lobby on the floor above and went to the registration desk to check in.

I stood up close to the desk so the clerk would not see the putter. The golf balls were in my coat pocket. He took a card off the rack for me to sign.

"Is this a large room?" I asked. "I'm looking for a very large room."

He peered at the card. "It's got two single beds. You'd rather have one with a double?"

"No," I said. "It's a question of the dimensions of the room itself."

He tapped a tooth with the end of his pencil. "Well, I wouldn't know offhand, but this room must be, oh, fifteen by fifteen. It's in the modernized wing of the hotel."

"I'd like to exchange it if I could," I said, "for something in the forty-foot-by-forty-foot bracket. Or even larger if you've got it."

He looked surprised. It occurred to me the notion might cross his mind that I was going to conduct an "experiment" of some sort in there—that equipment was going to arrive in large wooden boxes.

"How about a suite?" I asked. "Is there something of that sort available?" Of course I understood there would be a difference in price which I was willing to pay.

He looked in his rack. "Well, yes, you can have a suite here in the older part of the hotel — the rooms are all large — Suite 4G."

He reached for a key.

"It's not L-shaped, is it?"

"I beg your pardon."

"Well, what I'm looking for," I said, shifting my feet uneasily, "is a large *square* room. Or rectangular. Or even, come to think of it," I said, laughing hollowly, "an *oval* room would be O.K. But I'm afraid that a room that goes around a corner..."

The clerk took off his horn-rimmed glasses which he put down on the counter and he massaged the bridge of his nose.

"No sir, I think you're safe," he said. "Suite G, to the best of my recollection, is not L-shaped."

He handed me my key and banged on a schoolbell for a bellboy. I kept my body between his vision and the putter as we left for the bank of elevators, holding the putter hard against a leg as I walked somewhat stiffly, the bellboy alongside carrying my suitcase.

In the elevator the bellboy caught sight of my golf club and gave me an odd, noncommittal smile, his head bobbing swiftly and politely. He looked at the bank of floor numbers above the elevator door. We got off on the fourth floor. The corridor had a palm in a pot at the end. The bellboy swung back the door of Suite G.

"Oh Lord!" I said. The room was enormous — very much as I remembered — but the floor was not covered with the large rug appropriate for putting practice. It had a polished fine parquet surface dotted with a number of small rugs.

The bellboy heard my exclamation. He was putting my bag up on a luggage rack. He watched me shove at one of the little rugs with my putter.

"Yes?" he said. He had a tremendous smile.

"Look," I said. "I don't want to cause any more...well, confusion downstairs. Perhaps you can help me. Simple matter of changing rooms. You see, I'm playing in the golf tournament starting tomorrow out at Harding Park and the fact is, I'd like a room where I can practice putting—y'know, when I get up in the morning, just for keeping my hand in." I gestured with the putter. "This room is great for size, but these little throw rugs make it impossible to practice putts."

The bellboy looked puzzled and somewhat nervous. He had pleasant dark features—from the Philippines, I judged. Again, a sudden bright smile materialized on his face and then disappeared instantly. "Yes," he said, more tentatively.

"Well look," I said. I reached in my coat pocket for a golf ball and dropped it on one of the small rugs. I stood over it with a putter and stroked it toward a distant corner. It went off the rug and rumbled across the floor loudly, then silently across a rug, and noisily across another stretch of floor, up onto another rug, and disappeared under an armchair.

The bellboy stared after it. He made a gesture suggesting he was willing to retrieve the ball. "Yes?"

"No, no," I said. "It's O.K. Just leave it lay." I dropped another on the rug. "You see it's a question of having a room with a uniform surface—a large uniform surface like you'd have in a room with wall-to-wall carpeting. That'd be exactly like a putting green. But here, you see, the ball rolls from rug to floor to rug…no good." I stroked another shot off. Solemnly we both watched the ball disappear under the armchair and rattle up against the wainscotting.

"Bobby Jones had a feeling that the putt should be what he called a 'long sweep.' Well, you can't get the feel of a 'long sweep' on a wood floor."

I gestured at the floor. He looked down.

"Do you have a large room on this floor with wall-to-wall carpeting? The rugs here in this room are no good."

His English was apparently negligible. "Rugs no good," he said. "Ah, cleaning lady? Mop? Broom?" A brilliant hopeful smile lit up his face.

"No, no," I said.

He looked miserable.

"Is there a room like this down the hall with big rug?" I asked. "No floor. No floor."

I made a flopping motion with my hands.

"No floor! No floor!" he repeated. A bruised look of great confusion crossed his face, and he peered this way and that, with the brief vision, I suspected, perched in his mind that what I wanted was a room without a floor, a sort of shaft that led for miles down into some infernal region.

"Never mind," I said, moving forward and pressing an enormous tip into his palm. "Everything very good. Floor excellent."

I showed him the door, and then flopped back on the bed and listened to my heart pound. Lord, I thought, how does one get into these gentle nightmares.

Our family seems susceptible to them—particularly in hotels. I remembered an experience my grandmother had had staying at a fine hotel in Paris—the Continental, on the rue Castiglione. She had come home from a long walk in the Tuileries and on reaching her room she decided she needed some refreshment. A glass of sherry, namely, and she went to her telephone and called down to room service. A man's voice came on.

"Apportez-moi un sherry," she said carefully.

My grandmother had studied her French some fifty years before, and while her vocabulary had suffered the ravages of time, her accent hadn't. She was proud of it, and, in fact, it was her strong accenting of the word *"sherry"* that got her into trouble and afterward caused the hotel staff to give her quick darting looks when she walked by in the lobby.

"Apportez-moi un chéri" is what the room service man heard over the phone. My grandmother repeated her request a number of times in her clear boyish voice. After a few muffled explanations into the phone, the room service man scratched around and sent up his most ancient servitor to see if matters somehow could be clarified. He came in, my grand-

mother said later, a really frightened man, as if he expected a mauling. He had a menu under his arm. My grandmother looked for her sherry. She stood up and asked him disarmingly, "Chéri?"

The waiter took a quick step backward. My grandmother felt she could only pursue her order by pointing it out on the waiter's menu. When she approached him, holding out her hand and smiling, the waiter began to back up to the door and it was only with a swift far-reaching grasp that she was able to hook the menu out from under his arm.

"The man bleated when I reached for his menu," my grandmother said of all this later, "and it was then that I knew something was really wrong."

After inspecting herself in the mirror for a time to see if there was any indication as to what was upsetting the hotel staff, my grandmother shrugged her shoulders and turned open the menu. There were two sherry brands: Jerez and Amontillado. She hoped that using the name of the brand might bring results. Choosing the Amontillado, she picked up the telephone and reached room service again. It was the same man answering at the other end.

"Allo, Allo," she said, and she gave her room number. *"Apportez-moi un Armadillo. Armadillo."*

She could hear the man breathing at the other end.

"An armadillo, an armadillo," she repeated and then suddenly realizing she had got it wrong, she caught her hand to her mouth and laid the telephone back in its cradle.

That was as much as my grandmother could stand. For her refreshment, she drew herself a glass of water from the tap.

Lying in that San Francisco hotel I took a certain amount of comfort in remembering that the episode had not bothered my grandmother for more than a minute or so. She blamed it on the hotel staff. "Imagine," she said. "All that furor. Why a great hotel, if a guest wanted a gigolo and armadillo for some reason, why, they would have had those items up to the room in jig time. Now the Ritz would have done it, and no pussyfooting around about it, either."

The phone rang. It was the front desk. The voice was that of the receptionist I had talked to earlier. Was there some trouble, he wanted to know. Some rugs that needed to be cleaned? There was a report from a bellboy...

"No, no," I said. "Everything's just fine up here. Incidentally, it's a fine big room."

But wasn't there some problem about dirty rugs, he persisted. The bellboy had reported. What was this about a floor? The receptionist barked something abruptly in Spanish. I could hear the anguished voice of the bellboy in the background—oh Lord, he was doing the best he could.

"Absolutely," I said loudly into the phone to get the receptionist's ear. "One of the rugs could stand a cleaning. Absolutely. Spotted it first thing. Soon as the door was opened. Pointed it out. Bellboy absolutely on the job."

I could hear the receptionist breathing at the other end. "I'll send someone up right away," he said rather icily.

They arrived within five minutes, two large men, one of them with a leather sling over his shoulder for moving heavy objects. A rug was to be removed? Or was it a bureau? They were not sure.

"A rug," I said. "To be cleaned."

There were about six rugs in the room. I picked the largest one. "It's that one over there."

One of them went over and rolled it up swiftly and stuck it under his arm like a map.

The other looked embarrassed at being empty-handed. He shifted the sling on his shoulder. I turned away and opened the French doors and went out on a balcony which had miniature gargoyle heads at either end. Some pigeons were cooing on the ledge above and I could see their tails sticking out.

CHAPTER 27

All the golfers I talked to on the tour agreed that the most unfortunate position out on the course was to play immediately in front of Arnold Palmer and his Army. If one had to play in front of one of the superstars, Jack Nicklaus was the golfer one would hope for, because he was slow, so that however large a following he had, one could move on ahead of him and open up space between his gallery and one's own group. As for playing *behind* golfers like Nicklaus and Palmer, well, that was simply a matter of patience—waiting until their cohorts had moved their easy, elephantine meanderings beyond range.

At the San Francisco pro-am, I and two other amateurs were to be partnered by the professional Rod Funseth. I noticed in the evening papers, which published the starting times for the next day's play, that our foursome was scheduled to tee off immediately in front of Palmer's group.

It was overcast the next day, but Palmer had a big crowd with him. As I had been led to expect, golfing that day was not like playing in a tournament at all, but rather like being in a migration, the Great Trek, during which, because of some odd ceremonial ritual, one was asked to carry along a golf club and strike at a golf ball from time to time. One stepped out from the multitude to knock the ball along the line of march, standing and concentrating on the shot while the oblivious crowds rolled along beside the fairway, like the slow flow of a stream around a rock in a riverbed. There was only one person they had come to see hit a golf shot, and that was Arnold Palmer.

On the 14th at the Harding Park Golf Course I was nearly engulfed by the Army. The hole is a long par 4. On the golfer's left as he stands on the tee the fairway slopes sharply into gullies covered with heavy brush, and after a bit the hill drops off abruptly to Lake Merced, sparkling far below. When I stepped up to drive, the advance elements of Arnie's Army were streaming along the fairway, the mass of them on the right getting themselves into position for his appearance immediately behind us. I hit my drive off the heel of the club, perhaps compensating, wanting to keep my ball away from the crowds on the right, and it shot off at an angle and into one of the gullies on the left, not more than 50 yards or so from the tee. I sighed and went down there with my caddy to look for it. The rest of the foursome, Rod Funseth in the fore, continued down the fairway. I called to them that I would catch up if I could. My caddy and I both took clubs out, smacking through the underbrush in the hope of uncovering the ball.

In the meantime, Palmer and his group had finished the 13th and they had come up on the elevated 14th tee. I found my ball after a long search, and I was thinking about how to play my shot when I happened to glance back up at the tee behind me. There was Palmer looking intently down the fairway. I was so far down in the gully that I could only see the upper part of his torso. From the set of his shoulders I could tell that he was braced over his ball and that the rest of my foursome was now far enough away for him to lace into his shot. He had not noticed me; if he had, I doubt he would have taken me for a member of the team in front, since by now Funseth and the rest of them were more than 300 yards away down the fairway. He would have taken me for a grounds-keeper, perhaps, clearing out underbrush with a scythe.

"Wait!" I called.

He looked down, almost directly it seemed, off that high tee, as if he were peering over the edge of a large container. I thought afterward that he had the abrupt look of someone sitting at his desk who sees something move in the bottom of his wastepaper basket.

I raised my driver and waved it, so he could identify me as a fellow golfer.

"Down here," I called. "I'm sorry." I shouted, "I'll be right out," as if in reply to someone pounding on a washroom door.

The caddy handed me a club. I settled over my ball, my back up against a bush, and was about to thrash at it when I discovered that the caddy, in his confusion and in the awe of the moment, had taken my driver and mistakenly handed me a putter.

I tossed it back to him. "An eight," I called. "An *eight* iron."

I took a quick look back up at the tee. Palmer was looking on, and behind him were the other members of his foursome and their caddies and a few officials and a back line of spectators, all grim as they stared down. I hit a shot that bounced up out of the rough onto the fairway.

"Let's go," I said. We ran up after the shot, the caddy trotting hard, the clubs jangling thunderously in the bag.

I barely got my feet set before hitting the next shot—ripping up and letting it fly on down a fairway by now thickly flanked by Arnie's Army waiting for his drive.

I hurried down between those lanes. Some cardboard periscopes came up from the back ranks of the crowd and peered. I could catch the glint of glass. A couple of hundred yards ahead I could see the rest of our foursome on the green. Behind, Palmer was still waiting. We were not yet out of range.

"Lord," I said. The clubs jangled furiously. Fleetingly I thought of a *Golfer's Handbook* record I had noted the day before—a speedy round by an Olympic runner from South Africa who was able to whip around the Mowbray Course in thirty-odd minutes.

"I'm going to pick up," I called to the caddy.

I scooped up the ball on the fly like a centerfielder bending to field a hit, and we veered and headed off the fairway for the Army, stepping in among them. There were a few stares but then the heads began craning for Palmer's shot. We walked along with the crowd and I joined the others on the 15th tee. Funseth and my partner looked up when I climbed over the restraining ropes to join them. I apologized and said I had picked up. I was doing so badly. They said, never mind; one of them had birdied the hole, and the team was all right.

I was telling a friend about the experience later that morning. "I didn't see what else I could do," I said. "Picking up, I mean." I described what had happened, playing the shots in front of that grim gallery on the 14th tee: Palmer and the rest of them — a tableau of generals, with their staffs, they might have been, surveying the pageantry of battle from a hill, except that immediately in front of them something had gone wrong: a soldier's drum had fallen off, rolling down a gentle slope, and he was rushing after it, his cockade askew, and the drum was beginning to bounce now and pull away from him...

"You did the right thing," my friend said. "Picking up."

"I think so."

"That was not a pleasant experience."

"It certainly wasn't," I said.

He cleared his throat. He said that well, nothing could compare with an experience *he* had had with Palmer and his Army. I've forgotten what tournament he said it was, possibly the Masters or the PGA, one of the great championships, for sure. He was a spectator on the golf course at a position where the big-name players were coming through. While waiting, on the side of the fairway, he had stepped into one of those sentry-box structures called Port-O-Let, chemical toilets that are set about courses during tournament week. After a while he opened the door, which made a shrill squeal, and he stepped out into the bright sunlight. When he had stepped into the Port-O-Let there had been quite a few people trudging by, the advance guard of Arnie's Army. Now, he said, with himself and the Port-O-Let at its apex, an enormous fan of people had materialized that stretched away toward the distant green, a double line of faces — thousands, it appeared — all straining to see. And there, not ten yards away, standing over a golf ball that he had hit nearly out of bounds, and getting ready to swing, was Arnold Palmer. At the creak of the hinges Palmer looked back, and he saw my friend standing in the door of the Port-O-Let.

"What did you do?" I asked.

"Well, my gosh," my friend said. "I stepped right back inside and pulled the door shut. It was the typical reaction, I mean, stepping out and seeing all those people. It was like slipping through a door and finding oneself alone on the stage of a fully occupied opera house. What happens is that your eyes pop and you back up right through the door you came out of."

"Of course," I said.

"I really slammed that door."

"What happened then?"

"Well, after a second or two, there was this knock on the door of the Port-O-Let, and it was Palmer. 'Listen,' I heard him say, 'come on out, there's no hurry.' Well, I thought about that great mob of people out there, all looking and maybe getting ready to laugh and all if I stepped out of the Port-O-Let. So I said through the door, 'No. You go right ahead, Mr. Palmer. I'm in no hurry either. I don't want to disturb you.' Well, I heard his footsteps in the grass, moving away, and the increasing quiet of the crowd, which had been murmuring, and I knew he was standing over his ball and they were settling down for his shot. But the murmur started up again, and I was surprised, because I hadn't heard the click of his club going through the shot. Then I heard footsteps and there was this knock on the door. 'Listen,' he said. He sounded very apologetic through the door. 'I find it's hard to concentrate on my shot thinking about you shut up in that box. I'd appreciate it if you would come out.' Well, I did, of course. I pushed the door open with that big screech, those damn rusty hinges, and I stepped out. It was very bright in the sunlight after the Port-O-Let, and there was Palmer looking worried and serious, and he said he was sorry to have inconvenienced me. I said, 'Oh no, not at all.' There was quite a lot of laughter, and I sidled off and tried to get lost in the crowd. But people kept grinning at me, heads turning, you know, 'There's the Port-O-Let guy,' so finally I hurried across a fairway and watched someone else, Kermit Zarley, I think, someone like that, where there weren't too many people around."

"That's something!" I said.

"Yes, I think so," he said.

"Some terrible things can happen out there in tournament golf," I said.

"You're right," he said. "Terrible things."

CHAPTER 28

Almost by coincidence, I met a golfer that evening who admitted to a spectacular embarrassment during his own morning round. He had stepped up to the ball-washer just off a tee on the second 9, the type (as he described it) like a milk churn with a handle that pumps up and down and the ball is scrubbed and soaped against stiff brushes in the cylinder underneath.

"Yes, I've seen that sort," I said.

"There's a towel hanging off the bottom of the cylinder and you mop your ball with it."

"Yes, I know," I said.

He went on to say that every particular of the ball-washing apparatus was very vivid in his mind, and would remain so, he reckoned, for some time because that morning he had *lost* his ball in the bottom of the machine.

"Well, that can't be easy to do," I said.

"I've never heard of such a thing," he said, shaking the ice in the bottom of his glass. "But it happened. As I was pumping away, the ball slipped from its holder and somehow got down into the bottom of the cylinder. Lost ball. Well, it wouldn't have been a damn thing worth worrying about if there'd been another ball available there on the tee. I mean, I could have called to my caddy and asked him to fish out a fresh Maxfli from the bag. But he was down the fairway, with my bag, and with the other caddies, over the brow of a hill to spot our drives when we popped them out there.

"But what made it bad, a really serious problem for my addled brain as I stood there looking at the ball-washer, was that the foursome I was playing in hadn't exactly been the chummiest of groups. It just wasn't the bunch of guys you could turn around to and say, 'Hey, guys, guess what? I've lost my ball in the ball-washer.'"

"What was wrong with them?" I asked. "Had your golf been that bad?"

"It wasn't the golf," he said. "Somehow we didn't hit it off from the beginning—right there, meeting for the first time on the first tee. No one of us knew any of the others when we met, you know, just shaking hands and saying hello and going off as a foursome. Perhaps it was the pro's fault. He didn't help. He avoided us. If he had anything to say he said it to his caddy. He was a gloomy cuss, a Mister Melancholy, and he looked *whipped,* like maybe he hadn't made the cut in ten straight tournaments. Boy, did he keep to himself." My friend shook his head thinking about it.

"What about the other two?" I asked.

"Well, one of them was a candy manufacturer. I found that out about him. Hell, I *asked* him—politely, on the first fairway, as we were setting off after our drives—you know, what he *did* for a living, and he said, just snarling it out like he wanted me to make something of it, 'I make *candy*.' He was a very thin man, with this thin mustache, like a pencil line, and we swerved away from each other, heading for our shots, and that was about the extent of it—I mean, I don't think we spoke again. Do you want to hear something else about him?" he asked me.

I wanted him to get back to the ball in the bottom of the ball-washer, but he had settled on a framework for his story, and he was going to stick to it.

"Certainly," I said.

"Well, he had the most exaggerated swing I've ever seen on a golfer. He'd set there over the ball, swaying, and then he'd start his driver back—an outsized driver, it seemed to me, too long for him—and he was so thin that the club seemed to control him, y'see, so that once he got the club head moving back and around he had his troubles keeping himself from winding up on his backswing like a pretzel. Well, he'd get the club head stopped, just before it pulled him off balance, way behind his neck, and then he'd get it moving forward again, his face strained with this great determination, his eyes popping like a guy throwing a hammer, and the odd thing was that it took so much strength to control the great sweep of this swing that there wasn't hardly any muscle left at all when he got everything around to hit the ball. I mean there'd be this terrific effort and then this little click and he'd get the ball out there regular about one seven oh five. Period. But what a swing! Same with every club except the putter. No wonder our pro spent his time looking off in the distance."

"Now what about the other fellow?" I asked.

"Well, the other fellow was a good golfer, damn good golfer. Big man, and one of those cheery people, Mister Hearty, great big 'Hello, hello' on the first tee, the grand handshake, and the steady sincere look in the eye. But if you don't hit it off with him right off, come right back at him with that great frankness—if you don't say something to him like 'Hey, weren't we in the Fifth Marine Division together?'—you begin to lose him, and finally you can tell the idea has crept over him that you're snubbing him, that you think you're *superior* in some way. He'd like you to call him 'old buddy'—something cozy and crappy like that. Well, I couldn't think of anything to say right off, just stared at him, and this quick moment went and then the suspicion began to hit him and by that time it was too late. Hell, I didn't mind the guy." He shook his glass loudly.

"No," I said. "He sounds O.K. to me."

"We just didn't hit it off right there at the beginning."

"Perfectly understandable."

"So this guy went off and communed with his caddy. Called him by his first name, 'John.' He'd make a great shot and then he'd say that it was duck-soup easy 'cause *John,* his old buddy, showed him the shot. 'John, old buddy, you're a great son-of-a-bitch,' he'd say, and he'd amble over with this big grin and he'd give the caddy a big friendly punch that rattled all the clubs in the bag. He did that quite a lot. He was a damn good golfer."

"What about the ball in the washer?" I asked.

He wasn't ready yet; his eyes had a reflective cast; he leaned slightly forward and delivered himself of the following observations:

"Y'know I've played in a lot of pro-ams. I got them in the blood. I can't turn the invitations down. Here in San Fran. The Crosby. The Hope. The Las Vegas tournaments. The Thunderbird Classic. I go to 'em all. And yet, I'll tell you something. I don't like them. Pro-ams are the *loneliest* places—I mean, unless you're a gregarious sort and you don't care what sort of hours or company you keep. To begin with, you take a three-thousand-mile plane ride across the country to get to the tournament—all that money for your ticket and the overweight for your golf bag, and then you've got to rent a car once you get there, and the accommodations are overpriced, and you've got the entry fee to pay, and the caddies... and, of course, all of it would be worthwhile if you played good golf on a great course with interesting people. Well, there's the hang-up. Your golf is off. The golf course looks defoliated. Your pro doesn't turn out to be Nicklaus or anyone else, or even anyone you've ever *heard* of. He can't play *house*. His name is Pep Irving and he came in thirty-third in the Cajun Classic that year they had the bad tornadoes, and he's the pro at the Canoe Lodge Country Club on the Montana-Canadian border. And who are your partners? They're those guys you never liked at school and they've turned up on the course, twenty years older and twice as objectionable. Sometimes one of them is a celebrity. In some of the well-known pro-ams—y'know, like the Crosby—they try to spread celebrities through the field, but if you've got one in your foursome, who is he? Well, you're not sure. He looks vaguely familiar, Mister Nice Face, and so you ask one of the caddies and *he's* not sure either. He's the nice-guy brother, he thinks, of the fat kid in that big-family TV western—the one that gets in trouble? Oh, yes, you say vaguely. He doesn't look quite so nice you'd like to *ask* him who he is. Sensitive sort. So you don't. If the celebrity's a comic, he's one of those neurotic ones who needs big crowds to warm him up. He doesn't make any effort, y'know? Mister No Effort—just a sour bunny out there on the course with a tight little pokey constipated golf swing and he mumbles a lot, working up a routine that you got to reckon is composed solely of sharp answers to hecklers."

"You've had terrible luck," I said.

"Never fails," he said. "And the hours," he went on. "The sort of foursome I play in gets sent off in the morning during the false dawn— the first or second foursome out, with just enough light to tell you're not teeing up the ball on the toe of your golf shoe. Everybody's in a rotten mood, and, if you count the caddies, there are eight hangovers in the crowd, and they're all bad ones. So for the first five or six holes you just hear people *breathing* in the darkness. The 'Dew Sweepers.' Or if you don't go out early, you go out late—the 'Litter Brigade'—with a professional named Pogo Something, a Chinese kid, and two amateurs who've had five cocktails apiece for lunch—to 'quiet their nerves'— and it turns out these guys can't hit the ball out of their own shadows. You play up through the debris that's been left by the afternoon crowd—huge newspapers picking up and sailing around, and old picnics, and clusters of beer cans, and every green's got a ring of programs and Dixie cups and tubes of sun-tan oil. You got to admit it," he said suddenly.

"Admit?" I said vaguely.

"You got to admit that playing rounds with guys like that, you can't say 'Hey, guys, I just lost my ball in the ball-washer.'" He rattled the ice cubes in his glass.

I said, "Oh, yes," startled by the abruptness of his return full-circle to the ball-washer incident.

"We were all so goddamn formal and withdrawn from each other."

"Yes, well what did you do?" I asked.

"The ball was in there, and I didn't have another one—the caddies being down the fairway and all—so I decided the only thing I could do was to get the ball out of that damn washer, even if I had to break the ball-washer apart. So I got up close to the thing, my back to the others, y'see, to shield them from what I was going to do. They were all standing on the tee waiting for the O.K. from the caddies to drive over that blind hill. I could feel them watching. I got that plunger and with a good grip on it I gave a terrific up-jerk on it to see if I could pull it right out of the cylinder. I'm a big guy, as you can see, and I used to play varsity ball at Maryland. Man, did I put my back into it—a little knee bend and then *up*. Nothing the first time. Just a big *clonk* sound. So I tried again, man, like pulling a goddamn oak out of the ground— Mister Mighty Effort—and there was this great *clonk* sound and the top came off the cylinder and the water went up in a nice geyser. Boy!" he said, remembering it.

"Well, I looked down the cylinder and between those brushes was my ball, sure enough, and I reached in and removed it. Those bristles are *steel*. Got a good painful hand wash going in, and not a bad one coming out!"

"What was the reaction?" I asked.

"Well, I've got to tell you, I *averted my eyes,* as they say, when I turned around—I mean, I didn't challenge the three of them to make any comment. No one said anything. We were all so damn uncommunicative anyway. But they must have *thought* something. At the very least, seeing all that commotion, someone must have laughed to himself if he knew what the trouble was; or if he thought I was busying myself with the machine he would have remarked to himself, 'Boy! that guy sure likes to get his golf balls clean—Mister Meticulous.' But we were a goddamn forlorn group. We kept everything to ourselves. It was just forgotten. Damn surprised I remembered it myself."

CHAPTER 29

I also met Jack Nicklaus that evening. He has a sharp, high voice—something quite tough about it, and assured, and yet it turned out he could josh with others and about himself easily and without being arch. When I was introduced, he motioned me to a chair and to ease me into the conversation he said that the group at the table had been talking about superstitions among athletes.

I said that was a fine topic, and one which had always interested me.

Had I any, he wanted to know.

Well, no, I said. I was too scared to have them, I said, at least any serious ones, because they were apt to be time-consuming. Sidewalk cracks, I said; I avoided them.

"The bears get you," he said.

"That's right."

I said I hadn't meant to interrupt. Was he talking about his own superstitions?

Oh anyone's, he said. "Leo Diegel," he said, "he was one of the great players of the thirties—he was the guy who invented the elbows-out style in putting—well, he had the interesting superstition that he was invincible in the state of Maryland. He said no one could ever beat him there, and he believed it, and he was upset, hell, understandably, when they never scheduled the Open there."

"That old-timer Long Jim Barnes?" someone said. "He used to look for clovers, and if he found one he'd keep it in his mouth right through the round."

"How about your own?" someone asked Nicklaus.

He said that if things were going right, oh, he'd go out a certain door, and turn around a corner and head through *this* door, then *that,* and, of course, he'd take the same route to the golf course, and he'd keep to the same breakfast if his game was going strong.

"How about clothes?" I asked.

He said: "In 1962, the year I came onto the tour, just out of Ohio State, I'm telling you that you'd've found a better dressed guy out of a refugee camp than what I was: I was some sort of bad dresser. In the Open I was wearing a pair of twelve-dollar retail pants, iridescent olive-green-blue — like the belly color of a bottle-fly. It might have been all right if I'd thrown them away after the first round, but they were good luck pants, so I wore them for the entire tournament, including the last day. In those days you played thirty-six holes on the last day. Terrific heat that year. I'm telling you…" He turned the coffee cup in his hand. "I found out that superstition wasn't all you had to think about. You had to think about how you looked. There were those guys who'd come up who *knew* — I mean, they wanted to tell you that for, hell, for *sanitary* reasons — you couldn't wear the same trousers day after day. They had these pained expressions, but that was because they didn't quite know how to come up to a guy and say, 'Hey, listen, you got to change your pants.'"

Everyone around the table laughed.

"Of course, every year I carry a buckeye," he said.

"I've never known what that is — a buckeye," I admitted. "Other than the state symbol for Ohio."

"It's a poisonous nut," Nicklaus said.

"Oh."

"Squirrels won't fool with it. It's nothing. But I'll tell you what is good for me. The songs are helpful."

"The songs?"

"I do a lot of humming out on the course. I tend to stick with one song, you know, the sort of song that sticks in your mind and you can't get it out. I find my whole game shifts and becomes involved. I shot a 66 to 'Moon River.' You remember 'Georgy Girl,' that great song, how does that line go, 'Why do all the fellows pass you by?' I did pretty good with that one. Once in Chicago, playing with George Archer and George Knudson, I changed it to 'Georgy Boy.' I don't know what they made of it."

"What sort of a voice does this stuff come out in?" I asked.

"A flat monotone," Nicklaus said. "You remember 'Please Answer Me My Love'? Well, we won an awful lot on that one too."

"What else works from the outside—like the songs?" I asked. "I mean, do you ever get advice from unexpected quarters?"

"You mean from the galleries? Oh, I get these letters. 'Jack, I was sitting at the 4th at Bermuda Dunes and when you came through today, I noticed your elbows were *lower than they were yesterday.*' That sort of thing. I once got a letter from a woman, with illustrations, all diagrammed with arrows, that had fifty-five ways suggested as to how I could improve my game. Or a letter will come in, and the author will say very simply: 'I will fix your putter.' The best one I ever got was from someone who wrote in after I had played a real bad couple of days. The message was: 'I know why you didn't make the cut. You snubbed me.'"

Someone at the table said: "Lawson Little tells that story about the 1940 Open—the playoff against Sarazen—and how this guy comes up to him on the 5th and asks if he inhales or exhales on the backswing. It's a miracle he took Sarazen after that...but he did."

"How much psyching goes on?" I asked. "Are there players who go out of their way to unnerve their opponents?"

"There's not so much of that," Nicklaus said. "After all, there's so little match play these days. Your opponent is your golf course—he's the fellow you're struggling against. Of course, on a practice round players will have fun with each other—give each other what are called 'Dutch Harrisons.'"

"What is a 'Dutch Harrison'?" I asked.

"Dutch Harrison was a great needler on a golf course, a guy who'd throw you off balance with a comment or two. I'll tell you who's good at it these days: Chi Chi Rodriguez. Little guy, you know, big as nothing, but a long, long hitter, who, if he's got a sun-hit course, can expect a long roll for himself. Well, I'll hit a drive, and mine are high shots, big trajectory, a ball that doesn't gain much advantage from a roll along the ground. So then Chi Chi, if he feels he can outdrive me, if he's got the right sort of golf course, well, he shakes his head, oh very sorrowfully indeed, and he says, 'I don't know how the golf ball can *take* a shot like what you give it,' and he shakes his head again like something awful has happened, like maybe something's been *broken*. And then he steps up and hits *his* drive, which is patterned to take advantage of hard ground, and he's *by* you with a shot, a good way out, and if you let this sort of thing bother you, well, you can press, and find yourself in trouble."

"You have busted them, though," someone at the table said.

Nicklaus looked puzzled.

"A ball, I mean."

"Oh, when I was an amateur. When I was thirteen I exploded a Maxfli 3 at the 5th hole in York Temple. I hit an eight iron and the ball went forty yards. I went and looked at it and it was squashed, just there at the foot of the lake."

Someone at the table said, "You know there was this time before the Portland Open when Tom Weiskopf broke his driver on the practice tee, damn thing just disintegrated. He had to play his round with a three wood. Talk about superstition! From that day to this he doesn't warm up with his driver—goes right out into the tournament with it cold."

"How much ribbing goes on when you play with Arnold Palmer?" I asked Nicklaus.

"Not too much," Nicklaus said. "Oh, we kid around a bit. Arnie'll come in with a 75 and I'll say, 'Gee, where'd you get all those birdies?' Or when I come in he'll say, 'Nice round. What'd you shoot?'—in that order. We give nicknames to the girls in the gallery sometimes. We found a great one in Paris—'Blackie' we called her—and she turned out to be the daughter of a four-star general."

"It sounds like a lot of fun out there," I said.

Someone hitched his chair at the table and there was a perceptible pause. Then Nicklaus said, "You see me down on the practice tee today?"

"Sure," I said.

"I'm about five thousand shots away from being right."

"I see."

"But there's got to be a moment or so when you can relax."

"Sure," I said. "Absolutely."

CHAPTER 30

One evening in San Francisco I heard for the first time about the "yips"—a phenomenon talked about rather uneasily by the pros, and with wary respect, as one might talk about a communicable disease ravaging the neighboring township. The yips (a name invented by Tommy Armour, who had them) was the term given the occupational malaise of golf—a nervous affliction that settled in the wrist and hands, finally, after the years of pressure and the money bets and the strain. It was what ultimately drove the pros out of the game to the teaching jobs at the country clubs, setting the balls on the tees for the girls in the Pucci pants who came down for their two free gift lessons of the summer.

The legs don't give out, as in so many other sports, or the wind, or the sense of timing, or the power, but the *nerves,* so that one could see the hands of great golfers beset by the yips tremble visibly on the putting greens, the greatest names in golf completely at the mercy of short putts of 4, 5, 6 feet.

I said I had never heard of such a thing.

Dave Marr told me that he had seen Byron Nelson stand over a 4-foot putt at Florida's Seminole golf course, and, finally, after swaying back and forth several times, he had stabbed at the ball desperately and sent it *40 feet* past the hole.

At the same club, Seminole, Craig Wood had them so badly during an exhibition match, which should have relaxed the pressure, that he hit the first nine greens right on target in regulation strokes, but then putted so badly that his first-9 total was *44.* His dismay was such that he refused to putt out at all during the second nine; when he reached the greens he stooped and picked up the ball and stuffed it in his pocket and walked on to the next tee. The rest of his foursome, sympathetic, allowed him double gimmes, the regulation two putting strokes, and marked him down as such.

There was someone, a curious youngster, unaware of the ravages that the yips are capable of committing, who had gone up to the golfer and had the temerity to ask: "Why aren't you putting out like the others, Mister Wood? I mean, I don't understand..." and then he had stopped in mid-sentence because Wood had such a murderous look on his face.

It seemed to get them all. Leo Diegel had an awful time with nerves. He fussed around with a pendulum stroke with his putter but most people thought he was afflicted with a spastic tic. A great golfer, he never had the right mental equipment and he knew it: "They keep trying to give the championship to me," he once said, "but I won't take it." In the British Open in 1933 at St. Andrews he faced an incredibly short putt, just a foot or so, and he wandered up to it shaking like a leaf and stubbed it past the hole to lose the championship. Vardon, at the end of his career, in 1920, when he was in his fifties, got the yips. They were blamed on two attacks of tuberculosis. He called them the "jumps" and recommended putting in the dark as effective treatment. Apparently it didn't work. Gene Sarazen (he eventually got them, too) recalls Vardon as the most atrocious putter he had ever seen. "He didn't 3-putt, he 4-putted."

Rod Funseth, my partner in the Lucky, said that one of the saddest examples of the yips he had seen were those infesting the person of Jon Gustin, who was known for owning one of the prettiest swings on the tour. Funseth went on about him at some length. Apparently, he was a great dresser—he had been a former flag-bearer in the Honor Guards in Washington. Very snappy. "So you had," Funseth said, "the fine combination of a great swing, smooth and pretty as Snead's, and a guy who *looked* great as a golfer, like he stepped out of the advertising pages of *Esquire,* and yet what would happen, because of those yips, was that he would stand over the ball to swing—his irons, drives, putts, any shot—and his hands would come back, but the *club head wouldn't.* It would stick there right behind the ball like it was cemented to the ground."

"Lord Almighty," I said.

"He had to give up the tour."

"Well, I would think so."

"Worst case I ever saw."

"No cure, I don't suppose, for the yips."

"Golfers who have the yips *try* to cure them, God knows," Funseth said. "Gene Sarazen found one—at least one that worked for him. Watch him in the Senior tournaments. He steps up to the ball and hits it all in one motion—almost like he's hitting a shot off a polo pony. He doesn't dare stand over the ball, because he knows he'll freeze. Snead had the idea you could drift into a sort of 'pleasant daydream' to get back to the fundamentals of the practice swing. And then I recall that Bobby Locke had an idea that the yips could be cured by holding the club very loosely. If the yips had him bad, why you wouldn't be surprised to see his club just slip out and fall on the grass. Really no thing to have," Funseth said. "There's no sure cure. The yips can get so bad that you hate the idea of being in the lead in a tournament—where the pressure can bring on an attack. You begin to crave for a fair round, even a mediocre one, where the pressure isn't so stiff."

The great distinction to make was that there was no similarity between the yips and "choking"—though every once in a while the younger pros, who looked on the yips as something that couldn't possibly happen to them, would say that yips was just a fancy word that the older pros thought up to hide the fact that pressure gets to them too.

"Who told you that?"

"Oh, one of the younger professionals."

"That figures. If you want to see choking on a vast scale—I mean, what the caddies call the Apple Orchard for the big lumps that turn up in the throat—and if you want to see the eye-staring and those clammy foreheads, then you got to take in the qualifying tournaments that the rabbits play in. Ludicrous. Or you'll see one of those kids play in the high 60's for a round or so in the Open, and then what happens to him? The pressure gets to him. He skies to an 80. He chokes. He's so scared he damn near closes his eyes when he swings."

Someone said: "Pee Wee Reese, the shortstop, used to have a good phrase for the choke. He'd say, 'I know I'm choking when I'm chewing and can't work up a spit.'"

"Sometimes a particular hole will cause a choke—a choke hole," said Marr. "Like the 18th at Cypress. It's like walking into a certain room in a big dark house when you were a kid—you get this fear that hits you."

Johnny Pott said: "That's why we spend so much time on the practice tee. You're down there trying to groove the shot, to tone up the muscle memory, so that when you get out on the golf course and the pressure's really on—the choke at hand, and you can sense your eyes popping, and the jaw shaking—the muscles can still perform in their usual groove and you can get your shot off. You practice to get the muscles moving almost automatically."

"Doesn't that work for putting as well?"

"No, because muscle memory doesn't have anything to do with putting. Take Sam Snead. He's got the most famous swing in golf—you wouldn't find a differential of a millimeter in the circle of his swing if you took a thousand stop-action films of the guy. Perfectly grooved. Great on long putts, where the demands on muscle and swing are slightly more. But short putts! Give me someone out of kindergarten! His hands come back fine, but then the blade seems to go out of control just at the stroke. Sometimes he hits the top of the ball so that if it drops, it bounces every which way to get in there. Snead has had the yips for years. That's why he took that pro's job at Greenbrier way back in 1937. He thought he was going to have to quit the tour because he had the yips so bad. Or take Hogan, the most tragic case. Best tee-to-green player there ever was. Ever. I mean he puts the ball *there* off the tee, then *there,* just where he wants, then *there,* right on the green. You might as well *give* him those shots. But once on the green his troubles begin. He had those two holes to go at Oak Hill—just par-par, that's all he had to do to tie for the 1956 Open, but the yips got him. You know the guy got ten thousand letters from people trying to help him."

"Ten thousand!" I said.

"That's right."

I once asked Claude Harmon about those ten thousand letters, and whether he thought I would get an answer if I wrote Ben Hogan and asked him what the most ridiculous of the suggestions received had been—I thought that might be interesting.

"You wouldn't get an answer," Harmon said, looking at me sharply. "Because I'll tell you one thing. Hogan would have *tried* every damn one of them—I don't care how 'ridiculous'—to rid himself of those things." He repeated what I had heard so many people say: "If only Hogan could have putted—Jesus, he'd've made every record in the book look silly."

Hogan's miseries with the yips reached a climax in the 1954 Masters when, leading the field, he went to pieces on the final holes of the tournament. He 3-putted the 13th, missed a 4-foot putt on the 15th, 3-putted the 17th, and then came to the 18th needing a 6-foot putt to win the tournament. Claude Harmon said that Hogan went off to the side of the green and he made about one hundred practice strokes with his putter, all markedly different—changing his grip, the position of his hands on the club, the stroke itself. When Harmon asked him about it later, Hogan said that he had been trying to find a stroke, any stroke at all, in which he felt comfortable—a last-minute desperate search—and after the experimenting at the edge of the big crowd around the green, he had taken one of the styles back out on the putting surface and, perched over the ball, he used it, and not surprisingly he missed the putt.

Claude Harmon had an interesting notion that a golfer's control over those shots, putts especially, which were conducive to the yips, was at best fragmentary since the ball traveled over the *ground,* and was at the mercy of irregularities and worm casts and the rubs of the green and beetles sticking up their heads to look around and minuscule pebbles and so forth.

"Even a machine will miss half the time from six feet. It's been tried," Harmon said. "Golf is really two games. One is the game in the air. The golfer can lick that part of the game. It sounds like quite a feat—I mean, you've got to get all those parts of your body moving absolutely correctly to send that ball off the tee at over 200 miles an hour. But once the ball is up in the air, there's not much that can happen to it. The air is a medium a golfer can control, as easy as fish in water: he can move the ball in it just where he wants to—fade it, or hook it to his liking, if he's good enough—and he's never going to be surprised unless he makes a mistake himself. Or unless he hits a bird. But the other part of the game is across the ground. It sounds easy. You hardly move a muscle to hit a putt. A child can do it easier than nothing. But the medium controls the ball, that's the difference; the golfer can get the ball moving, that's all. After that, the ball moves and turns and dies by reason of the ground surface. What you can't control gets the best of you after a while—death and taxes, the old song—and that's what the yips are."

Harmon's story reminded me of Bernard Darwin's anecdote about the famous billiard professional who saw his first game of golf and remarked on it as interesting enough, but wondered why (as he said) "do golfers on the green first knock the ball up to the hole, and *then* put it in."

Some golfers felt that any prolonged absence from the game resulted in such a loss of confidence that an infestation of the yips would result. Bobby Cruickshank remembered that when his great rival Bobby Jones returned to competition in 1934 after a four-year layoff, his putting had deteriorated to such an extent that he wandered around the Masters that year asking his fellow golfers if they could spot what was wrong. "It looked the same," Cruickshank said. "I mean you'd see him address the ball, then set the putter in front of the ball, and then at the back of the ball again, and then the stroke—that was the famous procedure he went through. But you could see he had no confidence."

Claude Harmon told me of a more recent example of the damage a layoff could do—the decision of Mike Souchak to take his family for a month's vacation on the beach after he had a remarkable succession of wins and near-wins on the tour. "I told him he was crazy. You got to keep at it. When he came back it was gone—it had floated away on him, and what he had was like the yips."

Occasionally, though, one heard of cures. Roberto de Vicenzo, at one time afflicted with the yips so badly that he had the reputation of handling the spookiest putter on the tour, had been able to do something about it. It had not been easy. In the throes of the disease he had changed putters every week, picking out a new putter every time he went into a pro shop. He looked in a closet at home in Argentina not long ago and found fifty putters standing there, a total not counting many he had given away. No one of the putters seemed better than another. Each seemed utterly unreliable. In 1967 in Australia he blew an eleven-shot lead in the last fourteen holes because of his putting and lost to Alan Murray in a play-off. He talked about an occasion in England when his putters had let him down—his accent heavy, his big hands moving artfully in the air to describe his meaning, his chair squeaking under him, his face expressive under the white baseball-style golf hat he wears to cover his thinning hair.

"In the British Open, in 1965, I think, we are playing the final day, which is thirty-six holes, and in the morning I am leading. I have had one bad green, number 9, which I three-putt in the morning, but I still in very good position. So we come to number nine in the afternoon and I say to myself, 'Roberto, you no three-putt this green this afternoon, do you?' I didn't. I make *four* putts. I was so mad I wanted to break all my clubs and quit the game and never play again. I had no confidence. I look at the cup and she look like a little spike mark. I tell myself, 'Roberto, you no can put the ball in there.' So I lose my confidence and I lose the tournament right there."

Vicenzo's cure turned out to be a matter of self-application — finding the right type of putter, the correct style of hitting a ball with it, the regaining of confidence, and practice, endless practice. Many golfers go through an equivalent regimen of experiment and practice without finding the answer: Snead had tried a number of putters and such grotesque putting styles — the "sidewinder" in particular, in which he faces the hole and strokes the ball just off the outer edge of his golf shoe — that only his great grace as an athlete keeps him from looking ludicrous. Vicenzo was lucky. He found his putter two years ago. A mallet putter that he says is appropriate for his big hands. He watched other golfers' putting styles and decided that all the good putters (with the exception of Billy Casper and Doug Ford) use their *arms* primarily in the putting strokes, not the wrists, which had been his style. So he changed his style and found his sense of "feel" increased immeasurably. His confidence began to return. He practiced endlessly — especially to get what he refers to as the "head in rhythm...to work the heads and the hands at the same time." He began to collect some tournament wins — notably the British Open, and then a close run at the Masters which he would have taken to a play-off had he not handed in a mistotaled score card. But he was phlegmatic himself about the future. "The putt is a funny game. You can't think you got it for always. You can lose it tomorrow. But for the moment," he said, "I feel better when I step onto the golf course. I no feel scared to step onto the green. Not any more. Or maybe for the time being, eh?"

Another older player I talked to about the yips was John Farrell, once the great rival of Bobby Jones and now a teaching professional in Florida. He said that if you play in competition long enough you're sure to get the yips. "Walter Hagen," he said. "If you had to vote for the player with the best temperament, well, you'd *have* to vote for him. Hell, he had such confidence that there wasn't a shot that held any terror for him: they used to say that when he had a particularly tough shot to make, and he'd stepped up and made a great one of it, why then he'd whisper at his caddy, 'Did I make it look hard enough?' and give him a wink, y'see. Well *he* got them. The yips. He got them so bad that he tried strokes and grip styles you could scarcely *believe:* cross-handed putting; or sticking the elbows way out so that the wrist action was throttled down and his whole body moved as stiff as a derrick. He even tried putting in the dark—thought that might cure him. Nothing did. Or look at Ben Hogan. Take a player like him. The 'Iceman' they called him. *He* got the yips. And Bobby Jones. Finally he began to miss putts two feet long, and he quit because he couldn't keep oatmeal on his stomach."

Farrell told me that he himself had them, but he had an interesting variation of the disease. Though the yips most invariably affect the more delicate shots of the game, Farrell discovered that in time he began to tighten up on his *drives,* which in theory are the golfers' easiest shots because, as I had heard, the swing becomes grooved as the years go on. Yet Farrell found himself *steering* his shots off the tee in his later years, losing distance and accuracy, and he was totally unable to cure himself.

I asked the question I had put to the others—if there was any connection between the yips and losing one's nerve.

"It's that you lose *nerves,* not nerve," Farrell said. "You can shoot lions in the dark and yet you can quiver like a leaf and fall flat over a two-foot putt."

"I would think," I said, "that years of experience standing over two-foot putts, and gaining all the know-how of reading greens and distance, and the competition—that all of that would be to a golfer's advantage...confidence."

"Oh, I wouldn't want to be so sure as that," Farrell said. "I always remember Waite Hoyte, who pitched for the Yankees, you'll recall, and what he used to say about 'experience.' He said experience *punishes* you.

A veteran player *knows* what can happen to him: he comes onto a pitcher's mound and he knows the batter waiting for him can pop the ball right back to the bullpen where he's just come from for a home run. He's gone through it before. So he's something of a fatalist. It's the same in golf. 'Experience' punishes you as you continue with the game. That's why in golf we speak of someone being 'competitively young' or 'competitively old.' Craig Wood, you see, he was 'competitively young' at forty-three because he started playing serious golf when he was well into his thirties. Then on the other hand Bobby Jones was 'competitively old' at twenty-three—he had started at fifteen, you see, which gave him early 'experience' but it aged him good and quick as a golfer.

"Experience," Farrell went on ruefully. "I won the Open in 1928 at Olympia Fields, and then in 1929 I missed the cut at the Open at Winged Foot. Dropped from the tournament I had *won* the year before! D'you think *that* experience did me any good! Well, I'll tell you. The next year at Interlachen, Minneapolis—in the 1930 Open which Bobby Jones won to fetch himself the Grand Slam—I stepped up on the first tee with the 'experience' gained from those bad rounds the year before, and what did I do but get myself an *8* on that first hole. I managed to pull myself together after that and I finished eighth behind Jones, but don't talk to me about *experience*. Snead can't win the Open because of his memories—missing that two-footer in the 1947 Open. Palmer won't win the PGA. He has that block. No; it's the kids, the strong young golfers who have it all. They make great big errors—I mean, a kid like Marty Fleckman coming up with an 80 after leading the Open into the last day in 1967—but he's at the age when mistakes are easily forgotten; those kids' imaginations aren't jumpy with crucial flubs— y'know, disaster, that's what they don't know about. Not yet. It'll come. They'll get there. Experience will come. Oh yes."

CHAPTER 31

San Francisco has always been a favorite town—but I saw little of it this time. My round in the pro-am had been dismaying. I stayed over in San Francisco for the four additional days of the Lucky tournament, but most of that time I spent on a driving range endlessly poling shots into a vast bowl from the range which was set along one section of the rim. It was an interesting place—with a spectacular view south to one of the city's hills, with its rising layers of white stucco houses, like an Italian hill town. The bowl must have been nearly a quarter of a mile across, fashioned from a deep cuplike gully, and any ball scratched off the driving range would roll a couple of hundred yards down its slopes. The arrangement was satisfying to one's ego, perched as the place was on the rim of the bowl where one could enjoy the same aesthetic pleasure of abandonment one would feel by driving a golf ball off the stern of an ocean liner, or off a high cliff into the treetops of a forest far below.

The place had a restaurant with a jukebox and music was piped out along the length of the range so that the sad Bob Dylan ballads of the time became the background for the golfing activity.

I would arrive in the morning and stay through the afternoon. Over a small lunch I got to know the manager of the range—a middle-aged man who chewed tobacco and said he had been in the driving-range business for nearly twenty years, ever since the end of the war. He got around a golf course with a score in the mid-70's, he told me, and there was a sign in the restaurant that reported he was the range professional and was available for lessons at six dollars a half-hour. He preferred driving ranges, though; he felt they were the most interesting phenomenon in golf. "What happens on a golf course is predictable," he said. "People behave in a certain way. They're conditioned. But not on these ranges."

Weren't most ranges about the same, I wanted to know.

His eyebrows went up. "Hell, in the east they have double-decker ranges," he told me. Some of them were truly enormous. There was one beyond New York's La Guardia Airport, where he had put in an occasional summer's work, which was called Golf City. A five-million-dollar operation it was, and it included two nine-hole miniature courses done

George hits a few practice shots at the range. Bob Bruno and George's caddy, Abe, observe him keenly. (*Russ Halford*)

in "Disneyland Style"—which is to say, as I understood it, that one ventured onto an obstacle course of Disney props, such structures as miniature lighthouses, windmills, and so forth, with one's play surveyed by the round vacant eyes of human-sized statues of ducks and mice.

There were nearly 100 tees on the driving range at Golf City, 70 of them covered to give fair protection against the rain, though each stall was open enough so that a right-handed golfer's left side got fairly soaked in a good rain. Apparently, the customers came out in the most intemperate of conditions. Golf City remained open the year round, and when the temperature dipped to five degrees, many of the customers wore shoveling gloves.

"You look down the row of stalls," the manager recalled, "and see the steam of the golfers' breaths coming out, like engines were working in there."

He shook his head. "Man, that place is what the ranges of the future are going to be. Y'know what the advertising for the place says?"

"No," I said.

"It says, 'Don't Bend. Just Swing.' The driving range is automatic: as soon as the ball is whacked off its tee another ball gets pushed up by air pressure from below."

The manager explained that the system was expensive to install, but management found it a worthy investment, since customers had no way of keeping track of the number of balls they hit, and thus were likely to over-spend. Besides, it was very hard to turn away from a ball perched up on a tee waiting to be hit. To further entice the customer, an occasional gold ball popped up on the tee which entitled him to a prize—a transistor radio, a golf hat, a bag of gold-colored tees.

I asked him how many balls most people at golf ranges hit and the proprietor said he reckoned it worked out to an average of 150 balls per customer. He remembered that the record at Golf City belonged to a Korean who hit 750 balls a day, at 3 cents a ball. Asians make up an astonishing percentage of people who go regularly to driving ranges—not surprising in the San Francisco area with its large Asian population, but certainly so in the New York metropolitan area. No one in the business was quite sure why. The proprietor felt it was because golf is a game which does not handicap a small player.

"You know something odd about them?"

"What is that?" I asked.

"They come in small groups and they always pay with brand new bills."

"Really?"

"Invariably," the manager said. "So new they still crackle."

I asked if he had any other comments to make about life at his range. The manager grinned. "You know the joke about the pro asking this pupil of his who's topped 20 or 30 shots along the ground? He suggested the guy take off his shoes."

"Oh."

"Well, I've seen it actually done out here on the range, and you know something? It worked. I never saw this guy top another after he took off his shoes."

The manager laughed. "I'll tell you another one. You get these cats, beginners, who come out here with a full rig—new bag, the gold shoes, the cap, the works, and a golf cart that they wheel right up to the mat where they'll take out the club they'll use. The whole ceremony. And then they'll stand up there and whiff six times in a row before they hit the ball. The beginners are crazy. Sometimes you wonder about the mentality of people. I remember one night a couple of years back, down at a range in Southern California, an elderly man stopped in with his wife and rather than buy a bucket of balls—we had buckets then, forty-five balls to each—why this guy bought six balls. Cost him about eleven cents and I had to work it out on a piece of paper. He kept promising he would return them. Well, I kept an eye on him. It was about 7:00 p.m. and the range was jammed with people. What does this guy do but hit out his six balls—he must have mentally marked where they had come down—and then saunter out there to pick them up. He thought that was what you were supposed to do. Pick up your balls as soon as you hit them. Thousands of balls lying out there, and he was peering among them to get back those six. Someone yelled for the customers to stop hitting. Hell, that's quite a barrage going on out there from the driving mats, but that guy never paid it any heed. He thought he was doing what he was supposed to do."

"What did his wife do?" I asked.

"Well, she stood and watched him, wringing this handbag she had. I suppose she thought it was part of the *game*—the *danger* of the game, I guess."

Just then the door to the luncheonette squeaked open and shut and one of the players from the range came in. I had noticed him down the line from me—grunting each time he punched stiffly at the ball. His style was a beginner's, for sure, his legs spread too far apart, the toes out, and his stroke a quick scoop.

The manager looked up. "You ready for that lesson yet?"

"Lesson?" The man shook his head and swore. "Look at these hands." He held them out. They were raw and blistered.

The manager whistled and said he had some stuff back in the kitchen in a first-aid kit he thought might be helpful. He left to get it.

The player sagged down in a seat at our table. "Y'mind?"

"Hell, no," I said. "You want a beer?" There were a couple of opened bottles on the table.

He nodded. He took one by the neck and took a long drink and slapped the bottle down on the tabletop. He exhaled comfortably. "Jesus!" He looked back at his hands. "These things are as weak as a woman's. What I get myself into? You wanna know? On television I see these guys hitting golf balls, and I watch, and I can't figure it. A guy would hit a big shot and then the guy hits a little shot. So how do you figure it? Hell, I couldn't figure it. Like all those words the guy on TV says, in that low voice so he don't disturb no one, like 'that's about a five from there,' things like that. Five *what*? How you know if you don't play the game? Or words like birdie, and wedge, and the grain of the grass, and the breaks. Like he says it breaks just a bit to the left, and so I say to myself like I *got* to work this thing out. So I buy a set of clubs off a guy and yesterday I come out here and I buy a bag of balls and out there on those rubber carpets I hit maybe half of 'em along the ground and I can't figure it out until that guy, the manager, he comes aroun' and says I got warped clubs, and not only warped clubs but they're *lefties*—clubs for a left-handed golfer. Well, I feel pretty good to find *that* out. I wasn't hittin' the ball, and I couldn't figure it, because when I was a kid I played polo a coupla times with a no-good pony and a no-good polo stick down in South America where I come from as a kid, and I could hit the ball a shot. Well, so I had these wrong clubs. So I shift aroun' and try the other way, y'know, lefty? The manager—nice guy, real nice guy—he says, 'You wanna lesson?' I say, 'What the hell, I can figure it.' Already I figure what that guy on the TV means when he says, y'know, 'A five, that's about a five.' He's talking about a *club,* for Chrissake! The club's got a five written down there on the head. So I figure that; maybe I can figure the rest. So what do I do? I am out here today and this guy's breathing down my neck trying to get six dollars outa me..."

The manager was back with some salve and a tin box of Band-Aids.

"I'm a case for the hospital," the man said. "You know what? I'm going home to my wife and she is looking at my hands and she is saying what is with your hands, Harry? And I am going to say what? Golf? You kidding? She's seen those TV programs with all that whispering, y'know, the announcer, and these guys bending over the ball and taking these little tiny strokes with these clubs, and she is going to say, 'You son-of-a-bitch, you been *fighting*!'

"And so I am saying, Sophie, you don't *blister* fighting, you get things broke, Sophie, like a nose. *This* is what golf does to you, Sophie, I swear. It gets you in the hands, it can put you in the hospital, Sophie...."

The manager was grinning. He sat down and tipped back in his chair. He was going to crowd in again with the six-dollar offer, I could tell.

He did so: "Six dollars."

"You kiddin'? Six dollars to learn something to get your wife all crazy?"

He stood up and grinned. "O.K.," he said. "I'll come back maybe when I can catch hold of somethin' with my hands without it making me yell...." He gestured with his hands. "Jesus!" He pushed open the screen door with his elbows. "Man," he said, "I'm a hospital case."

The manager shook his head when he had gone. "You get some crazy ones. He's a good man, that guy—crazy, but funny crazy, y'know, not *nuts* crazy. He comes out of Argentina, I think, when he is maybe nine or ten, and he has this big business of bringing cowhides in from down there. Import business."

"He's something," I said.

"You get some crazy ones...I mean the other kind, the *nuts* kind. You want I should tell you the strangest..."

"Sure," I said.

The manager hitched himself around in his chair.

"This didn't happen in this place I got here. This was when I had the smaller place down the coast, way down, Southern California. Little place, just when I was starting out. Big field in front, couple of archery targets out there, lights for night, maybe twenty mats—and the best thing I had was this jeep with a wire covering like a cage for protection from the guys hitting on the range, and you drive out on the field and it picks up the golf balls, like those hay things, y'know? Hayers?"

"Yes," I said. "I've seen those things. You've got one here."

"That's right," he said. "I used to drive the one down there myself. I'll tell you something. When you're getting low on balls and you got to drive out and collect a big batch while you got customers on the mats, I'll tell you there isn't a golfer on the range what is not going to try and hit you with his shot. You get that jeep out fifty yards in that field and you can see them back there on the range reaching in their bags for two irons to drill these shots low at you. 'Course you got this wire cage around the jeep which is supposed to keep you protected, but a ball can get through maybe, and for sure it makes you a mite uneasy about human nature. They really pepper you. Know what I mean?"

I said I did.

"Well, this one time," he went on, "I had been out with the pick-up jeep and picked up the balls. It was a July night, very late, with everything damp and sticky. There was just this one customer out on the firing line. He had come into the place — I could hear his tires screeching in the parking place out back — not so long before closing time. Very late. An odd kind of cat. He took his pail of balls and they were gone in no time at all — he just ripped them out there, hardly taking the time to tee up his shot. Some he'd really *sock*. He was a big man. But he never took the time to see them sail out there — he'd be bending over the rubber tee with his next ball. Then when he'd done with his pail he came back to the window, y'know, of the little office where I was, carrying this club in his hand, and he looked in, fierce as all get out, and he said, 'Gimme another *pail*!' real tight.

"Well, I set him up with his pail and he went on out and got rid of them quick. Of course, closing time was coming up, midnight, y'know, but I didn't like the *looks* of this cat. He just wasn't someone you could just announce, 'Closing time, buddy,' without maybe his getting real fierce and upset. So I gave him some extra time. I thought maybe I'd wait until he finished the last pail of balls, and then when he turned up at my window I'd say, just as cheerful as I could, that the place was closed up for the night but for sure we opened good and early in the morning and he could start right up fresh *then*.

"Well, I waited there reading a mag in my little office. But the odd thing was he didn't turn up for another pail. Strange, y'know. So I looked out and there he was, hitting the balls all different. Before he'd been ripping them out as fast as he could; now he was pulling a ball out of the pail and looking at it very carefully, turning it in his hand, and *talking* to it, and then he'd set it down on the tee. Then he'd talk to it some more, really giving hell to the ball, because I could tell from the way his lips were moving. Sometimes he'd lean down and take the ball off the tee and talk to it some more from close up, just an inch or so away from his mouth like he was going to bite it. Then he'd set it back on the tee and after a while he'd rear back and really *sock* it — he'd put everything into really riding that ball out of there. He must have been a good golfer—I mean, those drives of his were getting out to that big archery target that is three hundred yards off. And y'know on golfing ranges we use these very low-compression balls with wire in them, which makes it hard to give them a long ride. Of course, we bring in the targets to compensate, y'know?

"But this guy really poked them out there. Each shot, what with all this jawing and talking, took so much time that the dawn would be coming up before he got down to the bottom of his pail. So I moseyed on out there from my office, y'know, to say it was quitting time, just saying something like, 'Hey, buddy,' nothing sharp or *controversial*... and you know what this guy did?"

"What?"

"Why he angled around on that tee, moving like a quick crab, and he lined his shot up on *me*. Lord *Almighty*. I mean, there I was, right in his sights. He kept shouting at me, 'Get back!' You know what I did?"

"What?" I asked.

"I put my hands up in the air like I was being *held up* with a pistol."

"No," I said.

"I'm not kidding. I mean that guy facing me with those wild eyes and that driver in his hands and just twitching to hit—man, I'd druther of faced a guy with a shotgun."

"Well, then what happened?"

"Well, so I backed up, y'know, and I flash him this sort of nice smile, and I say, 'No sweat, man, you just keep on with what you're doing. I'll be just closing up and getting on home and you just keep right on...' well, that was the sort of thing I was telling him, and then I turned and went out back toward my car, just leaving him in charge of the whole place. Man, what a walk! I had that itchy feeling like he was going to drill a golf ball right between my shoulder blades. I tell you I never looked back. Never, 't'all. Fact is, I came in late the next morning. I open the place at eight—that is, I do usually—but this next morning I turn up maybe at nine, maybe later. And I look around there pretty careful, sort of peering around corners, and it is all very peaceful, no sign that the big guy had been there at all.

"But, you know something? It was *creepy*. Like I felt the guy was around somewhere. I felt it in the office, this little place I used to sit, with the pails of golf balls under the counter, this little window like a wicket. Well, there's this big closet off the office in which I keep the clubs and the pails and a lawn mower and some stuff like that back in there. I had this feeling this guy had been in there. The door was open, y'know, not like the way it was the night before. I take a look in there, pulling open the door very fast. Nobody there. But you know what I see when I turn around?"

"What?"

"Well, I see these two pieces of paper on the office table. One of the papers, when I look, is a check drawn on an Illinois bank and it is made out to the name of my place—man, in this terrible neat handwriting. You know what the amount of the check was for?"

"How much?"

"One thousand dollars."

"Come on," I said.

"In this very neat hand. And there was this other note with it—the other piece of paper. It said: 'This is for the jeep.'

"So I said to myself, oh shit, he's taken the jeep. And I run out by the mats down by the end where I keep the jeep, and it's still there—just sitting there where I left it. But the key's in it—it has the big wooden tag on it. He must have seen it in the office where it hangs on this peg. And when I go up and look in the jeep, I see that the key's bent almost double in the lock...So he tried, didn't he..."

"I guess so," I said.

"He must have gotten in there and not pushed the key in far enough and when he turned it to get the thing started, well, it bent—bent damn near double."

"That sounds right," I said.

The manager clinked the beer bottles in front of him.

"Well, what would he want that damn jeep for—that crazy machine with a cage around it that he couldn't have driven two blocks in town without someone saying, 'Y'know, Jesus, that thing belongs on a golf range.' I mean the police..."

"Damned if I know," I said slowly, thinking about it.

"He had this perfectly good car out front. I'd heard him come in with his tires screeching."

"Was it there?"

"No. He'd driven off in it. I guess he changed his mind. Hell, he'd broken the key to the jeep."

"What about the check?" I asked.

"Aw, that check wouldn't have been no good. I kept it around for a while, like a souvenir. But then I threw it away. Some crazy nut, that's all."

CHAPTER 32

The next stop on the tour after the San Francisco tournament was the Bob Hope Classic, which is held in the Palm Desert–Palm Springs area — known as the Golf Capital of the World. There are over twenty golf courses in the vicinity, not counting the pitch-and-putt layouts or the innumerable driving ranges — one of which I frequented every morning on my way to the country club where my round was scheduled.

I never quite got adapted to Palm Springs. It is a community set down in a forbidding corner of the desert under the flank of a bleak mountain range with humped hills as desolate as slag heaps. A city ordinance forbids the building of homes over a certain height (presumably to ensure that the inhabitants get an unimpeded view of their raw surroundings), so that, seeing the identical low buildings with flat roofs and stucco walls, one has the sense of being in a vast adobe housing development.

"Wait for the sunsets," I was told. "You've heard about our great desert sunsets."

I had heard about them, but they seemed to hold off most of the time I was there. Night fell quickly but not mercifully. It was then that the bonanza of artificiality and gimmickry became most evident. To ease the gloom of the landscape, water pipes have been run part way up rock piles and mountain slopes to create artificial waterfalls and streams.

In the daytime the water tumbling down those barren slopes looks oddly unnatural, like a freshet gushing out of a window halfway up the facade of the Chrysler Building. At night, colored searchlights are brought into play, turning the waterfalls orange. Many of the palms of the area have tiny spotlights set about them; the trees glow blue and red, and one often feels surrounded by the garish props of an opera set. "It's all so fake," a golf writer said, staring up moodily from his drink on the terrace of one of the country clubs. Bells were ringing from a carillon tower, echoing against the bleak hills washed by searchlights. "The whole place seems to have been doused with Jade East."

On the golf courses the same quality of artificiality seemed to prevail. At the Crosby, one was always conscious of the natural surroundings—even with the big crowds in attendance—emphasized by the deep forests, the deer moving through the green shadows like phantoms, and the sea shifting against the rocks and beaches of the ocean holes.

At Palm Springs the atmosphere was urban—heavy traffic, the courses crowded with gaily painted golf carts, with surreys—and they run on macadam walks that lace the fairways. A golfer can get an extra breathtaking hop and run if his ball hits the pathway surface. The carnival spirit abounds. The crowds are noisy and colorful. Promotion effects seem everywhere. On the third hole of my first day of play I looked up from my drive and saw two figures dressed in black-and-white bear costumes ride out on the fairway in front of me in a golf cart.

"Wha'?"

"Those are the Hamm's Beer bears," I was told. "The company's involved in the tournament promotion."

Quite a few of them were positioned around the course, the implacable bear heads staring at one from the crowd.

The Dewar's whisky people were taking part in the promotion, too, and they had a special honor guard of six-foot Highlanders dressed in the full Scottish regalia—kilt, busby, and all—and they seemed to materialize at awkward and startling moments, appearing suddenly over the brow of a bunker and staring down as one was settling in for the shot with the sand-blaster.

Then again, with the exception of Bermuda Dunes, even the architecture of the golf courses seemed as forced as the surroundings—the water hazards were man-made, with smooth cement contours and an attending flock of Muscovy ducks gabbling at one end. Often the fairways were lined with bungalows, so that the golfers seemed to be playing down a green boulevard with the people on either side having their evening cocktails on the little flagstone terraces. Many of the houses have small, beautifully groomed gardens out front and occasionally a sign that tells you that the bungalow is called Par-a-dise or Birdie-House or Shankri-La. Four or five are called The 19th Hole. Usually there is also a sign requesting golfers not to play out of the flower beds. Iron statuary is sometimes set about—flamingoes in the petunias, heavy twenty-pound stone frogs peering out from under the boxwood, and in one garden I saw iron stands with two- and four-line poems on them—little homilies, Edgar Guest verses, I suppose. There was one I jotted down which addressed itself to proper behavior in a caddy's presence:

> *Mister Golfer, I should warn you*
> *There's a youngster at your side*
> *And if you are fit to be with*
> *He will very soon decide.*

The bungalows are faced with big plate-glass windows, which are often kept barred against the fine desert air. Air-conditioning units hum. One can look in and see the tall-necked vases in the corners of living rooms with bright-colored artificial dust mops stuck in them. The floors are marble or parquet. No rugs. The tables are glass-topped and bare. The sofas are white, with round cushions set about on them embroidered with such messages as DON'T BUG ME. The telephones are white and have long white cords. Some of the better-appointed places have swimming pools fronting on the fairways, one of them, I noted, with a *Manneken-Pis* at one end. At night the spotlights are turned on, and the gardens and pools glow in rose-red.

I was told that there are 3,500 swimming pools in the vicinity, which works out at approximately one pool for five persons. People don't go in very often because of the nippy desert nights. Often, the pools are heated, and sepulchral fog drifts off them like a cauldron's steam. Some pools are built in the shape of monograms. At one of the cocktail parties I was told of a circular swimming pool with a flagpole (flying a cocktail flag) rising out of the center—representing a massive cup and flagstick.

The shops were full of golf novelties. In one of the shops off the main street of Palm Springs I asked the proprietess which the more popular items were. "Oh just about everything to do with golf," she had said. "Look around." Every shelf displayed items with a golf motif—tableware and glasses, pillows, and then, of course, the novelty items: trick balls which "exploded," or "smoked," or were specially weighted so that they sashayed off the tee in wild hooks or slices; an apparatus called a Golfer's Crotch Hook, an icetonglike arrangement that one strapped on and which certainly looked as if it lived up to its corrective promise to "Keep the golfer's head down." I noticed a shelf of Kneel 'n' Pray putters which were each about seven inches long; there were boxes of Goofy Golf Tees and bags of trick clubs that looked harmless enough but that bent insanely during the backswing, convoluting, so that it was like trying to hit a ball with a fur boa. There were shelves of club covers—one set, I noticed, shaped like owl heads, with eyes made of buttons that bobbed, so that out on the fairway the clutch of owls must have seemed to be staring out of the bag, loopy, their eyes lolling, from motion sickness. In the next bin were additional models: rabbits, with ears to hold to pull the covers off the clubs; a set of mink covers for fifty dollars apiece.

"Aren't those fine?" It was the proprietess. "Here's a cutie," she said. "This Goofy Golf Tee." She held a small package in her hand. She had on bright orange lipstick.

"What's in there?" I asked warily.

"Can't set a ball on it," she explained. "It looks like any other tee, but it's built so that a guy could spend a week trying to set a ball on it—a real cutie."

"Oh yes," I said.

"Now over here," she said, pointing at a shelf of large boxes, "are the Big Boy Tees."

"What are they?" I asked.

"They are to tee a ball up over a water hose—jokey tees, y'know. It has long legs and the tee sets up on the top of a sort of structure. You want I should unwrap it for you. So you can take a look?"

"No thanks."

"Have you seen the Kneel 'n' Pray putter?" she asked.

"I certainly have," I replied. "Yes, indeed."

"Nothing caught your fancy?"

"These 'jokey' items really do well, do they?" I asked.

"At Christmas time," she said, "why, you can't get in this place. Have to stand in line."

I had a sudden vision of a Palm Springs Christmas—a tired man in an armchair surrounded by Christmas wrappings and string (looking not unlike Dwight Eisenhower, the most famous resident of the area) being approached by an eight-year-old niece holding her present for him, and he can tell because the package is about seven inches long and she has a somewhat tentative smile as she comes toward him, that he's about to receive yet another "Kneel 'n' Pray" putter, his fifth of the day.

"Nothing you can't find for the golfer in this shop," the woman was saying. "Don't forget," she said, lifting a finger, "this community is the Golf Capital of the World."

That was the common denominator of the Palm Springs area—that its residents were great boosters. They were always asking visitors what they thought of the sunsets, and the quick desert climate, and wasn't the verbena in bloom fantastic, and wasn't the city ordinance that kept buildings' heights down a fine one, and weren't the golf courses terrific?

I went out for a practice round the day before the tournament. One of the players in our foursome was a doctor from the area. He took what seemed almost a personal pride in his surroundings. We rode the first couple of holes together in a yellow golf cart. He was a good player and he hit a series of fine shots. He kept inhaling deep loud breaths as if draughts of desert air were essential to his skills. "It's great, isn't it?" he asked. We were going down a macadam path that cut diagonally across a fairway. Two people in Hamm bear costumes were riding in the cart in front of us.

"Well, I'm sorry about that shot of mine," I said. I had picked up. My fourth shot off the tee had ended up in a little garden fronting a fairway-side bungalow—the ball lying immediately under an iron flamingo as if (I had remarked to myself at the time) it had just been laid by the bird.

"Hell, never mind that," the doctor said expansively. "The great thing about this area—" he made a sweep with his arm—"is that it's such a damn fine country that if you do miss a shot all you got to do is raise your eyes and *look around*. Best medicine there is for what ails—even a shanked shot."

He stopped the cart and got out. He had a wood shot from the fairway. The ball was sitting up prettily for him. "O.K., baby," he said to it. He had a smooth swing, but on this occasion the ball rose off on a long slice, and it sailed and landed, and bounced a few times, and ended up in a swimming pool. There was something genuinely funny about the way the ball, bouncing toward the distant pool, took one last big hop and went in—almost in the same rhythm as a diver taking his steps and going off a board.

The doctor compressed his lips. "Son-of-a-bitch," he said. "God-damn son-of-a-bitch."

He raised his club and hit it brutally against the ground. I thought he was going to kick the cart. He drove off in the cart without me. As I walked along behind I felt a surge of good humor. There was good-natured hee-hawing and joshing among the rest of the foursome as we went up to the edge of the pool and looked in. We quieted down for the doctor's shot. He had taken a penalty drop just by the pool. He made the shot and drove off toward the green. His face was grim.

There were two balls there in the pool besides the doctor's. The owner of the property came out of his bungalow. He looked in the pool and shook his head. "Three," he said. He told me that he had a rake especially constructed with a long telescoping handle to fish the balls out, but it had disappeared. Most likely, he said, it had been borrowed by someone down the line who also had a pool and the same problem with errant shots popping in.

"How many golf balls does your pool collect, say, during the course of a month?" I asked.

"Oh, she pulls in maybe six or seven a week. We've had 'em drop in while the missus and I were swimming, you know."

"Oh."

"Of course, we're more worried about the windows. And the roof." He pointed up at the roof, which appeared to be made of red chimney tiles laid in rows. "That gets hit pretty constant."

George gets wet to retrieve a wayward shot from a backyard pool during a tournament in Palm Springs. (*Russ Halford*)

"What is that like?"

"Well, it makes a 'bong' sound."

"You're under pretty heavy bombardment being where you are," I said.

"On the weekends it can be fairly rough," he said. "After all, you know," and it was hard to tell if his smile was rueful, "this is the Golf Capital of the World."

CHAPTER 33

In Palm Springs the cocktail parties after a day's round were enormous. In the unfinished clubhouse at La Quinta, where nearly a thousand must have been packed in for a tournament eve party, the pitch of noise got to be awesome.

I have always had a theory that yachtsmen in convocation produce the highest decibel count of noise. After a rough day's sail, or a race, and having berthed their craft safely, they carry their sail bags ashore and then their subconscious relief at being back on land and turning a cool martini glass in their fingers results in a bray of sound like a cannonade. But these people at La Quinta made me revise my opinion. It may have been because of the acoustics in the barnlike place, half-finished, with patches of sawdust and wood chips on the floor, and the bars set up on planks laid on sawhorses. The golfers and their wives seemed to set back a bit on their heels to give themselves room, so to speak, to yell merrily at each other, their eyes very large with effort. I did not see any of the professional golfers there. Some of them may have looked in and backed away in awe. The voices, any one of them loud enough to carry across a meadow, became in concert a sheer wash of sound. Wandering through the crowd, it was hard to sort out one conversation from another— snippets, usually, of triumphs recounted. "My God, Harry, on the fifteenth..." And always the ubiquitous habit of trying to enliven the story by shifting it to the present tense. "So I am lying fifty yards from the pin and I am taking a wedge..." Perhaps the key to all that noise was somehow connected with the loneliness of the golfer out on his round, and the frustrations, and the relief of being able to put the clubs away and change his socks and no longer have to bear his own iniquities on the golf course.

Many of the guests wore big alpaca golf sweaters. Some wore their golfing hats. The girls' cocktail dresses displayed golf motifs—designs of red tees and flagsticks. The orchestra played the big tunes of the thirties and forties. "Somebody Loves Me" was struck up and there were shouts of pleasure. "Where is Farwell Smith?" A group looked around, their faces flushed. "Hey, where *is* Farwell Smith?" The band played. "Nothing could be finer than to be in Carolina..." The voices rose, the crowd joining in. Rippling applause came at the end. Shouts for Farwell Smith rose. Someone shouted that Farwell Smith had gone home. Cries of disbelief and woe. Beyond the bobbing heads, and the trays going by aloft, the drinks swaying in the glasses, one could see the brown wax mountains through the plate-glass windows.

I found myself packed in against a couple: a girl who wore a little mink stole across her shoulders, and her husband, Harry Something-or-other, who wore a golf cap and held two drinks to keep himself in store (the crush around the bars was thick), drinking from the glasses alternately to keep the "balance" right, as he put it. "It's a diplomat's trick," he said. "If you have two glasses you can always excuse yourself from a conversation by holding one up and saying you're carrying it to someone, and you can smile and walk on."

They were a friendly pair and they asked me if I would join them at their cottage at the Indian Wells course for a buffet dinner afterward, which would be followed by what they referred to as a "Silly Putting Tournament," or the "Sillies."

"We have it every evening," the girl yelled at me. "We have a course that would knock your eye out. Don't we, Harry?"

"It's not a bad course," he said. "For the Sillies, that is. It goes both indoors and out. It starts in the kitchen—a good opening hole, tough, with a couple of door sills to putt over, a par 5, to the base of that god-damn umbrella stand with those pussy willows standing in it. Then from there you putt to this grandfather clock down the hall, a par 4, no nonsense, a straight, easy birdie hole..."

"Harry, what are you goddamning our furniture for?" She smiled at him brightly.

"Who wouldn't?" he answered. "That pussy-willow container—all those damn stalks flown in from God knows where, Old Westbury. Listen," he said to me, "I'm a Wabash kid. I like the simple things. Give me a pussycat; I can take a cat. But those stalks, those goddamn stalks flown across the country and stuck in an umbrella stand made of fake Chinese porcelain..."

"What about the grandfather clock?" she shouted. "The Wabash Sundial. Right out of grandpa's den. On the face it's got a sun with a smile painted on it that rises out of the left and sets on the right."

"It's a great timepiece," he said. He took a swift drink out of one glass and then the other. "Just to let you in on something," he said, leaning in toward my ear so I could feel the pop and hiss of his breath. "We've laid the Silly Putting course through the goddamnedest hodge-podge of furniture—half of it Palm Beach modern that her family gave us and the other half Wabash, which comes from my folks. In-laws. Damn cottage is a highly polished junk yard."

"It's laid out," she interrupted, "from one piece of junk to the next...."

"Alternately! Alternately!" he shouted. "From her family's stuff, to mine. The course goes from the Wabash kitchen table to that fake Chinese umbrella stand to the grandfather clock (that grand ole timepiece), then on to this green Palm Beach frog that sits in the living room—useless goddamn thing. Weighs a ton. Big enough to sit on but you can't because it's got a big cavity in its back to stick things in—artificial flowers or big feather dusters. Lord! From there you've got an interesting hole, the fourth, par 5, through the bedrooms to that wastepaper basket..."

"*That* wastepaper basket," she cried. "It's an elephant's *foot*—the most atrocious piece of junk. It's an effort just to throw anything into it!"

"It's a little rough on the eyes," he admitted.

"Those toes!"

"Yes. Yes. But look what your family have done to the next hole. You've got to come back through the house, a very tough par 4, to the left back foot of a piece of sculpture we keep in the front hall, which is supposed to be a horse and looks more like a goddamn *house*." His voice rose. "Jesus, Lucy."

"It's a super piece of modern sculpture," she said.

He said, "Three men carried that thing into the house one day and they took that big matting cover off it and stared at it and in one breath they all said, *'Jesus.'* Her mother gave it to us for Christmas."

His wife had turned and was talking to a man who had joined us. Her husband glanced at her; he sampled from each of his glasses, and then once again he leaned in and shouted into my ear.

"The last three holes are outdoors. We slide the patio door open and you have to punch a little putt over the door sill out to a birdbath that used to stand in my uncle's front yard in guess where?" He looked across at his wife. She was still occupied.

"From there," he continued, "it's a little delicate par 3 across the garden walk to the right leg of this goddamn iron flamingo. But I'll tell you," he said, "it's the last hole of the course, the 9th, which is the great one. Because we go from the garden out to the real golf course. Right out to the fairway of the 16th hole and then to the green. It's dark out there, so if the moon isn't out you have to have a flashlight with you. So you can see the flag. It's a great finishing hole."

The wife had turned.

"Did he tell you about the course?" she asked. "Did he tell you about finishing out on the *real* course?"

"Yes," I said.

"You going to join us tonight?"

"Sure," I said. "I'd like that."

"Cool," she said. "It's not a bad course. But we have a *better* course—that is, it's cozier—where we live, out on the coast at San Diego."

"The course here is better," her husband said.

She ignored him and leaned forward. "In the summer months we live in a high-rise condominium just north of San Diego," she said. "A great view *down* on the Pacific. The Sillies course is indoors. It doesn't have the outdoor holes like this one does. But the reason I like the San Diego Sillies..."

"I know what you're going to say," he said. "That goddamn elevator."

"Right," she said. "Part of the third hole...it's *rich*...just super...because the Barclays..."

"The Barclays are a family downstairs," he explained. "They live on the third floor. We're on the eighth."

"You see," she said, "part of the 4th fairway is the elevator. You putt down the corridor, ring the elevator bell, and take the ball down to the third floor, and go from there into the Barclays' apartment. The rule is you have to putt into the elevator when it arrives at your floor no matter *how many people* are in the thing when the door opens. I mean you have to face the music. No fair cheating and waiting until you can get an empty elevator and...not have to be embarrassed. And, oh my!" She began to shout with laughter. She had these perfect teeth. "Oh, Harry." She leaned her forehead against his shoulder. "You ought to see the expressions of people in these elevators, all facing front, and then the doors slide open and there you are out in the corridor bending over a ball with a putter. And then you *hit it*. I think that surprises them the most. To have that ball roll in among them."

He began laughing. "You remember the woman who screamed when the ball came over the elevator door sill?" he said. "She was standing there and I hit this putt and the ball hit her foot. She didn't move. She just froze in panic and watched that ball come at her as if it were some sort of animal—a white mole, perhaps. What a scream she let out!"

We drifted away after that. I tried to find them a half-hour or so later. I liked them—their crazy house of disparate furniture styles, the way they jawed at each other, in humor, the cheery badinage that was a prop for their lives together apparently. The girl was awfully pretty. She was the youngest girl I had seen with a mink stole over her shoulders. I could not find them.

On the way back to the motel from the cocktail party I tried to remember the hole on the Indian Wells course where they had mentioned they finished out their Silly Putting course. I thought perhaps I would just arrive there and wander around the fairways until I heard them laughing or saw them through the big picture windows putting through their house.

Night had come by the time I left the cocktail party. I passed a Polynesian restaurant with flames pouring out of a decorative fountain pillar set in front, lazy looping flames like those from the great Olympiad saucer. Illuminated purple palms stood in groves. I drove slowly. Cars whipped by. The air was very clear and dry. I slowed down coming up to the entrance of the Indian Wells golf course, but then I drove by and kept going. I decided I had the tournament the next morning to think about.

CHAPTER 34

The Bob Hope Classic is a five-day event. The amateur teams play with the professionals for four of the five days. Three men make up the amateur team, and they are joined each day by a different professional. The four pros who were assigned to our group were Larry Mancour, from Lake Tahoe; Bill Martindale, a tall, gum-popping Texan; Bruce Crampton, an easy-going Australian; and Joe Taylor, an older pro who saw my cramped stiffish swing and kept telling me to forget about everything and really "belt" the ball. "Big tall guy like you," he kept insisting, "you should really poke it out there."

In the Desert Classic the partnerships move in succession to the four major courses in the area: Bermuda Dunes, Eldorado (where Eisenhower has his bungalow adjacent to one of the fairways), La Quinta, and Indian Wells.

On the first day of the tournament we went off at 10:15 at Indian Wells—our foursome of three amateurs and the professional, Bill Martindale. The foursomes walk up a red carpet, past a gold cord, where they are met by their official scorer, a young lady got up in a white outfit with a sun hat with ribbon. Each group had its flotilla of golf carts; one of ours, I noticed, had a simulated leopard-skin seat cover.

I was the last of our group to tee off. My first drive was topped; it bounced once and went into what is called the Phil-Bing lake. Absolutely no sound greeted the shot, just the clicking of clubs back of us somewhere as a caddy set a bag into the racks of a golf cart. I called for another ball. "Swing easy," I told myself. The ball hooked slightly and stopped short of a grove of palms.

"Accuracy is what counts out here," said the doctor. He and a businessman from Mexico City were the other amateur members of the foursome. Both were low-handicap players. We got into the carts and set off down the macadam paths.

The pressure did not seem as intense with three of us and the professional playing as a team. One of us, setting together a series of good shots, always seemed to be attacking the hole for a birdie.

My play continued to be erratic. The fairways were carefully defined and narrow, and after two or three good shots, I would press, and the ball would catch the out-of-bounds. I picked up on a number of holes.

The play was slow despite the carts and there was time to meander along the side of the fairway—to look in people's front gardens and into their houses through the big plate-glass windows. The rooms always seemed impeccably neat—never a newspaper or a book open on the table. Once I saw a maid working a vacuum cleaner across a marble floor. She pulled the plug while I looked and she carried the vacuum cleaner out to a golf cart in the driveway and I saw her drive off, presumably to another job.

I found myself grading the houses as we went down the fairways—whether I would like to own this one or that one. There weren't any that I was particularly keen on. I was reminded of summer evenings walking the wharfs of the big marinas, the bulk of the yachts in the darkness, and the sift of dark water below, and how one compared them, criticizing them, oblivious that perhaps the owner was lying in his bunk, the air close and smelling slightly of paint, with a little fan going somewhere, a faint whine, and he was staring at the bulkhead and trying to sleep, but hearing the squeak of duckboards outside and someone saying, "A tub. A tub. But look over here. Oh God, what a beauty! Zookers!"

I rarely saw anyone in the fairway-side houses. Once I saw a man, just a glimpse of him, moving from one room to another carrying a martini shaker, which he was pumping up and down as he walked. I couldn't hear the sound of the ice.

There were refreshment stands set about the course. When I hit the ball out of bounds and picked up, I would wander down to them and have a soft drink. Once, I was standing at the counter, and one of the Hamm bears came up. He unzipped the front of his costume and skinned himself out of the bear head. He ordered a hot dog. The bear head lay upside down on the back of his shoulders.

"That thing must get hot," I said.

"I suppose you thought the head lifted off," he said. "Like a diver's helmet."

"It's a very sensible arrangement," I said, looking at the costume. I told him that down on Broadway once, in New York City, in a pizza parlor, I had talked to a Planters Peanut man encased in a peanut outfit sitting on the next stool. "He wore a solid peanut outfit," I said. "I mean, you could rap your hands on it. It fitted over the body, so just the feet showed, and there were holes for the arms to stick through. It wasn't pliable like yours. To get it off was a big effort. So he had a little mesh screen in front where the mouth was and which he looked through when he was out on the street walking up and down on the job. To eat he'd lift this mesh up and you'd see this face come up from inside the costume, and *accept* the pizza in this damnedest way, like the Planters Peanut body was a container, like a goldfish bowl, with this poor guy floating around inside."

"These bear mouths aren't built for eating," the Hamm man said, gesturing back at the head collapsed on his shoulder. "Too small. You have to take the head off to eat." He bit into his hot dog.

"Yes, I see."

"You talked to this guy?" the Hamm man asked.

"Well, it was irresistible," I said. "The guy was in there—I could see him through the mesh."

I turned from the refreshment stand and looked over to see where the rest of my group was. They were still idly standing by their shots, waiting for the group ahead to clear off the green.

"I spoke to him through the mesh," I said. "I called to him in there. He told me he saw all sorts of things. While he was on the job, you know. Purses snatched, and pickpockets at work, and muggings, and such things going on. People just didn't think of him as a witness, they thought of him as part of the scenery, like a tree or a hydrant. He would yell at them, this muffled voice, shouting at them, you see — these muggers and purse-snatchers — and they would turn around and see this big *peanut,* and they'd go right back to what they were doing."

"He's probably had a lifetime at it," the Hamm man said defensively. "It's no wonder he's seen things like that."

"You haven't got anything to compare with it?" I asked. "I mean wandering around the golf course?"

"Hell, no," he said. "I've only done this for two days. I mean, I'm not in this line of work — wearing a bear costume — *regular.*"

He finished his hot dog. "This is just part time. I'll be going to law school next fall." He mopped his mouth. "Back to work," he said. He shrugged the bear head back over his head and zipped up the chest. "See you around," he said.

I looked at the Hamm bears afterward as they moved around the course, usually two of them to a golf cart, looking for some signs of recognition, but the big heads turned impassively, and I don't know if I ever saw him again.

I walked back up toward my partners. They were still waiting. "What was going on down there?" the doctor asked.

"I was talking to a Hamm's bear."

The doctor grunted. "You know what a good golfer does?" the doctor asked. "He'll study his next shot while he waits."

"Yes, you're right," I said. "The trouble is my next shot's in my pocket — I mean I picked up back there."

The doctor pursed his lips. "Jee*zus,* those guys are slow."

I looked up at the foursome in front. "I've always liked that story — I think it's Vardon's," I said—"about the foursome agonizing over the slow play of an old gentleman in front. He won't let them through. So they begin to pop balls around him in frustration. He sees them, and he sends a card back to them via his caddy. The message reads: Mr. So-and-so presents his compliments, and begs to say though he may be playing slowly he can play a devil of a lot more slowly if he likes."

The doctor was not particularly amused. "Slow players—punk players—they're a damn nuisance," he said. He was very serious about his golf.

CHAPTER 35

Of the vague record of holes played on my tour—described in a notebook as I finished each hole, usually scribbling as I waited on the next tee, in handwriting often sour and loopy with frustration—my most embarrassing string of holes on the tour seems to have occurred at Indian Wells. The difficulties began with an odd altercation with the Bob Hope team, which was playing immediately in front of us. With Hope was Phyllis Diller, the comedienne, outfitted in an outlandish Scottish golfing outfit with checked plus fours. She was a queen of the tournament, and her group had a large gallery following it. Here's how my notebook reads concerning part of that day's play:

Thirteenth hole. *Nightmare. Drive went off heel of club, bounded away, yards at a hop, and caromed into golf cart on the adjoining fairway containing Bob Hope and Phyllis Diller. Latter's laughter had been booming across golf course most of morning. I hurried over. She was laughing no longer. Shot was really quite close. Another foot or so up on the side of the cart and it might have cleared both comics off the seat. Their golf cart had stopped, my ball lying 10 feet or so from rear wheels. Both Hope and Diller wore slightly sullen frowns, as did the crowd with them, not unlike the looks received when demitasse cup is dropped on crowded patio floor. Apologized, smiled wanly, and shook head disconsolately. Everyone was waiting for me to shoot. Noticed that Diller was wearing tartan hat with outsized red pompon. Propped up beside her in the cart was a gag-sized brassie, about 6 feet tall, for use in funny photographs. My caddy hurried up. I leaned over to*

George sizes up his lie from the fringes of the parking lot. (*Russ Halford*)

inspect the ball. I said: "Yes, it looks like mine." Both Diller and Hope look-
ing back to watch me make my shot. Played quickly with three wood, too
quickly, and again hit shot off heel. Moaned. No reaction from crowd. Ball
bounced across the 14th fairway into parking lot. Disappeared from view.
Called out loudly after caddy who was hurrying after shot: "Lay it leave!"
Meant to say, "Leave it lay," or better, "Don't bother about it, I'm picking
up." But in confusion words came out, "Lay it leave." Heard Diller whisper,
"Lay it leave?" Hope said, "Who is that guy?" Hurried off.

Fourteenth hole. *Still shaken. Tee shot hopped off heel of club — went*
no more than 30 yards. Feel like throwing in towel. Sloughed gloomily
through grass toward ball. Good eight iron over tree back into fairway. Fine
brassie to green, but it's all too late. Team bogeyed hole. No one looks at me,
not even caddy. Approaches sidelong, like a crab, to hand me next club.

Fifteenth hole. *A short little par 3. Shanked three shots in a row!*

Utterly lost. Caddy offers condolences. "It'll come," *he says, referring to the return of my skills. His conviction is not particularly strong. That strange cry:* "Lay it leave" *haunts me. What must they have thought?*

Sixteenth hole. *Hit tree! Let out strange cry. Ball playable. Hit a fine recovery, then a good approach, but the team did not need my putt. About an 88-footer anyway.*

Seventeenth hole. *Sliced drive under tree. Hunched over ball like mushroom collector and punched out with three iron. Lobbed seven iron into clump of trees. Popped ball into trap next to green. Blasted out of trap and damned if my ball didn't hit the pro's ball lying on the green. Apologized and picked up. Doctor annoyed.*

Eighteenth hole. *Large rockslide on right. Drove into rocks. Fortuitously, ball ricocheted out. Not a bad lie. Good piece of work. Handed brassie. Gave up. Long walk to green. Spectator. Watched everyone hole out.*

CHAPTER 36

———

O ur foursome finished up the day about halfway down the pack.
We would have to make an enormous run the next three days. I
apologized to my teammates. I felt the usual doldrums of having had a
bad round. Someone had told me that there was a cocktail party for the
professionals at the Bermuda Dunes club. I thought I would drop in
there for a while. It would do me good. On the way over in the car, the
thought kept crossing my mind that I was having a rotten time — the
steady humiliation of playing awkward and poor golf...letting my
teammates down, the endless practice and reading to no avail. I felt
weak — not only physically but mentally. I understood what Judge
Learned Hand meant when he said he had given up golf because he felt
his difficulties with the game indicated not a physical inability but a
lack and weakness of character.

A. A. Milne once wrote that golf is popular simply because it is the
best game in the world at which to be bad. I read that passage after my
unfortunate San Francisco round, lying in that enormous suite with the
little throw rugs dotted here and there, and I remember snorting loudly,
and thinking, well, he has an expert to convince here.

I snorted again on the way over to the Bermuda Dunes, though it
was true that Milne did have some interesting points: first of all, he
pointed out that the bad golfer gets a chance to use almost all his clubs.
If he buys a new five iron or a sand-blaster, the chances are that he will

surely use these clubs the first time he gets out on his golf course. A great golfer—a prodigious smiter like Jack Nicklaus—will use a wood, a pitching wedge, and his putter, and these clubs will suffice to see him through seventy-five percent of the holes he plays during a round. The other clubs will stick neglected in his bag. Variety is rarely his pleasure.

Another point was that the bad golfer gets a chance to use his clubs far more *often*—very often a large number of them to get through just a single hole. Where Nicklaus will only swing in earnest, not counting the thirty-odd putts of a round, about thirty-four or five times, if not less, a really bad golfer can get in over a hundred strokes, and a few more possibly, which he won't count. And, of course, naturally, the bad golfer sees much more of the terrain than the expert. He has the greater opportunity, if he should be so inclined, to indulge in horticultural or even ornithological practice: his chances are far greater than the professional's of running into a chestnut-sided warbler, for example, which is shy and tends to flit around in the lower branches of heavy shrubbery—familiar duffer's territory. Because of my errant shots I could enjoy the pleasure of peering into people's homes along the fairways of Indian Wells. Perhaps, with my usual luck, at Eldorado, where Dwight Eisenhower had a house, I could pump a ball into his front yard, and peer into *his* front room. Perhaps I would catch him practicing his putting. The good golfer rarely has a chance at this sort of thing. He sticks to the open country of the fairways and greens—not unlike someone sailing down the middle of a river who never drifts over to the banks and strikes inland.

Perhaps the most important joy that the amateur has over the professional, Milne points out, is that he knows the greater pleasure of hitting a good shot because his feat is so markedly emphasized by the miserable succession of flubs preceding it.

That was when Milne's theory fell through—it occurred to me—at least in tournament play. One bad shot destroyed an individual's chance to help the team on a hole. If he hit a good shot, it came after a succession of poor shots that had put him out of contention, and it was hard to savor the pleasure of it. A good shot was usually followed by a side glance from a partner which suggested that it could have been made at a more expeditious time. I remembered hitting a tremendous brassie shot on the sixth hole at Indian Wells. The shot soared up toward the green, bounced, skidded, and kicked to a stop eight or nine feet from the distant pin.

The doctor called over. "Holy God, George, great shot!"

I was very pleased myself. "Wow!" I said.

"Damn, what do you lie?" the doctor asked.

The pleasure was extinguished.

"Hell, doctor, I had trouble back on the tee. I lie *five* up there."

"Oh yes."

I arrived at Bermuda Dunes early. The cocktail party was being set up. I went out on the lawns. The evening came, the only one that lived up to the promise the residents had put forward about their great desert sunsets. A gentle luminosity hung over the lawns and the distant mountains and muted the garishness so that one had the sense of looking out through delicately tinted glasses . . . iris and blue. I wandered out on the clubhouse grounds. A single golfer was on the practice range. A girl was standing with him. I moseyed down. The golfer was Rocky Thompson, a young Texas pro, who was hitting long practice woods from the tee that had a sweeping view of the course. Far below, on a massive lawn that stretched to a line of poplar trees, his caddy moved and stooped, as solitary a figure as a marsh bird. The girl was very pretty—a good golfer in her own right, it turned out, the daughter of a San Diego teaching pro. Thompson was showing her something about the hands coming through the shot—a subtlety I could not catch. "Watch," he said. He hit his drive, the little tee spinning out in front, and the three of us stared after his shot which soared out and hung briefly above the line of mountains in the distance and then dropped almost vertically. The caddy moved slightly and stooped. I said, "Wow!" The girl asked something about the distribution of the weight. Thompson said, "Yes," and he explained. As he was doing so, far below and fanning out across the golf course moved groups of people wearing Mexican hats and carrying long burlap sacks. They weaved back and forth in quick scurrying movements picking up the detritus of the day's big crowds. Thompson hit a few more shots and then he waved for his caddy. We walked up to the country-club terrace and had a drink.

We sat surveying the sunset. "Great life," Thompson said. He stretched and yawned. Behind us someone was hammering at the supports of a big garden tent. There would be a dance later in the evening. Lights were being strung under the canopy. A workman picked out a few chords on a distant piano.

"Well, I guess so," I said. "I was thinking about it on the way over."

"You had a rough round today?"

"Not so hot."

"Well, let's say if you're playing decent golf it's a good life. People are awful good to you. Moving around the country, doing what you do best. Like Nicklaus says: 'My desk is where I'm at.' All of that is pretty good."

The girl grinned at him.

"No regrets," he said.

"I guess not," I said. "If you do it right."

"You been playing the game long?" Thompson asked.

"Since I was ten or so," I said. "But very infrequently. I never really put my mind to it until a couple of months ago."

We sat with our drinks in our hands and watching the colors darken across the desert. The distances were immense. We were high over the countryside. Suddenly I remembered the first association I had ever had with golf—the image distinct in my mind of a man trying to hit low-flying airplanes with a golf shot. I had overheard my father talking about him. This fellow's property was a tremendous estate adjoining Roosevelt Field on Long Island, and he would take several balls down to the airport fence, positioning himself where the planes were coming in on their landing approaches, and then at the appropriate instant, he would loft up shots toward the bulk of the plane coming in, the minuscule Spalding Dot, whatever it was, moving up toward the plane in a long rising arc and then falling away. I don't think he did this very often — just a whim — but the picture was a vivid one... the two bodies moving on a converging course, one gigantic, silver I always imagined it, a silver biplane against a rich blue background of sky, with its propeller idling and its motor sputtering softly, the wings tilting in the air currents as it glided across the line of trees out onto the open area of the airport, over the fence; and then the other, the golf ball, infinitesimal, rising from its puff of dust and soaring up. And I occasionally thought of the pilot turning in his cockpit and catching a glimpse of the ball as it hung at the apex of its trajectory, not a definite sighting because the pilot was busying himself with his landing, but just catching enough on the edge of his consciousness so that afterward, walking toward the hangar with his leather helmet swinging from his hand, he might start slightly and think, "My God, a golf ball — was that? Well..."

"Even if you play bad golf," Thompson was saying, "I mean, there's nothing wrong with this." He waved his hand at the sunset. "I mean, you could be hanging to a subway strap."

"Sure," I said. I stirred my drink with my finger. I wanted to ask Thompson if he could remember the first instant when he was aware of golf — the activity which would eventually consume his adolescence and adulthood, but a wind, quite quick and cold, came up the long slope. The garden canopy behind us fluttered along its fringes and the guy ropes creaked.

"You want to go in?" Thompson said to the girl.

She nodded.

We went into the clubhouse. The cocktail party was in full swing. On the orchestra stand was Maury Arnold's band with its big beat muskrat ramble music. A girl was playing the bass. The golfers sometimes sat in with the musicians — Lionel Hebert on trumpet, Ken Venturi on the drums, and if he was in the mood and had had a good round in the tournament, Don Cherry, who is a singer of note besides being a top-flight professional golfer, would get up and deliver a song or two.

We sat at a long table with a group of golfers. They looked sleepily at Thompson's girl. They were talking about traveling on the tour. "The big thing to know about the motel you got a room in," one of them was saying, "is how far it is from the movie house."

The talk drifted on easily about distant towns, and what the entertainment was in them, and the eating places, and what the architecture was like in the hotels. One of the players said he had stayed in a hotel in Miami for the Doral in which the motif everywhere was balls. "Everything's balls," he explained. "Big symbol in that place. They got balls for the water faucets, balls for doorknobs, balls for chandeliers, balls on the four corners of the bed, the light cords have these little gold balls to grip, and in the lobby they have these big...well, obelisks with the big balls up there, man, on top, big goddamn *balls.* There's nothing you put your hand on in that goddamn hotel that isn't round—crazy round water glasses, lamps like basketballs, lights glowing in them, and then they've got round portholes down in the grill that look out on a swimming pool that is probably round, though I never got a look at the thing. I'm telling you, man." He shook his head.

Dave Marr cleared his throat and said that he was staying in a hotel somewhere in the Midwest once and he took a great fancy to the lobby furniture which he described as "modern Revolutionary." "I was sitting there long enough to get rather a liking for the furniture I was looking at—these round tables like Revolutionary drums, you know. You put your drinks down on the drum head. And they had furniture to match, chairs with sort of a military look, and I thought it was all pretty good-looking stuff. So I bought it. I worked out the deal with the hotel manager. He seemed surprised. He crated it up and sent it home, and when it got there my wife took one look at it and set it out in the garage. When I got home from the tour, she said: 'There's some sort of a mistake out there in the garage.' I went out there to look and it *was* a mistake. It didn't look the same. Susan kept saying it looked as though it came out of a hotel lobby."

Finally, the talk would always swing around to their profession.

They began talking about golf holes with a kind of quiet intensity that made me think of retired colonels recalling old campaigns on distant battlefields...names of the golfing holes, and then a story or two to go with it, so that one could almost visualize the terrain—the Soup Bowl at Rye, the Sandy Parlor at Deal, the Redan at North Berwick, the great 630-yard par 5 at the Williamsburg, Caroline's Arm at East Bournemouth, the 16th at Alema with the big pond, the Spectacles 18th at Carnoustie with the two big potholes in front of the green...

As I sat there, listening, perhaps taking a drink too many to dispel my gloom of the afternoon, the golfers seemed to take on heroic, if slightly tragic, proportions. Thompson was right only in a sense: golf had its compensations, perhaps, such as the easy evenings of hitting golf balls into a practice field. But the exercise of the game itself in top competition was an ugly combination of tension and frustration, broken only occasionally by a pleasant surprise, but more often by disaster. The game required a certain cold toughness of mind, and absorption of will. Perhaps it was only all right when you were done with it and could sit around and reminisce, with the music in the background, like the military people at the post dance after a hard day in the field.

There was not an athlete I had talked to from other sports—the roughest of them: football, hockey, basketball—who did not hold the professional golfer in complete awe, with thanksgiving that golf was not *their* profession. The idea of standing over a putt with thousands of dollars in the balance was enough to make them flap their fingers as if singed. They would have none of it. Golf was the only major sport in which the tension remained throughout—where each shot was far enough apart in time for doubt to seep in and undermine one's confidence, so that there was no way of establishing an equanimity of mood. Other sports were not similar: the tension would mount, but as soon as the first whistle blew, or the contact began, that was the end of it. It was the familiar business of jumping into cold water—it was all right once you got in.

For the professional golfer there is finally only one pleasure, which is to come in on the top of the field and win the big prize. The possibility consumed them. It often crept into their conversation. That evening they talked about the win which symbolized their own struggles perhaps more than any other — Ken Venturi's victory in the 1964 Open — the year he won in the great heat, overcoming years of vicissitude and personal difficulties, which included a circulation problem in his hand. The history of that win, and his difficult career, was dramatic stuff to hear — right up to the moment when Venturi, barely able to put one foot in front of the other, dropped his putter on the 18th, the realization flooding in on him, and he cried out, "My God, I've won the Open!" Many of the pros standing around watching at the Congressional broke down — Raymond Floyd among them. People stared curiously at him, rather hoping someone would come along and lead him away. They thought perhaps the heat had fetched him.

There were other great comebacks, of course, but somehow they didn't mean as much to the pros. Ben Hogan's recovery from the serious accident for example. On the operating table he had called out, "Back on the left! Back on the left!" referring to some crowd bothering him in a match he was playing in his delirium. *His* comeback was expected somehow, he was such a champion . . . it was part of the natural progression of things. But Venturi's was a rise from a background much more like their own — toiling away in the pack, agonizing, never quite able to come out on top, and finally, in Venturi's case, being overwhelmed by the pressure and the disappointments, getting into fist fights, domestic problems mounting, physical quirks assailing him — all the miseries magnified so that in him the other golfers could see their own tribulations and foibles on alarming display.

On the banquet circuit that year Venturi would tell the story of his Open win — always in the same words — and when he got to the part where he dropped his putter, his chin would tremble and he would break down, and down the length of the long table the other golfers would look at their plates and there was never one who was embarrassed for him.

CHAPTER 37

N ot far from Palm Desert I found a par-3 18-hole golf course that stayed open under the arc lights. I saw it advertised on a billboard. I played on it twice, giving up the evening festivities to do so. I was so damn ashamed of my golf. It was a long drive from my motel. I never saw anyone else on the course. There was a man wearing a French beret and cowboy boots in charge. The slight wind off the desert was chilly. The grass had an eerie silver quality under the lights, still and unnatural, like an enormous metallic expanse of carpet. The golf balls shone as bright as moths. Over the golf shack an illuminated sign turned. The "g" of golf was missing — *olf olf olf* it announced in its slow turns.

I played alone — trudging the course hauling a golf wagon after me. I played four balls. To keep from being too bored, I imagined each ball as having its own player. I wrote their names down in the score card. Each was a columnist. Leonard Lyons and Suzy Knickerbocker were two of the players, along with Arthur Krock of the *New York Times,* and General S. L. A. (Slam) Marshall, the military historian. Each had his (or her) own ball. For identification purposes in case I got confused I marked the brand names on the score card. I remember General Marshall started with a Titleist 8. Leonard Lyons had a practice ball with a red stripe.

Sometimes, if I was hitting the ball badly, I would give up the imaginary game and hit my shots morosely and tag after them across the course with my mind empty. But then a good shot or two, and I would pick up the game on the next tee. The competition was lively. Curiously, each player began to take on certain characteristics that remained constant. Suzy Knickerbocker (using a Royal 2) was a deadly putter. She had a tendency to shank, but was strong on recovery shots. Lyons was strong off the tees, though he had a propensity for landing in traps, and his putting was inaccurate and often hysterical. Arthur Krock was short but accurate. General Slam Marshall's game was disgraceful. He hit two shots in a row into a pond. He began to emerge in my imagination. His problem was a war wound acting up. His playing partner was Suzy Knickerbocker. "General," she would say, "you're bleeding slightly." "Yes," he would say, "but the pain isn't bad. I can shake it off."

The second night I played the course I got quite immersed with the fortunes of my imaginary foursome.

The Lyons-Krock team were pressing for a Nassau bet of five dollars — that is to say, five dollars bet on the outcome of the first nine, five dollars on the second, and five dollars on the winner of the match — press bets, of course, which meant that the team behind could accept a loss and renew the wager for the remaining holes. The Knickerbocker-Marshall team, not so sure of themselves by reason of General Marshall's severe hip injury (it was now vivid in my mind), felt that they would be better off at a *three*-dollar Nassau. Not only that, but they wanted a handicap of two strokes a side.

My lips moved briskly on the first tee as the terms were discussed. My voice rose somewhat sharply to identify Suzy Knickerbocker's complaints as she fought for the handicap of two strokes a side.

"I think you're unprincipled!" she shouted at Arthur Krock. "My partner's crippled!"

"Robbery!" he yelled. He emitted a fierce Bronx cheer.

I looked around. The course stretched silver and empty to the borders of the dark night. The man with the beret was out of sight, back in his fieldhouse. The moths, dazzled, circled the arc lights.

The controversy started up again. Leonard Lyons said: "I think General Marshall is fudging. Nothing wrong with his damn hip."

"Damn right," said his partner, Krock. "Absolute disgrace."

"What do you call all that *bleeding*?" Suzy Knickerbocker asked. My voice rose high and shrill. I looked around again. The *olf* sign turned eerily across the metallic lawns. "He's almost *dying*!" she said.

"A natural state with the military," Lyons said archly.

I hee-hawed at the Lyons pleasantry. The breeze was cool off the desert. The moths were huge around the arc lights. "Look at those moths," I said aloud. "Big as towels."

Who was speaking? I pulled myself together. The terms of the wager were finally settled. A four-dollar Nassau bet was established. The two-stroke handicap would stand for the first nine, and then there would be an adjustment depending on the nine-hole totals. No one was particularly pleased. I separated the four balls. The Marshall-Knickerbocker team won the coin toss and the honor. There was a short discussion between the two as to which one would lead off.

"All right, Susan," the General finally said wearily. "Let me take the honor and lead the way."

I drove his ball smartly into a water hazard.

The other three stepped up and I hit their balls more or less to character. Lyons had a shot that dropped six feet from the hole. The whole foursome was out of sorts, though, and there wasn't much mention of the feat.

Suddenly all around me, the ground seemed to shudder slightly, a sighing groan swept around like a wind, and I whirled, sand wedge in hand. "Wha'? Wha'?" From countless water points geysers of spray rose, and water began to spring up from the nozzles of sprinklers and work out across the grass and then sweep in great arcs covering the course. I ran for my cart, and pulling it after me I wheeled crazily through the maze of water and fountain, sprinting in front of long sweeps of spray as they came curving in their patterns. I reached the little clubhouse where the proprietor, the young man wearing a French beret, was leaning against the counter watching me come.

"That's a helluva trick," I said when I'd caught my breath. "A man could drown out there."

"Don't blame me," he said. "The whole system works automatically. The watering goes on even when it's raining. There's nothing I can do."

"There ought to be a warning device out there," I said. "A siren, perhaps. Or maybe you ought to fire off a cannon."

"It's late," he said. "You know what *time* it is? No one's *ever* been caught out there when the system went on." He was peeved. "You trying to win a bet?"

I paid him for the extra time. "There are four balls out there. They are yours to keep if they haven't floated away."

I drove back to Palm Springs. On the way I stopped in at the Polynesian restaurant. Dave Marr and some of the other golfers were off at a table in the corner. They waved and I went over. I sat down beside Marr. He asked where I'd been.

I told him that I had just finished playing golf — not more than twenty minutes before.

He was incredulous.

"No, honest," I said. "On a night course. I'm so horrified about my game."

Marr said, "Let me tell you something I learned from Paul Runyan when I first came out on the tour, back in my rabbit days. It's good advice, and, man, you can stand some." He grinned. "It is that on the tour you try to behave just the way you do back home. It doesn't do any good to get to bed at eight o'clock if that isn't your habit. Or sit in the motel and stare at the end of a light-bulb chain — unless one has a fancy for that. Or practice putts on the motel carpet all night long. You been doing that?"

I nodded. "I've done an awful lot of putting in hotels," I said, "except in San Francisco."

"It's no good," he said. "You got to live the same pattern. Go to a movie, if that's what you do normally, or a good dinner or dancing. There's no other way."

He looked at me. He shook his head.

"Who's out there on those courses at this time of night?" he asked.

"Well, no one," I said. "It's pretty nice. It's a little cold. You don't get held up, y'know. You've got the place to yourself."

"Do you play with anyone?"

"Well, no," I said. I couldn't bring myself to mention the four columnists.

"That's crazy," he said. "The best thing to improve your game is to play with professionals, the best professionals. That's the one other piece of advice I've never forgotten. Jackie Burke told me. He said never stick with the losers on the golf course. Stay away from the rabbits, if you can. No matter how nice they are as golfing companions, if they are perpetually rabbits, they've got a streak in them that's no good for you to be around too much. Always play with the winners."

"How do you go about that?" I asked.

"Well, when they're going out on a practice round, you ask them if you can play with them. They're not going to turn you down. Can you imagine Arnie turning someone down? Or any of the other great ones?"

"Yes," I said.

"Don't you believe it. Not if there's a place. There's much more camaraderie between professional golfers than you might think. They help each other. The two enemies in golf, in medal play at least, are yourself and the golf course. Another golfer, even though he may be beating you out of the prize money, you just don't think of him as an opponent—as you would in tennis, say, or poker. Now, naturally, if some young golfer doesn't come up and ask me for advice, well, I've got nothing to tell. I don't go out of my way to advise. But if he asks, I'm glad to."

I began laughing.

"What's wrong?" he asked.

"Well, with all this camaraderie and helping the other fellow, I was thinking...well, maybe you'd like to go out and play some midnight golf tomorrow. Maybe with Palmer and Casper. I could stand a few tips. Besides, it's sort of interesting out there. The water-sprinkling system goes on automatically."

"Man, you really think them up," Marr said. He was grinning. "If you want my advice, a good evening on the town and something with some *rum* in it is what you need for what ails you."

"All right," I said. "You've persuaded me."

CHAPTER 38

Just about the liveliest place to listen to golf talk, though of a slightly different nature, was along the rail fence where the touring caddies gathered out behind the clubhouse—just off the practice putting green—where they perched upon the fence between the big golf bags they tended, many of them in white coveralls with the identifying numbers and names of their professionals across the shoulder blades. Their rialto was here, and they rocked back and forth on the fence and compared notes and swapped yarns and gossip, and talked of their rounds, particularly about money and how their pro had let them down: "Oh my, we're doin' jes' fine and then my man he goes an' *dies* on me," etc., etc.

There are about forty professional caddies—touring caddies, they're called—some of whom, the fortunate ones, stay with one golfer throughout the winter tour (the PGA does not allow the touring caddy system during the summer months when the high schools are out—at that time a caddy must stick to a home course) while the others, less fortunate, travel uncommitted and hope to pick up a bag, or "pack a bag" as the phrase goes, when they turn up on the eve of a tournament and look to catch a pro's eye and sign up with him for that particular event.

The touring caddies are a wildly individual clan, not at all to be confused with the local caddies. They are a nomadic group (some of the more disapproving professionals refer to them as "The Traveling Brewery") that moves from tournament to tournament, usually four or five to a car, and they suddenly appear around the caddy shacks with the abruptness and aplomb of extremely competent men sent to do an expert job. The local caddies stare at them with as much awe as they work up for the professional golfers. Johnny Pott once told me: "I can't imagine what it's like to travel with the touring caddies. I remember once a car with six of them in it—going cross-country—came through my hometown, and they stopped by to pick up an open-faced driver I had promised one of them. Well, I opened up the trunk of their car to put in the driver and there wasn't anything in there at all—no suitcases, kits, anything. Real gypsies. They travel in just their shoes."

During the tour I got to know some of them by wandering down and leaning up against the fence and asking questions from time to time. It was very lively listening. Most of the touring caddies are Negroes, though there were exceptions, notably Arnold Palmer's caddy, Bob Blair, a loner I never saw with the others, and Jack Nicklaus' regular caddy, Angelo Argea, who was quite a different sort, being a soft-spoken Italian with a pleasant grin who was very popular with the others. In joshing him, they had a number of derogatory nicknames, which he took in good humor. The caddies, as a whole, owned a splendid variety of nicknames: Cut Shot, Violence, Texas Sam, the Wolfman, the Rabbit, the Baron, Cricket, the Rock, Big Ted, the Golfball . . . their names peppering their conversation, as in, "Hey, Cricket, you seen the Golfball?" "Hell no, ask the Wolfman."

Ted Randolph was the one called the Wolfman. He was given that nickname in the Boy Scouts where he had once made, he told me, a very impressionable imitation of a werewolf. The name stuck for a while and was about to fade away. "Then," he said, "I grew me a long beard and I damn near *looked* like a werewolf. So the name stuck for good."

Walter Montgomery was the one they called Violence. He had had his hair straightened. He kept it flattened slick against his skull, so that the sheen of black seemed newly painted on. He was named after his short temper—a characteristic he had worked in recent years at curbing.

"What did you use to do, Violence?" I asked, relishing the odd nickname and the strangeness of it on the tongue. "...Hey, Violence?" I asked, grinning at him.

"I've cooled it, baby. It don't make no sense. It don't do no help to the guys I was packing for."

"You mean you took it out on the golfers?" I asked.

"A cat'd make some crazy play like miss a putt of two foot. Now a cat like that, why he's cuttin' my money, making a bad shot, dig? So I go up and kick his bag. I really bang it."

"Well, how did they take that?"

"Like I say, it don't make no sense, 'cause it don't do no good. They start keepin' a side eye on me, like maybe I'm fixin' to lift a shoe into *them* the next time, druther than the bag. It don't do no good for their golf, and then I...well, they ain't fixin' hard to have me pack for them again."

"What else did you do?"

Violence frowned slightly. "Oh," he said, "I slam the pin back in the cup real hard, jes' to show the guy, y'know, what I think of his messin' up the shot. Threw my cap quite a lot. Once I sailed it across the green and it hit Doug Sanders in the back of the head. But then, like I say, I cool it. I pack for Julius Boros and he like me and he say, 'Man, act like me, very calm, all the time, and you do O.K.' So I do what he say. I'm goin' fine for a good long time now, and it pays good, it's an honest livin' an' I'm gettin' on fine. But the guys remember what I done—y'know, like in San Diego, when we go there for the Open, they say, 'Hey, Violence, baby, so you goin' out on the town? Well, you broke a guy's jaw in this town, you *re*call,' and they grin, and I say, 'Sure, man, but that was las' year.' They waiting for me to bust someone, they al'ays *lookin'*, but I ain't done nothin' like that for a time. 'Course I ain't sayin' when a guy messes a shot, the juices don' get worked up...."

I said that frankly I was glad he wasn't packing my bag, if he didn't mind my saying so.

He laughed and said, oh yes, he had heard about my golf.

Alfred Dyer, out of New Orleans, was called the Rabbit. He was very self-assured. "You talk to the Rabbit," he said, "an' you're getting the stuff straight from number one. If it's caddyin' you're talkin' 'bout, the Rabbit's your man. Why, at those big Jewish country clubs in the east, it's the Rabbit they's always calling for—'Where's the Rabbit? Where's the Rabbit?' They say, 'You think I'm takin' one step on this course lessen the Rabbit's packing my bag, you is loco in the *head*.' Why, I make forty dollars a day in the east jes' on my name alone. Autographs? Man, the Rabbit's always signing autographs..."

At this, there was a bit of good-natured hooting from the others down the fence. Someone shouted, "Rabbit, you can't write, man, an *X*, much lessen your name."

I asked, "Rabbit, what do you think you do best as a caddy?"

The Rabbit thought and he said, "Well, calm my man down, I think that's what I do very good. Pull him off to the side when he's got a lot of pressure on him and I tell him, let the Rabbit share it with you. Maybe I get him telling what he done the night before—jes' to get his mind off the pressure and make him relax. 'Course sometimes you got to do jes' the opposite—fire yo' man up. Now take Tom Weiskopf in the Colonial. We're comin' down the stretch with a jes' fine lead, but then Tom bogeys three holes in a row and he comes up on the thirteenth jes' 'bout ready to fall to pieces. He's chokin'. He's got this big ball in his throat. He says, 'Rabbit, we're going to have to play for second place. I'm playing it safe in here.' So the Rabbit says, 'Man, I'm dropping yo' bag right here if you don't go for the flag. You take a two iron and put the ball up there nice an' easy. Smooth,' I said. I can say 'smooth' like you never heard nobody say that word, like silk. Well, he done it."

Quite another sort of touring caddy was Dale Taylor, Billy Casper's caddy—a soft-spoken polite man in his forties, I would guess, and with very much of a no-nonsense attitude about his profession. He was an excellent golfer, I was told. He told me that he caddied for his man with pleasure because Casper always tended to the business at hand—their rounds together on a golf course had no other purpose.

"That's the point," Dale said. "If you're in the business and you want to make a dollar, you got to play with a man who's got a right attitude. Billy Casper's got a wife and two kids. He goes out on a golf course and he's got their support in mind. He isn't thinking about anything else but his business. That's the attitude I got to have too. We think alike. I'm good for him to have around. He keeps me on the payroll and I baby-sit for his children, things like that."

I asked: "But don't all golfers go out on the course with that same attitude — that they're going to win?"

"They should," Dale said. "But then you get a golfer like Ken Still who has this really great talent, this fantastic potential..." He looked around at the other caddies. "That's right, isn't it?" They all nodded. "And yet when he goes out on a golf course his mind just isn't on what's what. He's interested in sports, Ken Still is, and if there's a ball game going on somewhere, he's thinking about it. He's like to have a transistor plugged in his ear, and sometimes he yells things like, 'Come on, Duke, belt one for ol' Ken.' You ever see Ken walk down a fairway?" The caddies all rocked back and forth, grinning. "Why, he's got that radio goin' in his ear, maybe one in *each* if they got two ball games on, and his feet come down *plop plop* like he's dizzy, and you got to see him wobble from one side of the fairway to the other, his arms waving, and his lips wobbling, too, and then he wanders off, and then his caddy, he's got to say, 'Man, we're over *heah*', just to get his man back on the track."

"You jivin'," someone said. They were all laughing.

Doug Sanders' caddy, who was called Cricket, spoke up and said that he wished he had transistors to worry about with *his* man, because it was girls, which was worse.

"He looks for 'em in the gallery, and man, he spots one, we gotta lose three strokes."

"It don't take much to make 'em a duck," someone said.

"A what?" I asked.

"A duck."

"Duck" turned out to be a word they used a lot for the young professionals rather than the word "rabbit" which the golfers used. A caddy would say: "I got me a duck who *faints* on me at Napa—lies down on the course and goes to sleep with two holes to go and we got the cut made cold."

Some of the terms they used were rather arcane. One caddy referred to a golfer as a "Union Oil."

"What's that?" I asked. "A Union Oil?"

"He's like those speculative oil stocks," I was told. "He goes up and down jes' like they do—man, he's a sixty-nine one day, and the next, he shoot up to a eighty-nine. So we call him a Union Oil. Or a 'drugstore pro.' Sometime we call him that."

From the earliest days of golf, caddies have been the originators of golfing terms, and also masters of the quip, the laconic remark that seems so often the legacy of menial jobs. I particularly like the caddy's retort to the novice golfer who slices an enormous divot out of the ground, and asks, "What do I do with this?"

"Take it home," the caddy says, "an' practice on it."

Or the golfer who hits his drive toward the end of an imperfect day and peers off into the gloom.

Golfer: "Did that go straight, boy?"
Caddy: "Couldn't see it, but it sounded crooked."
Or this one:
Beginner (after repeated failures): "Funny game, golf."
Caddy: "'Taint meant to be."

Traditionally, caddies have been great showboat characters. In recent times when Johnny Pott sank a chip shot to win the Crosby in 1968, his caddy, Scott, flung his arms up and fell down in a heap. The television cameras caught him in his prostration of pleasure, and he told me that his mother had seen him on national television, and most of the neighborhood, and he had become a celebrity with people coming around and knocking on his mother's window, and smiling in, some of them complete strangers, to indicate they'd seen him and now appreciated his status.

When I spoke to him, and he was reminiscing, he said that he thought he might *patent* his collapse and do it every time he came on the 18th with a tournament winner, or even with someone back in the pack if that golfer recorded a great shot on television. "Just throw up my arms," Scott said, "and fall in a heap on the green."

"Scott, do you ever throw up your arms and fall in a heap on an *early* hole—if your man makes a great shot on the third hole, say?"

I sensed his answer and was right: "Oh, I give a good yell," he said. "But for falling down, I save that for the finishing holes and the television. I mean it takes something out of you to fall down like that. It's a question of timing. Of course, the trouble is," he said, "you got to find someone to pack a bag for who's goin' to do *his* side of the act. I mean, make that shot, baby. I been all set to fall down for some months now but I ain't had no *kind* of cat to give me the opportunity. It seem like I'm fighting to make the cut every time. I dunno," he said mournfully. "Maybe the next time we make the cut I'm goin' to fall down in a heap jes' to keep my hand in..."

I asked them about perhaps the most famous contemporary caddy—the one the golfing public would know about from watching TV—Arnold Palmer's Iron Man, the tall, gaunt dean of the caddies at the Masters in Augusta, the caddy everyone remembered for his long, slow, loping walk up the last fairways in the white coveralls, the old, thin face under the cap, and how he sat on the bag at the edge of the green with his knees drawn up under his chin, or stood out behind Palmer where he leaned over and spoke his notions into Palmer's ear as the two of them inspected the lie of the putt on those last huge greens.

A chorus of disapprobation rose, particularly from Scott.

"Iron Man? What he know 'bout packing a bag. He know nothin', man."

"That's right. You get the Iron Man offen the Masters course, an' he *lost*—why he stumble 'round like he gonna be *bit* by something."

Another caddy chimed in: "He been confused since he was two year ol'—shit, man, how you talk about Iron Man?"

"Well," I said, "what about all that advice he gives Palmer. On the green. You see him there, leaning over, advising...at least he's whispering things for Palmer to hear."

"He's jes' movin' his lips. He don' know what he sayin'."

"Why, he ain't *got* nothin' to say. He don' know golf enough to say beans."

One of them leaned forward. "I'll tell you what he's sayin', man. He's leanin' into Palmer's ear an' he's saying: 'Jes in case you wanna know, Mis' Palmer, it's gettin' on 'bout fo' fifteen in the afternoon."

The caddies all grinned and hee-hawed.

The one caddy all of them spoke creditably of—a hero among them, apparently—was Hagan, semiretired now, they said, who worked out of the Riviera Country Club in Pacific Palisades, California. They spoke of him as being the first caddy who made a scientific art of the craft—checking the course early in the morning for pin positions and packing off the course and marking distances on a card so that if a golfer asked what the distance was, Hagan would say, looking at his card, "Well, from that tree it's exactly 135 yards to the center of the green." All of this, when Hagan began the practice, was unknown, and was now widely practiced, not only by the caddies, but by the golfers themselves. Nicklaus relied largely on a card he pulled from his hip pocket with the distances carefully tabulated.

"Tell me more about Hagan," I said.

"He really knew what he was doing," one of the caddies said. The others nodded. "Big pride in his work. There was this time he was working for Tommy Bolt. So Bolt says, 'What do you think?' and Hagan says, 'It's a six iron.' Bolt says, 'No, it's a five.' Hagan says, 'No, it's a six and when you hit it, just hit it firm and don't press.' Bolt says, 'You're crazy, Hagan,' and he takes a five iron and hits it twenty yards over the green. So Bolt takes the five iron and he breaks it over his knee. Well, Hagan, who's been holding the six iron, *he* breaks *it* over *his* knee, and he drops Bolt's bag right there and begins striding off down the fairway. He's done with him. But Bolt comes hurrying on down after him and he's all full of apologies. He says, 'Wait for me, Hagan, ol' Tom's right sorry. You was right. Listen, I'm on the tournament committee and I'm fining myself $150 for what I done."

"Do caddies ever get fired?" I asked.

The caddy called the Baron spoke up and said that Bob Goalby had fired him three times on one hole.

"He says to me, 'How far is the flag?' I tell him, and he says, 'You're fired.' Well, I stand around and he comes up with a bad shot and he sees I was right and he looks around and he hires me again. But he's all riled up inside, and when he misses his next shot he bangs his club around and his eye lights on me and he fires me again. So I drop his bag. I stand around. I don't know who else he can hang the bag on. A couple of grandmothers. He don't have this big gallery. His wife maybe. She was there. Or maybe he'll pack the bag himself. He must be thinking the same thing, 'cause after a while he says, 'Hey, Baron, pick it up,' which means he's hired me again. We get up to the green and we confer on a putt and he misses it real bad—he don't *begin* to do what I tell him. So he wheels around and he fires me again in this big loud voice. That's enough for me. I drop the bag and I head for the caddy shop. His wife comes running after me. She don't want to pack the bag. She says, 'Come back, Baron, please, Bob don't mean none of that, he *needs* you.' She's a great girl. I know he don't mean no harm. Golf does things to people. So I tell her that and I go back and I pick up his bag."

"Does one ever really drop a bag on a pro?"

"Who was it—Tony?—who dropped Finsterwald's bag on the 13th at Denver in the Open in '60."

They nodded.

"Yah, Arnold Palmer won that one with a little short white caddy. You recall?"

I never could get a word out of Arnold Palmer's present caddy— Bob Blair. He reminded me of a rancher—quiet, strong-faced. I asked him a few times if he would talk about his job but he always declined, very politely. He kept to himself. The other caddies knew very little about him. Palmer had had some strange ones, one of the caddies told me. For a while he had a caddy who was a Marine Corps colonel on the lam—his wife was trying to sue him. The colonel thought he could lose himself in the nomadic life of the touring caddies—which he imagined, I suppose, as the American equivalent of the Foreign Legion. It worked for a while, until suddenly he was Palmer's caddy, appearing on television, and it rather went to his head. "He tried to pass himself off as a big shot," the caddy said. "Man, he had a terrific wardrobe. Then he begins signing Palmer's name to checks. I don't know what happened to him. He was a big good-looking guy. He turned up at the country-club dances in a tuxedo—man, he was more at home in a tuxedo than Arnie, the guy he was caddying for."

"Maybe his wife caught up with him," I said.

"Well, it was sure a funny place to hide," the caddy said. "With the touring caddies. I mean, every Sunday, if his wife catches a look at her TV set, there her husband would be most likely—standing in the background there."

"Maybe she never made the connection," I said. "Maybe she saw him and said, 'Well, that reminds me of somebody, that guy...' like that theory if you're going to hide something, set it right out in the middle of the room where it's so obvious everyone walks around it and ignores it."

"Well, I don' know about that theory," the caddy said. "More is likely she took one look at the TV set and said, 'So there you is, you mother,' and she jumped in the family car and took off after him. Hell, man, if my wife run off and I look in the TV set and there she is caddying for Jack Nicklaus, I ain't going to be saying to myself, 'Now let's see, who that remind me of?' Hell, *no*."

"Well, you sound very convincing," I said.

When I asked the caddies along the fence if there were any players they were not particularly anxious to caddy for, there was a quick reaction.

"Oh my!"

A chorus of dismay went up.

"Frank Beard!"

"Man, Bert Yancy's got to head that list."

"Baby, I'll tell you, Bobby Nichols sure on that list, and there don't have to be no squeezing to get him on!"

"Cupit!"

"Tommy Aaron!"

"Shut yo' mouth. Richard Crawford, he's the cake. That man, why he's as tight as beeswax!"

"I'm telling you Frank Beard! Nobody's alive like him—why I'm telling you he pinches a penny and right between his fingers that thing turn into a BB pellet!"

"You know what Deane Beman give? Why, man, he give ten dollar a day and *three* percent of his winnings. And when he han' that ovah, he look at you like you done stab him in the knee!"

"How about the caddy's friend?" I asked.

The mood grew respectful.

"Dan Sikes, he's sure one, I'll tell you."

"Nicklaus. You know what he did for this caddy, this guy called Pappy?"

"What was that?" I asked.

"Pappy took his winnings at this Las Vegas tournament and he got hot on the crap tables and he had a pile—$22,000—sitting in front of him. He thought his luck was never going to stop. He was going to take that entire town and stuff it in his back pocket. Well, someone run and get Nicklaus and he come on the double and there's Pappy, the big crowd around him, with this big gleam in his eye and rolling the dice like crazy. Nicklaus says, 'O.K., hand it over, Pappy, 'fore it's gone.' He leaves Pappy $2,000 and he takes that twenty grand and invests it for him in Arnold Palmer's equipment company. I tell you that fellow Pappy's sitting pretty these days."

"Dean Martin's a great caddy's friend," one of the others said. "There were these two guys last Fourth of July up to Bel Air Country Club, and they find Dean and they say, 'Dean, we got a good drunk goin' and we ain't got enough to *finish* it.' He looks 'em over and they were telling the truth, you could tell that right smart, and so he reckons twenty dollars ought to be enough to finish what they begun, maybe much less, maybe *two* dollars by the looks of them, but he takes out the twenty and he forks it over."

"I tell you my man Doug Sanders is a caddy's friend," Cricket said. There was general agreement.

"I tell you," someone said, "the caddies' best friends are the golfers who finish in the top fifteen. You don't pack a bag for one of those cats and you like to have troubles."

"You're talking," said Cricket. He reported he had made $2,700 in a month of Florida tournaments packing Sanders' bag.

They told me that if they finish out of the money caddies get paid $100 to $150. Usually, they can rely on ten percent of their professional's winnings.

The caddy called Doc stirred and said that when it came to money they were all spoiled. He had been on the tour for twenty-two years. When he started to caddy he was lucky to get two dollars for packing a professional's bag for 18 holes. Out of the first prize for tournaments in those days—maybe $3,000—why, a caddy'd be pretty lucky to clear $150. Doc's real name was Foster Eubanks. He was called Doc because he carried all his gear—his rainhat and so forth—in a doctor's satchel. He was one of the caddies with a car. Five other caddies drove with him—spelling each other at the wheel. He shook his head thinking of their conduct. "They don't know what a dollar is. The gambling! Those boys from Dallas, I tell you, they'll bet you a hoss fell out of a tree."

Most of the caddies certainly had first-class ideas about high living. Jack Nicklaus told me that Willie Peterson, who caddied him through his first Masters win in 1963, had suddenly, on one occasion, turned up in Columbus, Ohio, the golfer's hometown, to see him to borrow money—traveling first class on the plane and arriving at Nicklaus' door in a taxi with the meter ticking over and the driver waiting—very nattily dressed, according to Nicklaus, in an outfit which included a silk shirt in the twenty-dollar price range, with a straw boater set at a debonair tilt over one eyebrow. "Mister Jack, I'm here for a loan," he said, just as easily as he might have said "good morning."

Nicklaus paid off the taxi, invited Peterson in, and sat him down to talk finance with him. "I told him I had some friends in Cleveland who could give him a hand, give him a good enough job to keep him going, and that I'd let them know. I suggested he cut down on his standard of living since he just wasn't in the financial bracket to keep it up. He nodded and he said certainly, but he'd better be hurrying on up to Cleveland to see those people I'd told him about. Well, he took a *taxi* to Cleveland — 149 miles."

Nicklaus laughed and shook his head. "A great character. He was sort of a cheerleader for me — jump up and down and try to get some reaction from the crowds if there had been a good shot. He loved to get his picture in the paper and he was very proud about caddying. He'd say, 'Mister Jack, I gotta have more than anyone's *ever* been paid.'"

The caddies themselves kept track of each other's fortunes. "You can tell if a caddy's doing O.K. on the tour by his shoes," one of them told me. "If he ain't wearing rubber-sole shoes to get a grip on the hills, and he's wearing his regular shoes with wax paper in them to keep the wet out of his socks and slidin' under those big bags — those big Haigs, hell, they'll weigh over a hundred pounds — and he's wearing a quarter in each ear to keep out the cold out there on the dew patrol — first golfers out in the mornin' — well, you got a caddy who hasn't got a deal, an' he'll be thinking real low. He'll be starvin' in *Florida,* man, packing for ducks who can't play the game, who won't stand up for you nohow."

A "deal" is what the traveling caddy craves — a steady arrangement with a golfer who finishes consistently in the high money.

I asked how they got started with their pros — those who packed for a pro regularly. One of them, called Leroy, who had talked about being fired, spoke up and said that he had been with Bob Goalby for nine years. He had gone through some tough times with him. And then, this one time, Goalby had this 60-foot putt to win his first tournament. Goalby said: "Leroy, what do you think?"

"I took a look," Leroy said. " 'Bob,' I said to him, 'I think it's goin' to double break, this way, then hump over that way, but you got to make sure it *gets* there.' "

Goalby followed his advice. The putt dropped, and he leaped for Leroy and gave him a big hug, near hauling him down to the green. "You got a job for life!" he shouted.

Some of them got involved just by chance. Angelo Argea, who has been with Nicklaus pretty steadily since 1963, was assigned to him at a Las Vegas tournament in which Nicklaus was not expected to play because of a bursitis attack. Argea was assigned "just in case." Nicklaus did play, and won the tournament.

The two had a ritual. Argea was always supposed to say, "Good luck," on the second hole. Sometimes, particularly if they started a round on the back nine, and the second hole was the 11th, Argea would forget, and Nicklaus would fret, and ask leading questions, until finally Argea would remember and say, "Oh God yes, good *luck*!"

One of the main topics that the traveling caddies talk about is the "Rule." They inveigh against it at any opportunity, and one can hear such odd legal phrases along caddies' row as, "I'm telling you, baby, it's restraint of trade . . . and besides it ain't fair practices."

The Rule is the condition enforced by the PGA that touring caddies cannot work the tour from June 1st to September 1st when school is out and the caddy forces are largely made up of kids caddying for their summer jobs. The PGA is sympathetic—excessively so, the professional caddies feel—to this group, administering, for example, a scholarship plan known as the Chick Evans Award, which benefits top caddies from each club; of particular dismay to the touring caddies is the PGA's insistence that when the tour arrives at a club in the summer season, its own club caddies should benefit.

Tommy Brown, a caddy they called the Kid, who had been on the tour for three years, said, "Yeh, it's a good life. You travel. You sit around in these nice country clubs. The company is good. You have just about everything. When the Rule hits, though—why these thirteen-year-old kids are depriving me of this good time, and my income. The summer months—well, it's hard to sit in one place, in the east there; you count the time when you can get back moving."

"Those kids snap up our bread," the Rabbit said. "Why in San Francisco this one time when they play the tournament there in June, this kid from the Stanford University packs for Billy Casper who makes the playoff and wins it. Kid's name was Stark. Casper says, 'Stark, what's your fee for packing?' And the kid says, 'Seven dollars a day. Five dollars for the playoff 'cause that's extra.' Billy gives him two thousand dollars."

A moan went up along the fence, and the clicking of tongues.

"What can you do to better your cause?" I asked.

"Well, let me say this," one of them said. "Them players, those cats who calls themselves the caddy's bes' friend, what they can do is say that if they can't have their own caddies for the summer months, why, they'll *strike*. Won't play. That's what those cats could do, dig?"

They all nodded their heads. "Man, you jivin'," one of them said.

"We're treated like dogs," one of the caddies said. "We got to park fifty miles over in the woods. The public don't understand this. We got a lot of trouble. We should have credentials just like the touring pros. We're worth it to them. In the seven years I been a touring caddy I can't think of a touring pro who's lost a penalty shot 'cause of some mistake."

It was true that many of the golfers were sympathetic to the caddies' woes. When I asked Doug Sanders about the Rule, he was very insistent.

"I wish they'd waive it," he said. "You have to be lucky to get a good caddy in the summer. I'd as soon put $100 in a kitty for the high-school kids for the chance to have a touring caddy packing for me. You don't want an intern operating on you; you want a doctor. A great caddy can help you maybe only one shot a week—but that adds up. Try that on the money list. It makes a big difference. An amateur caddy will lose you strokes. I don't mean that he's going to rake a trap with your ball in it, something against the rules that'll penalize you, but you can lose strokes worrying about him. Particularly if you're near winning a tournament. He's never been through an experience like that. It's like combat. You want someone you can really depend on."

Rod Funseth agreed. He said: "You get scared around a trap if your caddy doesn't know the rules. It's a two-stroke penalty if you hit your own bag. Most caddies don't know that. Two strokes if you hit an attended pin. Why I can remember T.B., who caddies for me a lot, having a pin stick on him with a long putt of mine rolling up toward him, and he wrenched at that flag, and he was so anxious he let out this yell, and finally he hauls the whole cup out, the entire metal thing, and just in time, too."

"The only thing one can say against the touring caddies," Sanders said, "is that they drink and carry on too much—a bit crazy. Like if a caddy has $500 a week, he'll spend $520. But then, that's *his* business. I tell you that for my business, which is golf, I want them around. Good caddies are confidence builders and great assets. In fact, if you've got a really good caddy you find yourself playing hard for him. My caddy, Cricket...you know him?"

"Yes," I said.

"...well, this one time I made this really great recovery shot. Cricket says: 'That's a great save, Doug!' I say to him, 'Cricket, I'm right glad to hear what you say 'cause that's the first nice word I've heard you say this round.' And he says: 'Doug, up to now you ain't deserved any comment.'"

Some of the golfers disapproved of the touring caddy arrangement. Tom Nieporte, for example, told me that he thought a team of a professional and his caddy, if they had been together for a long time, might be tempted, well, to "try something." To give an extreme example, a caddy, with or without the knowledge of his pro, might be tempted to edge a ball into a slightly better lie. Nieporte had never heard of this happening on the tour, but his point was that an arrangement should not be condoned that could so easily lead to such a temptation.

I asked the caddies about this, and they were scornful. Cricket said: "It never happen. Man'd be crazy to take a chance like that. You get caught, that's the end, baby. I never heard of such a thing, trying to help or hinder a golfer. You ain't goin' to find any long-toed boys on the tour." When I asked, he said what he meant by "long-toed boys" was in reference to the old-time barefoot caddy who could envelop a ball with his toes and move it to a better lie. "You see these cats at the private clubs. These boys work the eastern country clubs in the off-season, packin' those big-money amateur foursomes. You always give a good lie for those cats. It don't mean that much. If I step on a player's ball, man, I put it back. But you don' find nothing like that goin' on when the tour rolls aroun'. It ain't the same gig."

The main attribute of the caddy, almost all professionals seemed to agree, is to reinforce their pro's decisions, or even to dispute them, and make the golfer think hard before making his shot. Naturally, some golfers feel a caddy's importance is overrated.

Claude Harmon was scornful of a caddy's advice. He said his instruction to them was always very simple: Clean the clubs and the balls and show up on time and be in the right place and always be quiet. "My idea of a caddy is the one I won the Masters with. Never said one word. Hell, he won two other Masters that I know of—with Ben Hogan and Jackie Burke—and I think he won a fourth one. We compared notes and only Burke could remember him saying anything. That was on the 72nd hole, the last of the tournament, and Burke, who was looking over his putt, heard this calm voice just behind him say: 'Cruise it right in there, Mister Burke. Cruise it in.' And he did, too."

Harmon said he never could recall asking a caddy's advice. He said: "How can a boy know what you spend your life learning? Take a ball's lie. Just how the ball's sitting on the ground, whether it's hunkered down or sittin' up can mean a fifty-yard difference in a shot's length using the same club. How's the caddy going to know? Is he good enough to make the right allowances for the weather—that a ball isn't going to go so far in the cold...that it's going to die up there—he's going to know *that*? And how's he going to know about adrenaline—that great power you get under pressure, that strength, y'know, that allows one-hundred-pound women to lift Cadillacs off children? That's why you get such great pitching performances in the World Series from those speed pitchers—guys like Gibson of the Cards. Why he throws the ball faster than he ever *knew* he could. In golf the same thing…you come down those last fairways in contention and you find yourself hitting the ball thirty yards more than you know how. Well, how's a caddy going to judge *your* adrenaline quota? Think of Trevino in the '67 Open. He comes down the stretch just about ready to take the whole thing and he asks his caddy to club him and the guy suggests a five iron. Trevino's all hopped up, crazy strong, and he knows it, so he grabs himself an eight iron and hits the flag with it. Well, imagine where a five iron would have taken him. Right out of the whole caboodle, that's where."

I asked: "Are there golfers who don't have the courage of their convictions? Who really rely on caddies excessively?"

"Well, Sam Snead's too dependent on his caddy, and he's gullible—which is a combination that can add up to a couple of mental errors a round. I can remember once at Oakmont on a round we come up to the 13th hole and we both hit the middle of the green with six irons. Well, the next day we come to the same hole and Sam asks his caddy, 'Boy, what do you think here?' He hasn't got his mind on it, I guess. His caddy clubs him with a five iron and Sam flies the shot over the green. He stares after it, and then he says, 'Hell, boy, that ain't no five-iron shot!' Well, hell, it's Sam should have known about that shot, not the caddy. It's typical of him, though. I always reckon I can have a good time with Sam on match play. I work up a little conversation with my caddy, just pretending to be all-fired confused about a shot, and I take out the three iron, and then the two, and then finally I choke up and hit an easy two that just clears the river and coasts up the green. The fact is, the shot's a natural four iron. Well, Sam steps up and he says, 'Boy, what do you think?' and his caddy, who's been keeping his ears open, knows that I used the two iron, so he says, 'It's a good two, Mister Snead.' So

Sam laces out a two iron and it clears the river, and green, and maybe some trees beyond. And Sam, he stares after it, and he says, 'Hell, boy, that ain't no two-iron shot.' Well, the fact is, you got to learn to depend on yourself. Hagen had the great system for penalizing opponents who eavesdropped on him. He had a jacked-up set of irons — the four iron was marked five, and so forth, and you could get into big trouble relying on him."

Gay Brewer, the 1967 Masters champion, also felt a caddy's value was overrated. It was fine to have his reassurance on club selection, but a professional would be foolish to rely on anything but judgment based on knowledge of his own game. Brewer had a different caddy every week on the tour, never really trying to keep one on a regular basis, and indeed he had won tournaments with boys who had never been on that particular course before. He took the Masters in 1967 but he couldn't remember the name of the caddy with whom he won.

"But I'll tell you when the caddy *is* important," he told me. "In England. The caddy seems more devoted there, and God knows he *has* to be. The weather is such a factor — weird stuff — that the courses can change overnight. You'll have a hole which one day requires a drive and an easy wedge, and the next day it takes a drive and a *three wood* to reach the green. So yardage doesn't mean a thing — I mean, unless the conditions are absolutely perfect and static, which in that country is rare, hell, *unknown*. So you rely more on your caddy. They not only know the course but also how your ball is going to act in the air currents above, and how it's going to bounce and move on the turf. I think I was clubbed on nearly every hole in the tournaments I played there. Those caddies are incredible."

Certainly the English caddies were self-assured. Bobby Cruickshank told me that on his first practice round at Muirfield in 1929 he had a seventy-five-year-old caddy, Willie Black. Cruickshank hit a good drive on the first hole. "Willie," he said, "give me the two iron." "Look here, sir," Willie said. "*I'll* give you the club, *you* play the bloody shot." I've always liked the story about the caddy at St. Andrews who interrupted his "boss" (which was the current term) at the top of his backswing, and shouted, "Stop! We've changed our mind. We'll play the shot with an iron!" Frank Stranahan had a terrible problem with such caddies in one of the British Amateur championships at Muirfield. He fired a number of them, mostly because pride on both sides got the best of the situation. The caddies were furious and sulking because their advice was ignored, and Stranahan was upset and oversensitive because he could not, under the circumstances, keep his mind on his golf game. The climactic moment in their strained relationship came on a hole with the green hidden behind a high ridge. Stranahan sent his caddy up on the ridge to point out the direction of the green, indeed to place himself so that a shot soared over his head would be on the correct line. The caddy went up there with the golf bag, moving around on the ridge, sighting between Stranahan and the green, his head turning back and forth, and finally he waved Stranahan on. Stranahan hit directly over the caddy and then toiled up the hill to discover that the caddy had lined him up with a thick patch of bracken, waist-high, where it would be a miracle if he found the ball, much less knocked it out; the caddy looked at him and very carefully, like a dog laying down a bone, he dropped Stranahan's golf bag at his feet and set out for the golf house, saying over his shoulder, "Now, sir, if you think you know so much about it, let's see you get yourself out of *there*."

What a tradition caddies come from! I suppose the first of their number who achieved prominence was Scotland's William Gunn of the early nineteenth century. Caddy Willie, he was called—an odd and famous character referred to in the chronicles of the time as "peculiar but harmless." His habit was never to refer to those he caddied for by name, but rather by profession. Mr. Brand, for example, his landlord and an amateur gardener, he called "the man of the cabbage," as in "You'll be needin' a cleek, sure as not, man of the cabbage, to reach the green."

He wore his entire wardrobe on his back, one suit above the other— four or five of them at a time, including their vests. An old worn fur coat was outermost. He wore three bonnet-like hats, each sewed within the other.

He would leave his job for six weeks, hiking up to his Highland home, all those suits on his back, and the hats. One spring in the late 1820's he never came back. His one fear had been that he would end up in a pauper's grave—he had set all his money aside for a proper burial. Those for whom he had caddied comforted themselves that at least he had reached home and had his wish granted; they preferred not to think that he had succumbed on his long trek...a small tumble of clothes that could have been discarded from a passing coach.

There were others: "Big" Crawford, who caddied for "Wee" Ben Sayers and used to try to intimidate the opposition by rearing over them and making rumbling sounds in his throat. He once threw a horseshoe at Vardon. Pretense meant nothing to him. He referred to the Grand Duke Michael of Russia as Mister Michael.

Max Faulkner, himself one of the most colorful personalities in golf, had a series of memorable caddies—Turner, who had a long red beard, and then for years he had a caddy who traveled with him named Mad Mac, who wore three ties but no shirt, and a long shoe-top-length overcoat which he kept on during the hottest weather. From his neck dangled a pair of large binoculars from which the lenses were missing and through which he would peer at the line of a putt and announce, "Hit it slightly straight, sir."

Then, Eddie Lowery, age ten, who carried Francis Ouimet's bag when the young American beat Ray and Vardon for the U.S. Open at Brookline.

Or Vardon's caddy at Prestwick in 1893, who was so disgusted when Vardon disregarded his advice that he turned his back and held out the golf bag behind him for Vardon to choose from.

Or Skip Daniels of Sandwich, who was Walter Hagen's caddy when he twice won the British Open Championship. Gene Sarazen had him in the year 1932—a stooped man who wore an old cap, a celluloid collar and a black Oxford suit that had never been pressed. He was seventy years old when Sarazen won his 1932 Open with him at Prince's, a course next to Royal St. George's in Sandwich. He was almost blind and Sarazen didn't want to take him. He did more out of nostalgia than anything else, and when he won he had Daniels stand next to him while he accepted the trophy and he gave him a polo coat.

Or the caddy who is reputed to have said to Vardon when asked, "What on earth shall I take now?" "Well, sir, I'd recommend the 4:05 train."

My favorite caddy, though, is a Frenchman — Vardon tells the story about him — who packed the golf bag of an Englishman playing the course at Pau, just north of the Basque country. The Englishman made a particularly fine approach shot, and he turned to his caddy with a wide smile for some indication of approval. "Well, good heavens! What? What?"

The caddy's English was very limited. He struggled, and offered what he had often heard uttered but did not fully understand. He said, nodding happily in reply: "Beastly fluke!"

CHAPTER 39

Hey!"
I turned around.

It was the man from the Crosby who had told me about the three C's—control, concentration, and confidence. He was just down the practice range from me. He walked over.

"Hello, hello, hello," he said. "I've been thinking of you. What sort of a round did you have today?"

"The usual," I said. "It was our second round. Bruce Crampton was the pro. We're in the middle of the field somewhere."

"Have you got any tips for me?"

"Well, Crampton was pretty serious. He told me that he always looks up the year the golf course was built—it tells him little subtle things about the greens."

"I mean from your reading. You got anything I should know?"

I must have looked confused.

"You know, like Papini's *Life of Christ*—like Bobby Jones read that book to relax."

"I remember," I said. "Well, I don't know. I don't know if I can come up with something just on call."

"You haven't been keeping up on your reading?"

"I've been spending quite a lot of time on the night golf courses," I said. "How are your three C's? Let's see: control, confidence, and . . ."

"Yes...concentration," he interrupted. "Well, they seem a little dull after our conversation," he said. "To be frank. So you haven't got anything for me?"

"Well, let me see," I said. "Helen Hicks, who was a pretty fine golfer..."

"Yes, yes, I know about her."

"...well, she had the word 'o-o-o-o-o-m' stamped on the top of her woods so that when she addressed the ball, looking down, she'd be reminded to use the rhythm of that word with her swing. How's that?"

"Well," he said doubtfully.

"How about this one? There is a professional called Morrison, author of a book called *Better Golf Without Practice,* and his idea is that the golfer should lie in bed or sit in chairs and *visualize* the proper swing—a psychokinetic approach to the game. His biggest tip is to get his student to point the chin at a point immediately behind the ball. He used to get Joseph Grew, former ambassador to Japan, to call out loudly: 'Chin!' to remind himself of this. He also had him call out another, slightly odder phrase: 'Roll the feet.' How about that?"

"Yes," he said. "Roll the feet."

"I can tell you the history of the tee," I said. "I read about that the other day."

"Well."

"Well, the wooden tee was invented by a New Jersey dentist named Lowell. The old method, of course, was to hit the ball off sand, which was kept in a handy sandbox next to the tee, and fashioned, usually by one's caddy, into a cone-like structure with the golf ball perched on top. The wood tee was known as the Reddy Tee and it came into general use after a tour by Joe Kirkwood, the famous trick-shot artist, and Walter Hagen, the great glamour golf figure of the time. The dentist turned barely a nickel on his invention. Patent law suits cut into almost everything he made, and more important, even with such a simple device as an inch-long tee he was not able to protect its exclusivity."

"Oh yes," the golfer said.

"Over a hundred patents on tees were established — including one which was made of a composition of fertilizer, grass seed, and soil... on the theory that a split tee would go right to work and repair the ravages of nature caused by a divot. How about that?" I concluded.

"Well, that's interesting — that business about the tee," he said. "But I don't know if that's going to give my golf game much of a jolt."

"No," I said. "It's instructive, but not very practical."

"That's right," he said.

"You'll have to go back to those three C's," I said.

He started back for his pull-cart. "Keep your eye out for me, though," he said.

CHAPTER 40

The round the next day, the third of the tournament, produced an odd shot. Larry Mancour was our professional, and on one hole he drove a three wood on a line into a high palm just at the edge of the fairway. After we had trudged around the tree for a while it was apparent the ball had not dropped out. Mancour climbed the smooth bole of the palm some thirty feet up and discovered that his ball was impaled on a thorn. He took a swipe at it with an iron, leaning far out from the tree trunk to do so, and brought the ball down with the thorn and a network of fronds still attached. No one knew whether Mancour was allowed a free drop, or if he was required to scrape along with the original ball, its branches flopping, until he got to the green where he could presumably "lift" it and clean it. A marshal appeared and allowed him a free drop.

The rules were not always so lenient. In *The Golfer's Handbook* I discovered that one R. Andrew, playing for the Hillhouse Cup at Troon, found his ball impaled on a hairpin. He had to play the hole with the hairpin intact. It never came out during the play of that hole, and it was Andrew's estimate that the hairpin had cost him ten strokes.

As usual, the *Handbook,* under its heading "Freak Shots," had pertinent material to enjoy that evening, some of which made Mancour's shot seem pretty small potatoes. In 1953, for example, a Scottish golfer trying to sink an approach on the 5th hole at St. Andrews duck-hooked his shot which rolled up on the adjacent green, the 13th, and dropped into the hole. On that same round, obviously inspired, this same golfer sliced his second shot on the 18th so severely that it bounced off the roof of a lorry and sailed through the front door of the clubhouse and rattled around until it ended up in the bar.

Another example, one of the best from the *Handbook,* I think, reads as follows: "A member of the Wildernesse Club, Kent, drove a ball from the first tee through a window of the professional's shop, where it ended up in a cup of tea which the professional was about to pick up. The cup was undamaged, but the professional was slightly cut by broken glass from the window."

Much of the talk around the bar that evening—inspired by reports of Mancour's odd difficulty—was about freak shots. Bob Rosburg said that he had once hit a shot that went up a drainpipe into the men's locker room and rolled out on the carpet.

"I know a guy," said someone at the table, "who putted into his own hat. Guy called John Beck, an Englishman, a good golfer, and his hat blew off while he was making his putting stroke and damned if it didn't land out there where the ball went right into it."

But the golfers didn't seem at home with the subject—true duffer's shots were an indignity to their profession.

Johnny Pott leaned across and said to me: "I guess it's the 18-handi-cappers who are what you might call experts on such shots."

"I'll say," I said.

I began describing a shot I had seen my brother hit. We were in England on a vacation together, and on impulse had gone out to play a round at Sandhurst, one of the historic courses of England. Our caddy was an elderly, stooped man who expressed at the start his warm admiration for the United States and its golfers. He had caddied at one time for Bobby Jones, he told us. My brother and I are both tall and big, and he expected, I think, a powerful round from each of us. He handed my brother a driver, and then with a cheerful smile, standing off at right angles, just where a caddy should be while the golfer shoots, he recommended that my brother favor the right side of the fairway, not too much, just a wee mite.

My brother nodded and then hit the ball off the toe of his club, just ticking it with the rush of his club so that the ball went off nearly at right angles, on a line, rather softly because it had just been grazed, directly into the kneecap of the caddy. The caddy gave out the following sound:

"Awks!"

He sat down. My brother was very contrite, of course. He rushed up and did what he could. The caddy was unable to continue. He went back to the caddy house with this rather forlorn look, not of pain, but disappointment, as if my brother, as a representative of his country, had not lived up to... well, expectations.

"Yes," the golfers said.

"I wish I had had a tape measure there at Sandhurst," I said suddenly.

"What for?"

I told them about the statistics in *The Golfer's Handbook*—that one of the categories was the length of rebound shots hitting caddies. The record, I told them, was a 75-yard rebound off the forehead of a caddy on the Premier Mine Course, South Africa. The caddy's name was not recorded, but the ball was. It was a Colonel.

"The ball that my brother hit wasn't truly a rebound," I said. "It went a long way, but it was more a grazing shot. I guess it wouldn't have counted."

"No," said the golfers.

"In any case, I didn't check the name of the ball."

I was very enthusiastic that evening. I went on to describe another misplay. I told the golfers about a shot hit by Alex Karras, the Detroit tackle. They'd told me about it, his Lion teammates, maybe five, maybe ten times. He hit this shot on the first tee at Red Run Golf Club in Royal Oak, Michigan. He's a terrible golfer, Karras—almost all big football tackles and guards seem to be, I suppose because of the lack of suppleness in their upper limbs—and what happened was that he stepped up and smacked his drive off the end of his club, very much as my brother had, and it went right through the big plate-glass window of the clubhouse. The entire glass front disappeared—the glass simply dropped out of its supports with a roar, and Karras, with his club over his shoulder in the follow-through, and the rest of his foursome could look into the interior of the clubhouse front room. There wasn't anyone in there. Karras went up and looked in over the sill. Of course, the glass collapsing had made this terrific crash, and after a while down at the end of the room a waiter appeared in a doorway, balancing a tray with someone's lunch on it under covered plates, staring up the length of the room.

Alex couldn't see his ball on the carpet, but he yelled down to the waiter: "Hey, is this room out of bounds?"

The golfers laughed, or murmured, rather. They did not warm to the subject. One of them ordered a round of drinks. The talk drifted on to something else. I had a few more shots I could have described. I'd seen a Random House editor, Joe Fox, hit a drive off the heel of his club *between his legs* into a large shrub off the tee. I could have described that. Or a shot I had seen Peter Duchin, the orchestra leader, make from the flat roof of the Shinnecock Hills Golf Club at Southampton where he had skyed his approach. He climbed up a painter's ladder to get there, outlined against the sky with his putter, and he skillfully punched the ball from the roof over the drain gutter down onto the green where he got his putt down for an interesting double-bogey.

Then it occurred to me, sitting with half an ear to the golfers' conversation, that the ultimate in bad shots had been described somewhat tartly by Abe, my caddy. One day during the Crosby, I had asked him if he would describe what he considered the worst shot he had ever seen in the Crosby.

He thought I was speaking generally about bad shots, and after thinking a while, he said: "Well, the worst shot I seen, if you want it straight, are them that go nowhere. Them that sit on the tee."

I must have looked puzzled.

"The golfer swings and *misses*. That's the shot I'm talking about," Abe said.

"Oh, yes," I said. "You know what the *easiest* shot in golf is, Abe?" I had asked.

"What?"

"The fourth putt. Ring Lardner wrote that."

"Oh yes."

That night, just by chance, I looked into the book bag and found a story of Vardon's about the worst shot *he* ever saw. He had once seen a beginner at a place called Totteridge miss the ball completely and yet lose it. This fellow had lashed at the ball, his eyes apparently almost shut tight, with a lofted iron, and hitting far behind the ball he had lifted up a divot, a piece of turf, as large as a soup plate which had dropped on the ball. "Where is it? Where'd it go?" he asked, peering down the fairway, shading his eyes, and then someone said "ahem" and it was pointed out to him that the ball was directly under his divot.

CHAPTER 41

▬

As I stood on the 9th tee at La Quinta, the last hole of the last round (we had started on the back nine), I could see the big half-moon of spectators waiting up by the green. Many of them had come with lunches, and they sat there all day on steamer rugs with the open picnic baskets beside them.

Just as I had at Monterey in the Crosby, coming up to the 18th green there on the last day of the tournament, I hit a titanic slice, the last wood shot of the tour, the ball soaring toward the desert as if the crowd and that final green would not accept my approach but instead were waving me off like a plane from a socked-in airport. I wandered into the desert. It was quiet there, with a faint wind stirring the thin wire cage of tumbleweed, not quite enough to get it moving, so that it quaked slightly. Some blackened sand-blasted palms stood on a ridge. The dunes rose in abrupt slopes. I found my ball finally. From where I stood there was no sign of the golf course. The green lay beyond a sand dune, which I toiled up to get a line of direction and then half-slid down, the sand seeping into my golf shoes.

I dug myself in and flailed at the ball. It shanked and spun off toward the ridge with its forlorn palms. I stared after it. The mockery of it, I thought—to finish up almost a month on the pro tour standing in a wilderness beyond sight of civilization. A photographer took a picture of my difficulties in that forbidding terrain, and it has a surreal quality, as if a golfer had been dropped by parachute with a club and a ball into the depths of the Mohave Desert to play himself back to civilization.

I didn't bother to look for the ball. I put my hands in my pockets, the club under one arm, and when I breasted the dunes I could see the rest of the foursome up on the green putting out. I saw no reason to join them. I wandered around behind the crowd and headed for the clubhouse. If there was any celebrating being enjoyed on the 18th green, I didn't feel part of it. Ruefully, I remembered from *The Golfer's Handbook* an account of exaltation on the 18th when a competitor in an open tournament at Harrogate in 1926 was so excited holing a 60-foot putt that he flung his club into the air. It was very much like what had happened to Bobby Cruickshank. Everybody stood looking at him doing his jig of pleasure, the club sailing up above them, and when it came down it hit his partner on the head. This poor man heaved a little groan and sank to the green with a concussion.

I mentioned this to someone later, and I said that if anyone had thrown his club in triumph on the 18th at La Quinta, the way my luck was running, even though I was avoiding my team and heading for the clubhouse, skirting them by thirty or forty yards, still *I* would have been the one hit on the head. Absolutely.

CHAPTER 42

The temptation was to pack up and leave but I had very much wanted to talk to Arnold Palmer. Perhaps that would be the climax and the purpose of my activity on the tour—a compensation for my difficulties, especially my disastrous last round. I hoped to ask him just a few specific things—perhaps about the yips or what he thought of the traveling caddies, or about the great crowds he played in—but perhaps even more hopefully to get a sure impression of the titanic player who had been such a figure in the golf world. I knew something of him from afar, having played just in front of him in the San Francisco pro-am and having had the rotten experience below the tee, and then at the Crosby I had traveled in his Army on the final day of play when my pairing with Bob Bruno had not made the cut.

I found this latter experience—being in his Army—one of the most exhilarating experiences a sports enthusiast can have: I found myself transfixed by the excitement of it, scarcely believing that it would be possible to walk around a golf course and watch a golfer—if one was lucky enough to crane over the ranks and actually see him swing—hit a golf shot and wax enthusiastic over it. Of sporting spectacles a golf stroke is surely the one least adaptable to exhilaration. And yet Palmer made it an art of such excitement. The reasons were varied: Palmer's *attack* had much to do with it, as has been said so often, and I have always admired the golfing writer Charles Price's description of Palmer walking to a tee or green quite unlike any other golfer in that he *climbs* onto them, as if clambering into a prize ring.

I asked a sportswriter acquaintance if he had any suggestions as to interviewing Palmer, any hints as to what would make him, well, unwind, so that I could catch some essence of his charisma. The answer was not encouraging. Palmer had been asked everything, I was told. Questions seemed to bore him—the obvious ones to the point of annoyance. An interviewer, unless Palmer knew and appreciated him, had to be lucky to get much out of him beyond the usual platitudes.

Well, that put me out of luck, I said, because I didn't know him, and as for being appreciated, my only credential was that I had trundled around in his Army.

My informant, however, did have one suggestion: "What makes Palmer *unwind,* to use your word," he said, "is to be asked something that really catches his fancy—a question out of the ordinary, something unexpected which he hasn't been asked before."

"For example," he said, "I asked him once, just off-hand, about the rumors of odd deportment on the ladies' golf tour. You know, things like lesbianism. Well, that really sparked him; he stayed on that subject for nearly an hour."

"Oh," I said.

"That's how you can get him going, some out-of-the-ordinary question."

"Yes, I can see," I said.

He asked: "What had you in mind to quiz him about?"

"Well, I'm not going to ask him how he *feels,*" I said, "if that's what you're worried about. I wanted to ask him about the yips—unless you think that's a bad idea."

"That's tricky, of course. I mean it could be like asking a terminal case about his disease."

"Then I was going to ask him about crowds and nerves," I said, "and maybe what he thinks about when he hits a shot. You know, things like that."

"Oh, yes," he said doubtfully.

"Well," I said, casting my mind around, "perhaps I should pop him with a psychological question: is he ever struck by the *lunacy* of scraping a golf ball across the countryside and dropping it periodically into a hole. Is he playing out some internal frustration..."

"I wouldn't demean the game he plays—no," my informant said.

"Perhaps I could ask him about his dreams," I said, sticking to the psychological approach. "I mean, does a golfer have different dreams than, say, a dentist?"

"I'll tell you one thing," the writer said. "Palmer gets up at two a.m. every morning and without fail he goes to the icebox and drinks a Coca-Cola. Absolutely without fail. There was this one time when some of the guys he was rooming with on tour barricaded his room after he'd gone to sleep—they slid a bureau up against the door, and an armchair or two, and then they sat around and waited to see what would happen at two a.m. When the time came, they heard Palmer groan in there and stir around, and they heard the turn of the door handle behind the bureau and the creak of the door being tried. Then there was a crash and the scrape of the furniture they'd set up being moved back, the whole mass of it pushed aside as Palmer put his shoulder to the door—y'know, he's so damn strong, a bull—and he came through with hardly a glance at the golfers sitting around, on his way to the kitchen refrigerator. They said he looked half-asleep, a somnambulist, and the next morning he had forgotten it. He vaguely remembered the noise of the furniture scraping back across the floor. He said, 'What were you guys doing in there last night—throwing chairs around? Hell of a racket!'"

The writer concluded: "The fact is that the hardest thing is to get Palmer aside long enough to *ask* him something, much less to think up a worthwhile question."

He turned out to be right. I called Palmer once on the phone. Someone else answered and said he was not available. I heard the murmur of voices in the background, a loud, sudden laugh, and the clink of ice in glasses. The crowds were always there—even in his private quarters. As for his presence in public, a circle of people collected and moved along with him as soon as he appeared at the locker room door — the front runners of his Army, and they were with him at the end of his golfing day, accompanying him back to the locker room and standing around waiting once he had disappeared, as hopeful as dogs at a kitchen door, just in case he should turn up again.

One afternoon just after a round, I joined this group and leaned in among them to ask Palmer if he had a moment. He looked at me quickly. I explained I was a writer. He said he was awfully busy. I was surprised by his voice, which was very clear and loud, almost a honk, the sort many public figures seem to have, as if their interlocutors were a bit deaf. I was shoved at by some people trying to get pieces of paper at him to sign.

He looked at me again. "I'm going out to the practice range to hit a few balls," he said. "You can talk to me out there if you want."

"That would be fine," I said.

I trailed him across the clubhouse lawn toward the range. His caddy, Bob Blair, moved on ahead. The crowd moved with Palmer, the hands with the slips of paper out, and he would collect the paper and cup it against one palm, bending slightly, and sign it. He signed a napkin. "What can they want with them?" he asked.

The napkin began to disintegrate under the pen. Palmer turned his body to shield the paper from the crowd.

"I'm going to send this to my son," the man said.

We reached the practice range. He stepped across a retaining rope and motioned me after him. I stood in front of him with my notebook out. The crowd pressed up against the rope, very quiet now, and respectful — craning to see. His caddy tipped a bag of balls, spilling them out, and then walked out on the range.

I was unnerved by the crowd, which had about fifty people in it. The notion of asking some of the more particular questions — the one on dreams, or perhaps, as a last resort, the one about lesbianism on the women's tour — in front of that group was unsettling, particularly if the answers were to be delivered in Palmer's strong declamatory style. I stood shifting uneasily. I began writing busily in my pad, as if my function rather than to quiz him was to sketch a word portrait of him at practice. I looked at him only sporadically while he was concentrating on a shot, so that he wouldn't catch my eye and force me to ask something. I used up a number of pages, flipping them briskly. My notes read as follows:

He takes almost a minute between each practice shot—as if each is a separate challenge. He begins with the high-loft irons. He fishes a ball out of the pile in front of him, setting it up daintily with the toe of his iron on a raised lie.

When he hits, there is a rush of clothing in abrupt motion, a spray of dirt, and the ball soars. We all stare at its flight. The sun is setting behind us. Blair shades his eyes. Ball lands just beside him. He jumps. Could not have seen it. Pops ball into bag. Shades eyes. Palmer fussing around. Strips cellophane covering from new club. Hefts it. Has twenty clubs or so lying in front of him to try. Is his touch really so sensitive that he can tell one from another? Must ask. Clear throat to ask. Decide not quite right moment.

Man in crowd behind rope suddenly asks, "What do you think of the alums, Arnie?" meaning the aluminum shafts golfers are beginning to experiment with. Palmer's face lost in thought. Long pause. Palmer sets up ball. Then delivers opinion. Very clear voice. Says that aluminum shafts are an interesting development. Everybody reflects on his statement. He hits iron shot. Everyone stares at its flight fixedly. Soars out. Blair takes three, four hurried steps to left, and ball hits and bounces where he was.

"Yah, it's an interesting development," Palmer says. The same man ventures: "That an aluminum shaft you're using there?"

Everyone leans forward slightly.

"About half of these clubs are aluminum, the other half steel."

Everyone backs away, informed.

An airplane goes over, its motor very loud in the mist. Palmer looks up. Everyone looks up.

Time for another club. Strips cellophane wrapping. Hefts it. Motions Blair back.

All his practice balls are new and are marked Palmer 1. He strips glove off glove hand to get feel of club. His glove hand is dyed purple from the glove. Enormous wrists.

Another man asks: "That a four iron you got there, Arnie?" Perceptible leaning forward again.

A pause. For dramatic effect? Palmer says: "No, got a five here." Everyone sways back, satisfied.

I clear throat to ask about the yips. Decide not quite right moment.

Airplane going over. Big noise. We all look at it.

Palmer moves to wood shots. Blair is in the distance. He hardly seems associated with what Palmer is doing. Palmer compresses lips when he hits but there is no grunt. Only sound is rush of clothing, the click of the ball, and then the tee kicks up. The pile of tees in front mounts up. Big clutter. Cellophane wrappings. Clubs. Maybe thirty clubs. Piles of tees next to balls. Kicked up tees out in front. Tees all red.

Palmer muttering to himself.

Marty Fleckman just down the line, hitting out irons. Palmer stops his routine to watch him. Fleckman had a good day, sixty-nine, three under. Young man, beginning career. Small man. Dark tan. White Hogan golf hat.

Palmer says: "Well, what'd you do?"

"Three."

Palmer looks at him. "Three? Sixty-three?"

"No. Three under. A nine. A sixty-nine."

"Oh, sixty-nine."

Palmer had round of seventy-two that day. But no doubt who is who. Crowd grins and rocks back and forth, delighted with exchange.

Palmer goes over and looks in Fleckman's bag. Hefts some irons. Fleckman's woods have fur covers. Palmer impressed by weight of Fleckman's irons. "How you swing these things?" he asks.

Fleckman makes noncommittal murmur.
Palmer: "Well, you're young and strong... and healthy."
Fleckman: "... but not wealthy."
Palmer: "Haw! Haw! Haw!"
Crowd delighted. Everyone stares at Palmer to see if he has
answer for Fleckman's quip.
Palmer: "Haw! Haw! Haw!"

My notes from the practice range ended at this point. Palmer was done with his practice. He motioned Blair in and, turning, he hitched at his trousers in a quick, characteristic gesture, and stepped over the retaining rope. The crowd closed in around him immediately. I tried to keep close to him. I said I hoped he could spare me a moment or two in the locker room. I explained lamely that I hadn't really wanted to disrupt his practice with questions.

"Well, all right," he said. "I've had a lot today, though."

He kept signing papers as we walked for the clubhouse, the people calling to him, "Hey, Arnie," "Arnie," "Arnie." There was a big jam at the locker-room door, and he had difficulty getting through.

It was quiet in the locker room. "Boy, those crowds are something!" I said. "I don't suppose you ever get used to them."

He sat down on the bench and scaled off his golfing glove. The quietness was almost palpable and his voice was very loud in it. "There's one woman here in Palm Springs who embarrasses me half to death — she's always yelling these little endearments, 'darling,' 'lover-boy,' 'sweetie.' I come down the fairway thinking about my next shot and I suddenly hear her bellow out of the gallery, 'Go, lover!' It's not the best thing for your concentration."

"Are there people who follow you from tournament to tournament?"

"Yeah, yeah," he said, the honking voice somewhat mournful, I thought, and I said to myself, O my, this is familiar country and dull...

"There is a doctor from Pungsatin, Pennsylvania," he was saying. "He turns up at every tournament. He's retired, I think, getting on towards eighty years old by now, and he's always there — Japan,

Argentina—and I'll be walking through the hotel in one of those places—Buenos Aires, Kyoto, I don't care where—and there he'll be, eating a steak, alone, in a corner."

Someone, a locker-room attendant, I suppose, handed him a pack of letters. He removed a rubber band and began opening them, scanning them quickly and setting the ones he wanted to keep on the bench beside him. The others, the trash mail I assumed, he crumpled and dropped on the floor.

I was going to launch the question about dreams, but I thought better of it and asked about advice—did any of his admirers, golfers or not, the people who yelled "Sweetie," with all that concern they had for him to win, did any of them come up with advice?

Palmer looked up from his mail and said that a guy once told him that he was catching his elbows on a rather loose sweater he was wearing.

"But you know it's against the rules to accept information from people on the golf course."

"I didn't know," I said.

"A guy who could afford it might have four specialists, or a dozen, out there on the course advising him. That's why they have the rule."

"Oh, yes," I said slowly, my fancy rather struck by the thought of a convocation of advisers over a difficult shot—a clutch of them sitting around on shooting sticks, the binoculars out, the pencils and the slide rules working like military people studying maps on war maneuvers.

"The only intrusions I'm aware of," Palmer was saying, "are the cameras—the whir and click of them. Of course, these have been banned from the courses recently, so it hasn't been anything of a problem."

"Hi there, Arnie!" A man looked around the corner of the locker.

"Howzitgoin'?" Palmer said pleasantly.

"Great! Great! Great!" the man said. He fussed for another sentence, but nothing was forthcoming; he backed away and disappeared around the corner.

"Superstitions?" I asked. "Do you indulge in any rituals?"

"Oh, no," Palmer said, almost in disgust it seemed, in that loud honking voice. "Oh, sure, I wear certain outfits on certain days. I use the same marker to mark the ball."

"Do you stick to a ball throughout a round if it's going O.K. for you?" I asked.

"A golf ball loosens every time you hit it; even one shot loosens it. So your professional golfer'll change his ball every three holes or so — though, of course, he'll stick to the same trademark." He spoke as if by rote, or as if reading from a training manual.

I cleared my throat and asked him about the yips and the chokes.

He ripped open a letter and dropped the contents between his toes: "Well, I'd call them pretty close cousins. Choking is a stage of the yips. Both of them have to do with being unable to study, to concentrate. It's true that a golfer can get a nerve problem that can't be helped. Those are the yips. Hogan and Nelson got them; to say that Ben Hogan or Byron Nelson *choke,* I mean that's crazy. But both of them, the choking and the yips, I say, are connected with losing the ability to concentrate, and in various degrees that happens to all of us. But you can escape it, get out of it. When I'm working well, I just don't think I'm going to miss a shot or a putt, and when I do I'm as surprised as hell. I can't believe it. A golfer must think that way. He must say to the ball, 'Go to that spot.' The best players who ever played must have thought that way, *willing* the ball there, you see. I don't mean to suggest that it's easy. In fact, the hardest thing for a great many people is to win. They get scared. And they *doubt.* Which gets them into trouble. Of course, that's not Jack Nicklaus' problem."

"I suppose one big win gets you over that problem."

"No. Because you got to want to win more, fast. The temptation if you win is to coast for a while. You begin to think that to run high in the pack is enough. Well, that's the end of you." He rubbed his chin. He snapped the rubber band from his letter packet.

"The competitive thing in golf isn't for everyone. And it hasn't got anything to do with age or horsepower."

"I see," I said.

"Well," he said.

I could see that he felt he had talked enough.

"I had this question about dreams," I said hurriedly. "I wonder if you could talk about that...what you dream..." My voice trailed off. He seemed to be staring at me, but then I noticed his eyes were fixed at a point over my left shoulder. "Hey, Albie!" he shouted. I looked around. A man wearing a small green apron, the locker-room attendant apparently, appeared around the corner of the locker. "What you done with my shoes?"

"In your locker, Mister Palmer. You think I ate 'em?"

Palmer rocked back and forth on the bench. "Haw! Haw! Haw!"

The man in the apron grinned. "You think I don't take care of you, Mr. Palmer?" He turned away.

"Albie, you're a brother. Haw, haw, haw!"

I looked back at Palmer. His face was solemn again, his jollity as swift as a wince. He was sliding off his golf shoe.

"You wanted to tell me about some dream you had," he said without looking up.

"No, not exactly," I said.

His voice sounded very tired.

I looked at my notes.

"Listen," I said. "On the PGA tour, the WPGA is it? The women's tour, that is, there is this high incidence..."

"It's the LPGA — the *ladies'* professional golf..."

"Oh, yes," I said. "Well, on the tour, I am told, there is, er, this very high incidence..."

"Hi, Arnie!" Another man had poked his head around the corner. This one was wearing a straw boater. "Damn good to have you here in Palm Springs."

"Howzitgoin'?" Palmer said pleasantly.

"Oh, it's just going great, Arnie," the man said. He made an abrupt motion with his fist. "You're going to take this goddamn thing, Arnie... you're going to have one great day tomorrow, I'm telling you."

"We're going to sure give it a try," Palmer said.

"Well, great, Arnie," the man said. His face, so full of expression and concern, froze suddenly, and then went vacant as he gazed at the golfer looking sleepily at him; his eyes popped ajar slightly. "Well, so long, Arnie," he said. He disappeared abruptly around the corner.

Palmer ripped open his last letter.

"Well, how's that for you?" he asked. "That enough?"

I looked up from my notes. I wanted to say that I had just a question or so more, if he didn't mind, but I didn't.

"Oh, sure," I said. "You've been very kind." I stood up and shuffled my notes together. "Absolutely great." I began backing away. I wanted to shake his hand in gratitude for his time, but Palmer was staring down between his feet. "Great," I said. "Thanks." I backed around the corner of the locker.

I had the quick sense of failure—that I had been accorded valuable time and had not made the best of it. I walked from the clubhouse out into the afternoon. I began singing to myself—a manifestation of embarrassment that a friend of mine refers to as "the hummings"—making loud noises in one's head to drive out discomfiting thoughts. I often have them—the hummings—waking up in the morning and thinking back on the indiscretions of word or deed the evening before. The WPGA, I thought; boy, that wasn't so hot. Why hadn't I done better with him, I wondered. The confusion over the dreams. I had been just as clumsy and ill-at-ease with him as the two men who had come around the corner of the lockers full of things to say, and whose confidence had drained like meal from a split sack at the sight of him, his proximity. Perhaps one expected too much of such superstars—that one would sit in front of them awestruck and gapejawed and no effort was necessary: one would simply bask in their presence. Of course, Palmer had not been particularly easy. Driving back to the motel I began to take it out on him. Boy, he let me down! If he knew how I strained watching him on television to help him get that putt down; or how an evening was just a little bit off if that afternoon I'd watched him charge the leaders of the tournament and just fail; or the long gloom and worry reading in the paper that he hadn't made the cut of some tournament in the West, as if some prop had been knocked out of the great order of things.

Lord, I wondered, am I going to desert him for Nicklaus, or Casper, or someone....

I found out the last day of the tournament. The professionals were playing without their amateur partners. I had a chance to stick with whichever golfer I chose. I toyed with some of the others. But I found myself drawn inexorably to Palmer's Army. I joined them. I craned to see what he was up to. I agonized over his play. "Drop, drop!" I shouted, along with the others, at a long putt as it went for the hole, and when it did drop, I let out a great cry of delight. "Man, he did it!" I shouted hap-

As always, the enthusiastic fan. (*Russ Halford*)

pily at the stranger next to me. He was a man wearing a straw boater with a brim that read GO, ARNIE. His eyes were glistening with excitement. We pounded each other on the back.

"D'ja see him *will* that ball in there," I cried.

The other man nodded wildly. He seemed speechless.

"There wasn't the slightest doubt in his mind."

He shook his head vehemently.

We moved happily for the next tee.

"That fellow doesn't coast," I said. "He's got to win."

On my way my companion caught his breath. "He really *attacked* that hole," he said in a high wheeze.

"Damn right."

We were trading familiarities about Palmer.

"Guy's got a million-dollar jet," the man said. "He's got it all."

"Yes," I said. "I'll tell you something else. He has a Coke every morning at two a.m.," I said.

"Oh?"

I had him there.

CHAPTER 43

A couple of months later, when spring had come to the east, I went out on a Long Island golf course with a friend. It was the first time I had handled a club since the sands of La Quinta. He said, remarking on my tour, "I expect you'll be giving me quite a lesson, what with your being out there with all those golf people. I'll want a handicap. You'll have to give me, oh, maybe three strokes a side."

"Well, Fred, you're not getting them," I said. "Nothing's happened to my golf. It's the same old sloppy friend you know and cherish."

"I can't believe it," Fred said.

"Well, you wait," I said.

On the first tee, a long par 5, I won the honor and drove. I hit a tremendous straight shot.

"Holy smoke!" Fred said. "You really creamed that one. A sweetheart."

"Yes," I said easily. "I managed to get some hurtin' on that one."

"What?"

"'Hurtin'.' Well, that's how they describe a good drive out there... on the... ah... tour."

"I see."

"Sometimes we refer to it as putting some 'swift' on the ball."

"Oh, yes."

We set off down the fairway, the caddies striding purposefully ahead. I was wearing the Crosby golf cap, a little tight back of the ears. A large metal blue disk still attached to my bag identified me as a contestant in the Bob Hope Desert Classic. Alongside clanked the Crosby identification disk. The Hope disk was more distinctive. Along the upper curve it had the name of the tournament, across the center my name was superimposed on a caricature of the comedian, and along the bottom curve it read CONTESTANT. There was a San Francisco Lucky disk as well.

Two girls were with us—just ambling along. Neither was playing. They moved along the side of the fairway, both in Pucci pants, like tall brightly colored birds; the sheen of the silk material would shine and catch the eye like the blue of a teal's wing turning in flight. They paid no attention to the game. They looked into the yellow forsythia that paralleled the fairways sometimes as high and thick as the banks of an up-country river. They chatted endlessly, talking so hard that their long legs ambled them against each other, so that they bumped gently down the fairway, their laughter drifting back. My friend looked up from his second shot and saw them in his line. "Lord, Gail, fore!" and the two started and drifted back into the forsythia until just their heads showed, both dark-haired, like swimmers in that wash of yellow.

"Come along," their cry drifted up the fairway, "come a...long."

When Fred hit his shot, both heads ducked, though it was perfectly safe, so that there was just that tumble of yellow flower, until one head appeared tentatively, and then the other. "O.K.? O.K.?"

Fred waved. They stepped out of the flowers. "Like Indians," he said.

I came up to my drive. The girls had come back to join us. They stood with the caddies. I hit another long wood shot. "Holy smoke," I said. I stared after the shot. I let the shaft of the club slip down through my fingers to the club head, a professional habit I had developed for use after a good shot.

"Lord!" said Fred.

"It's hot. We're going to get some iced tea," one of the girls said. "We'll join you in a bit. We can see you from the terrace."

They started for the clubhouse. It sat on a hill with the course sweeping completely around it.

We strode along.

"Well, what happened out there? What'd you make of the golfers?"

"I did the wrong thing," I said. "I spent all my time worrying about my own game. Natural, I guess. I mean if the average person packed up his bag and did it, he'd do the same thing...golf ranges, putting practice, books to read, and the rest of it. Most of the talking and listening was in my own head—very mournful dialogues indeed."

"It's not like hanging around a football team, like your stint with the Detroit Lions?"

"There's not the same sense of camaraderie...and danger...and the drama, well, it's all *private* in golf. Which is its strength."

"So if you do a book it won't be the same."

"Well, the mystique of golf—I mean anyone can play the game, or try it—so it's not quite like the great arena sports, where people are really curious about what goes on. But maybe it'd be easier to write about—more fanciful, I guess. More fun."

"So maybe you'll do it?" Fred asked.

"Oh, I should hope so," I said.

A faint cry drifted down from the direction of the clubhouse.

"Jack-*son!*"

"Was that Gail? Who are those girls calling for?" Fred asked.

"Listen, Fred," I said. "What I'll do is give you one stroke a side."

"I should hope so," he said, "after those first two shots."

I knew it was an absurd arrangement; that nothing had happened to my game. But then again, perhaps something could have happened. Was it possible that the gears, after a deserving layoff, were now, after so much grinding and screeching in California, perfectly meshed? I could see my ball down the fairway—a fine lie. Another good shot, perhaps a two iron, would fetch the green. My fingers itched for a club. I hurried up to find out what was going to happen.

About the Author

G eorge Plimpton (1927–2003) was the bestselling author and editor of more than thirty books, as well as editor of the *Paris Review* for its first fifty years. He wrote regularly for such magazines as *Sports Illustrated* and *Esquire,* and he appeared numerous times in films and on television.